Make It Miami

A cookbook presented by

THE GUILD OF THE MUSEUM OF SCIENCE, INC. and

Space Transit Planetarium

Miami, Florida

The Guild of the Museum of Science, Inc. is a non-profit volunteer service organization within the Museum of Science and Space Transit Planetarium and is dedicated to providing assistance to the professional staff, and to giving financial aid through special projects.

The funds generated through the sales of **MAKE IT MIAMI** will support special projects and permanent exhibits within the Museum and Planetarium complex which, in turn, will benefit the cultural and educational conditions within the communities that it serves.

First Printing, November, 1987
Second Printing, April, 1990

TO ORDER ADDITIONAL COPIES OF **MAKE IT MIAMI**, PLEASE USE THE ORDER FORMS IN THE BACK OF THE BOOK OR WRITE:

MAKE IT MIAMI
3280 South Miami Avenue
Miami, Florida 33129

Library of Congress Catalog Card No. 87-82220
ISBN: 0-9619054-0-9

Printed in the United States of America
by
Moran Printing Company
Orlando, Florida

TABLE OF CONTENTS

HISTORY OF THE GUILD OF THE MUSEUM OF SCIENCE, INC.

The Guild of the Museum of Science was founded in 1953 by the Junior League of Miami. A need was recognized for a group of volunteer workers to increase community interest in the Museum; to give financial aid through special projects and to provide assistance, leadership and guidance to the Museum's professional staff. Mrs. Henry O. Shaw served as the Guild's first president.

The Junior Museum, which was the original name, was housed in the Miami Woman's Club from 1954 to 1960. Ground was broken on October 4, 1959 for the present Museum of Science building, and on September 25, 1960, the doors were officially opened. The Space Transit Planetarium was formally dedicated on November 4, 1966.

A Spitz Planetarium was presented to the Museum in 1954 by the Guild; and from 1956 to 1964, eight annual circus fund raising events were held to benefit the Museum. The Guild was recognized by the Miami News as the Outstanding Club in 1958, and in 1967, the Miami Herald's annual "Club of the Year" contest awarded the Guild first place in the Continuing Project Category.

A new committee took the Museum out into the community during 1979-1980. The committee, named "Know Your Museum," was the forerunner to our Community Outreach Program. This committee visited 2300 school children that year. During the 1986-87 year, the Community Outreach Committee visited 42 schools with over 7000 school children in attendance, giving lectures and demonstrations on science and native Florida wildlife.

During the 1986-87 school year, over 45,500 students, teachers and parents were guided through the Museum and Planetarium by Guild volunteers.

The Guild operates the Museum Store in its entirety and during the 1986-87 fiscal year, turned over $75,000 in proceeds to the Museum.

An average of over 11,000 hours of volunteer service is given annually in support of the Museum and Planetarium by the Guild.

During the past three years, the Museum has entered another phase of development with a completely new exhibits concept; and, a multi-million dollar fund-raising project is underway for the renovation and expansion of the Museum and Planetarium complex.

The members of the Guild are proud of the service they give to benefit the Museum and Planetarium. These dedicated women continue to play an ever increasing part in enlarging the scope of the Museum's educational and cultural contributions to the greater South Florida communities.

INTRODUCTION

MAKE IT MIAMI offers a wide range of culinary delights from the diverse ethnic cultures of our community. It features some of the exotic fruits and vegetables that are grown here. The book offers basic and easy recipes as well as delectable gourmet dishes that are clearly expressed for the beginning cook, and will also entice the experienced chef.

Although much has been written about Miami, Dade County, Florida, there are some very impressive facts about our area's agricultural production that many people do not know and some of these facts we would like to share with you.

The sub-tropical environment of Dade County provides the nation with much of its winter fruits and vegetables. Miami provides the nation with 95% of the mangoes produced in the continental U.S. and over 90% of the limes. About 70% of the fresh market avocados are grown and shipped from here from December through March.

A partial list of Dade County's exotic fruits include carambola (star fruit), lychee, mamey sapota and papaya.

The County produces more tropical vegetables — boniato sweet potatoes, malanga and calabaza — than any other county in the continental United States. Also, 50% of the nation's winter fresh market tomatoes and 40% of the sweet corn makes its way from Miami and South Dade County each year; hence, the name "The nation's winter salad bowl."

We are the largest producer of okra, snap beans and squash of any county in the state of Florida, and also have the largest ornamental nursery industry.

Dade County is one of 6 counties in Florida that ranks in the top 100 counties in the nation in the value of agricultural products sold annually.

MAKE IT MIAMI is full of helpful information and hints in the use of these exotic fruits and vegetables.

We sincerely hope you will enjoy the recipes that are included in this cookbook and that some of these will become a tradition in your home for years to come.

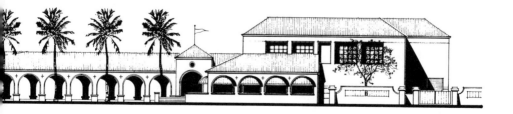

ACKNOWLEDGEMENTS

Our sincere appreciation to all Guild members, their families and friends for submitting and testing over 1500 wonderful recipes. Unfortunately, not all could be used due to lack of space or similarities. We have selected 544 recipes that we feel sure will please every cook.

A special thanks to the following people and organizations:

Margie Van Vliet Silvestri for her cover design work. Margie is a graduate of Ohio State University, with a major in Fine Arts. She has taught many classes in oil, landscaping and children's art. Oils are her favorite medium. Margie is an associate Guild member.

Liz Dee for her section designs of the beautiful palms that grow in our "Sunshine State." Liz is a graduate of The University of Florida in Art Education and holds a Masters degree in Education from the University of Miami. She teaches art and is a freelance artist. Liz is an active member of the Guild.

Edward C. Berounsky, of the architectural firm of Architeknics, Inc., Miami, Florida, for the designs of the planned renovation and expansion of the Museum of Science and Planetarium complex.

Dade/IFAS Cooperative Extension Service, USDA, and Florida Crop and Livestock Reporting Service, Orlando, Florida for all the helpful agricultural information supplied to us.

Brand names were used in this cookbook only when absolutely necessary.

Cookbook Committee
Betty Babitzke, Chairman
Betty Catlin, Co-Chairman

Donna Auger	Jeanne Harper	Nancy Perry
Lucille Bass	Jane Harrigan	Nan Russell
Ruth Bischoff	Joanne Karcher	Corrine Shilling
Mary Brenner	Carol Kuhnke	Jean Simon
Joy Cole	Tina Meyer	Mary Ann Stemples
Judy Dorn	Ev Milliken	Helga Wornick

Joan Hudiburg, President 1986-87, Advisor
Doris Blanck, Advisor
Nancy Herget, President 1987-88, Ex-Officio

Typists

Betty Babitzke	Judy Dorn	Carol Kuhnke
Betty Catlin	Maxine Dunlop	Tina Meyer

Research	**Indexing**	**Marketing**
Nancy Perry	Audrey Tallon	Mary Ann Stemples

Testing

Donna Auger	Betty Catlin	Joan Hudiburg
Betty Babitzke	Joy Cole	Tina Meyer
Frances Baboun	Candice Cosmides	Shirley Natuluk
Lois Bailey	Marianne Devlin	Nancy Perry
Lucille Bass	Judy Dorn	Sheila Revell
Mary Ann Bedingfield	Maxine Dunlop	Nan Russell
Ruth Bischoff	Carol Ezzo	Corrine Shilling
Doris Blanck	Jeanne Harper	Mary Ann Stemples
Carol Boyer	Diane Harrell	Carol Stokes
Mary Brenner	Jane Harrigan	Fran Towle
Connee Bretz	Nancy Herget	Kendra Townsend
Peggy Brodnax	Carol Hogan	Joan Welbaum
Diane Brown		Mattie Wessel
Ramona Busot		Helga Wornick

Editing

Donna Auger	Joy Cole	Ev Milliken
Betty Babitzke	Judy Dorn	Nancy Perry
Lucille Bass	Jane Harrigan	Corrine Shilling
Ruth Bischoff	Nancy Herget	Jean Simon
Mary Brenner	Joanne Karcher	Carol Stokes
Betty Catlin	Tina Meyer	Helga Wornick

CONTRIBUTORS

The following is a list of contributors who so generously donated their time, talent and recipes for the success of **MAKE IT MIAMI**.

Mary Alexander
Fran Alley
Marilyn Allison
Edie Altman
Doris Anguish
Yvonne Arch
Donna Auger
Barkley Averette
Betty Babitzke
Maggie Babitzke
Lois Bailey
Betty Barkdull
Ellen Barnes
Lucille Bass
Molly Baumberger
Mary Anne Bedingfield
Joan Bell
Nina Bell
Nancy Benouiach
Geri Berounsky
Sally Billingsley
Ruth Bischoff
Doris Blanck
Barbara Blankenship
Carol Boyer
Marianne Brauzer
Mary Brenner
Annmarie Brockmann
Peggy Brodnax
Peggy Brook
Martha Brook
Diane Brown
Karen Brown
Ramona Busot
Jody Byrne
Anna Cabral
Lila Campbell
Betty Catlin
Shirley Cochran
Caroline Coffey
Joy Cole
Jeanne Corlett
Sandi Corlett
Candice Cosmides
Ceil Cox
Ann Craig
Marty Crispin
Mary Cunio
Yolanda Daly
The Late Louise de Hart
Martha de la Vega
Marianne Devlin
Bob Devlin
Judy Dorn
Karen Dowling
Elaine Duncan
Jeanice Ewoldt
Carol Ezzo
Valerie Ferguson
Martha Fithian

Sue Forrest
Jean Foss
Lorraine Fulton
Beth Gardner
Carolyn Gardner
Diane Garrison
Frances Germain
Charlene Gilbert
Avis Gill
Ann Greenfield
Jane Greenop
Mabel Griley
Madeline Gruber
Pat Guernsey
Jeanne Haas
Gudny Hagestad
Barbara Hall
Bea Hammond
Mimi Hammond
Kristi Handley
Betty Harper
Jeanne Harper
Diane Harrell
Jane Harrigan
Mary Harrington
Sandy Harris
Judy Hasseld
Nancy Herget
Jean Hicks
Margaret Hobbs
Carol Hogan
Linda Hogan
Patsy Howard
Joan Hudiburg
Jo Ann Hudson
Carla Imbrie
Priscilla Jackson
Becky Jahnel
Voncile Janvrin
Anita Jenkins
Boots Jones
Joanne Karcher
Renee Karnegis
Hazel Karnig
Helen Kilmer
Geri Kirtland
Manya Kissanis
Carol Kuhnke
Jane Larkin
Marilyn List
Kathy Logan
Sharon Lombardo
Inez Luckett
Reva Luckett
Marigrace McCabe
Barbara McIlwain
Verna McLendon
Bobbie Meadows
Mary Meadows
Lou Melching

Nina Meyer
Tina Meyer
Ev Milliken
Carol Mitchell
Winnie Mitchell
Dolly Morrow
Jim Morrow
Pam Normandia
Cal Pappas
Sally Pearlson
Nancy Perry
Joyce Perse
Lee Peterson
Nancy Petillo
Angela Phillips
Linda Raatama
Charlotte Reeve
Sheila Revell
Astrid Reynolds
Carol Richards
Mary Ritchey
Debbie Ritter
Nancy Roberts
Hazel Rogers
Pam Roundtree
Nan Russell
Louise Schilling
Daisy Schmitt
Marilyn Schornstein
Sherri Sewell
Becky Shelley
Corinne Shilling
Zoe Sicking
Willie Siert
Jean Simon
Gerry Smith
Joyce Smith
Christine Sowards
Dottie Spillis
Donna Steele
Carol Stokes
Fran Stokes
Audrey Tallon
Frances Towle
Brenda Townsend
Kendra Townsend
Wescott Trinidad
Sally Tripp
Jean Van Hemert
Martha Vickers
Geneva Waldin
Ginny Ward
Marge Watt
The Late Claire Weintraub
Beverly Wilson
Peg Woodward
Helga Wornick
Sis Wyllie
Cicely Zeppa

BON VOYAGE BRUNCH
**Florida Summer Punch
Scrambled Eggs
Ham Broccoli Roll-Ups
Hot Curried Fruit
Citrus Lime Muffins
Best Ever Mango Bread
Strawberry Butter**

LADIES LITE LUNCHEON
**Pool-Party Mint Tea Punch
Microwave Strawberry Soup Supreme
Rain Forest Supreme Salad
Crab and Shrimp Quiche
Toasted Fingers
Mango Mousse**

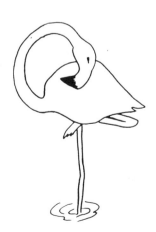

"ORANGE" BOWL DINNER
**Orange Cow
Chutney Fingers
Salad Mandarin
Miami Orange Chicken
Orange Rice
Orange Fluff Cake
Florida Orange Pie**

CARIBBEAN CUISINE
Trinidad Rum Punch
Conch Fritters
Wine-Gelatin Ring
Coconut Shrimp
Caribbean Pigeon Peas and Rice
Grapefruit Alaska

ELEGANTE DINNER
Champagne Punch
Bleu Cheese Mousse
Caviar Pie
Almond Soup
Brandied Roast Cornish Hens with Peaches
Green Bean Salad Provencal
Barley Pilaf
Chocolate Mousse Cake

CINCO DE MAYO
MEXICAN FIESTA
Jim's Sangria
Microwave Burrito Tidbits
Party Tapatia
Mango Salad
Chalupas
Chicken Enchilada Ole
Cheese Casserole Squares
Spanish Flan

POOLSIDE BARBECUE
Miami Moonlight Cocktail
Dilly Shrimp Dip with Crackers
Tricolor Salad
Barbecued Dolphin
Tartar Sauce
Bleu Cheese Potato Casserole
Herb Dressed Italian Bread
Key Lime Pie

SOUTH AMERICAN POTPOURRI
Yellow Birds
Ceviche
Guatemalan Stuffed Tomatoes
Cuban Boliche Roast
Spanish Rice Casserole
Cubano Buevelos
Tres Leches

SOUTHERN SUPPER
Iced Tea Drink
Chicken and Dumplings
Southern Green Beans
Southern Style Creamed Corn
Honey Buttered Carrots
Strawberry Pie

DOCKSIDE PICNIC
Windsurfer's Passion Fruit Quencher
Leek Soup Cheese Ball with Crackers
Chicken Curry Salad
Tomato Pie
Cranberry Relish
Pecan Pick-Ups

SEAFOOD DINNER
Calypso Cup
Pate of Smoked Salmon with Chives and Dill
Gazpacho
Snapper Parmesan
Spinach Topped Tomatoes
Wild Rice with Mushrooms and Almonds
Aerobics Drop-Out Cake

HOLIDAY SEASON DINNER
Cranberry Eggnog
Smoked Oyster Dip with Crackers
Mushroom Strudel
Wild Rice Soup
Orange-Mincemeat Congealed Salad
Roast Turkey with Giblet Gravy
Sicilian Broccoli
Creamed Onions
Sweet Potato Casserole
Brandied Cranberries
Refrigerator Rolls
Old Cutler Holiday Cake
Old English Plum Pudding

Appetizers and
Party Fare

DWARF PALMETTO

Hints For Appetizers and Party Fare

Always allow at least six hors d'oeuvres per person.

Figs wrapped in prosciutto ham make great hors d'oeuvres.

Cabbage is a very attractive centerpiece when hollowed out and filled with a dip. Arrange crudites around the cabbage.

Try dried fruit stuffed with a variety of fillings for something different.

Microwave stale chips or crackers 15 to 20 seconds to freshen them up.

To protect platters, use different types of lettuce as a base and then arrange various hors d'oeuvres on top of the lettuce.

To prevent tea sandwiches from getting soggy, butter the bread before putting on the filling.

Baskets make a wonderful serving device. Line the basket with different colored fabric according to your theme.

Offer dieters low calorie appetizers such as vegetables or fruits and consider using yogurt or reduced calorie mayonnaise.

Make sure that your hors d'oeuvres have a fresh appearance at the time of serving. If made ahead of time, wrap the serving tray in plastic wrap or waxed paper and place in the refrigerator.

Bread cutouts used for canapes should be no thicker than ¼ inch so they can be eaten in one bite. They should be easy to hold.

Arrange appetizers on trays by type and never crowd them. Garnish your trays with colorful foods such as parsley, carrot ribbons, cherry tomatoes, pimento or peppers.

Celery is delicious stuffed with Roquefort or cream cheese mixtures.

Edam or Gouda cheese may be hollowed out and filled with caviar. Spread crackers around the cheese.

If foods require only a short heating time, use your microwave to heat them right in their serving baskets or wooden serving ware.

BOURSIN CHEESE

Yield: 36 servings

3 (8-ounce) packages cream
cheese, softened
1½ sticks margarine or
butter, softened
1 (8-ounce) bottle Green
Goddess Dressing

4 or 5 garlic cloves, minced
Pepper and chives, to taste
¼ cup chopped parsley
Assorted crackers

Mix all ingredients (except crackers) together with hand mixer. May be frozen for future use. Serve with assorted crackers.

HORSERADISH CHEESE BALL

Yield: 3¼ cups

2 (8-ounce) packages cream
cheese, softened
2 tablespoons horseradish
1 teaspoon celery salt
½ small onion, finely diced

1 cup chopped dried beef
Dash Tabasco sauce
Waxed paper
¾ cup chopped parsley

The day before, or up to one week before serving, beat cream cheese until smooth. Beat in horseradish, celery salt and onion. Mix in dried beef and Tabasco sauce. Turn into a bowl lined with waxed paper, and refrigerate until serving time. At serving time, reshape cheese into ball or dome, and sprinkle with chopped fresh parsley.

NOTE: Can be prepared in a food processor.

BLEU CHEESE BALL

Yield: 1½ cups

3 (3-ounce) packages cream
cheese, softened
1 (4-ounce) package Bleu
cheese, crumbled

2 teaspoons bourbon
¾ teaspoon dry mustard
½ cup toasted sesame seeds
Sesame crackers

Recipe can be prepared in a food processor. Mix cheeses until soft. Add bourbon and mustard. Place in wax paper-lined bowl. Cover and refrigerate.

At serving time, shape into ball or dome, and cover with toasted sesame seeds. Serve with sesame crackers.

NOTE: Make the day before serving.

BLEU CHEESE MOUSSE

Yield: 12 servings

1½ envelopes unflavored
  gelatin (1½ tablespoons)
¼ cup cold water
6 egg yolks
2 cups whipping cream

¾ pound Bleu cheese
3 egg whites, stiffly beaten
2 tablespoons poppy seeds
Pepperidge Farm Butter
  Thins

Sprinkle gelatin over cold water to soften. Combine egg yolks and ½ cup cream in a heavy sauce pan. Over low heat, cook and whisk until mixture is creamy and slightly thickened. Add gelatin, and beat until dissolved. Pour into a large mixing bowl, and set aside. Process cheese in a blender or food processor until smooth, and add to gelatin mixture. Cool until partially set. Whip remaining cream, and fold into cheese mixture, then fold in egg whites and poppy seeds. Pour into a 2-quart, oiled mold, and chill until firm. Unmold on serving plate, garnish, and serve with Pepperidge Farm Butter Thins.

LEEK SOUP CHEESE BALL

Yield: 2½ cups

1 (8-ounce) package cream
  cheese, softened
1 (2½-ounce) jar softened
  dried beef, chopped
6 to 8 small green onions,
  chopped

½ package leek soup mix
3 dashes Worcestershire
  sauce
2 dashes garlic powder
½ cup chopped nuts
Potato chips

Mix first 6 ingredients thoroughly. Roll in finely chopped nuts. Chill. Serve with potato chips.

GUACAMOLE DIP

Yield: 12-16 servings

4 medium avocados
2 tomatoes, finely chopped
1 teaspoon salt
½ teaspoon pepper
Juice of 1 lemon
2 cloves garlic, minced

2 tablespoons vegetable oil
2 tablespoons chopped green
  onion (optional)
2 tablespoons chopped fresh
  jalapeño (optional)
Tortilla chips

Peel and mash avocados; add remaining ingredients. Place in airtight container and chill. Serve with tortilla chips.

NOTE: May be served as a salad on bed of lettuce. Will yield 8 salad servings.

MORE DIP

Yield: 12 servings

1 (16-ounce) can peeled tomatoes, drained and chopped
1 (7-ounce) can black olives, drained and diced
1 pound cheddar cheese, grated
1 (7-ounce) can green chili salsa or use 1 (4-ounce) can whole green chilies, drained and chopped
1 medium onion, diced
Corn chips

Mix all ingredients together. Serve with favorite dipping corn chips.

BEER CHEESE SPREAD

Yield: 3-4 cups

1 pound natural cheddar cheese, grated
1 pound natural Swiss cheese, grated
1 teaspoon dry mustard
1 clove garlic, minced
½ teaspoon Worcestershire sauce
1 cup beer
Crackers

Using a blender or food processor, grate cheese according to personal preference, coarse or fine. Add dry mustard, garlic and Worcestershire sauce. Add beer until mixture is of spreadable consistency. The amount of beer depends on coarseness of grated cheese. The finer the grate, the more beer will be needed. Serve with crackers, dark or light bread.

NOTE: Keeps a long time refrigerated in a crock.

HOT DIP

Preheat oven to 400°   Yield: 8-10 servings

1 large egg
1 teaspoon Cavender's
  seasoning (Greek)
1 (8-ounce) package cream
  cheese, diced

½ (16-ounce) can zucchini
  (see note following recipe)
Crackers

Using the metal blade of the food processor, mix the egg and seasoning. Add the diced cheese, mixing slightly. Put the zucchini on top, and process on and off several times. Put in ovenproof serving dish, and bake at 400° for 30 minutes or until brown on top. Test with a knife. Knife should come out clean or a bit moist. Do not allow to get too dry.

NOTE: Mushrooms, chopped chives, crab, tuna, etc. can be substituted for zucchini. Serve with crackers.

CHEESE SQUARES

Preheat oven to 325°   Yield: 24 squares

2 (4-ounce) cans green
  chilies, chopped
1 pound Jack cheese, grated
1 pound cheddar cheese,
  grated
4 egg yolks

⅔ cup evaporated milk
1 tablespoon flour
½ teaspoon salt
⅛ teaspoon pepper
4 egg whites, stiffly beaten

In a large bowl, combine chilies and cheese. Turn into a well-buttered 9x13-inch pan. In a small bowl, combine egg yolks, milk, flour, salt and pepper until blended. Fold in egg whites. Pour over chilies and cheese. Stir slightly with a fork. Bake at 325° for 1 hour. Cool, and cut into 1-inch squares. Arrange attractively on serving dish.

MICROWAVE BURRITO TIDBITS

Yield: 18 pieces

1 package (12 to 14-ounce)
chorizo sausage, if
available, otherwise use
pork sausage

1 dozen flour tortillas
3 cups Monterrey Jack
cheese, grated

Remove casing from sausages. Crumble meat into 1½-quart micro-wave baking dish. Cook, uncovered, in microwave oven 3 minutes on high, stirring 2 or 3 times until meat is firm and looks darker in color. Drain and discard drippings. Sprinkle about 2 tablespoons meat down the center of each tortilla. Sprinkle with about ¼ cup cheese. Roll up tortilla SNUGLY; place seam side down on a paper plate or serving dish. Heat 3 rolls at a time, uncovered, about 1 to 1½ minutes on high in microwave or until cheese is melted. Cut each roll into 4 slices, and serve warm.

SAUSAGE AND CHEESE TURNOVERS

Preheat oven to 350°

Yield: 10 turnovers

1 (10-ounce) can refrigerated
biscuits
½ pound Italian bulk
sausage, browned and
drained
¼ teaspoon Italian
seasoning
1 (4-ounce) can mushroom
stems and pieces, drained

4 ounces shredded
Mozzarella or Provolone
cheese
1 egg, slightly beaten
1 to 2 tablespoons grated
Parmesan cheese

Separate dough into 10 biscuits. Press or roll each to 5-inch circle. In a medium bowl, combine browned sausage, seasoning, mushrooms and cheese. Spoon about 3 tablespoons mixture onto center of each flattened biscuit. Fold dough in half over filling; press edges to seal. Brush tops with beaten egg; sprinkle with Parmesan cheese. Place on greased cookie sheet. Bake at 350° for 10 to 15 minutes or until deep golden brown.

SAUSAGE TIDBITS

Preheat oven to 375°   Yield: about 88

1 pound lean ground beef
1 pound hot or mild pork
  sausage
½ teaspoon garlic powder
⅛ teaspoon Worcestershire
  sauce

1 pound Velveeta cheese
2 loaves party rye bread or
  plain white melba rounds

Brown beef and sausage; add seasonings. Stir and crumble meats. Cook until browned. Drain off all fat. Add small chunks of cheese to mixture over low heat until melted. Mix well with meat. Spread on rye bread or melba rounds. Bake at 375° for 10 minutes.

NOTE: May be frozen after assembling but not baked. From freezer to oven, bake at 350° for 15 minutes.

BARBECUED SAUSAGE BALLS

Yield: 36 balls

1 pound bulk pork sausage
1 egg, slightly beaten
⅓ to ½ cup fine dry bread
  crumbs
½ teaspoon sage

½ cup ketchup
3 tablespoons brown sugar
1 tablespoon vinegar
1 tablespoon soy sauce

Mix sausage, egg, bread crumbs and sage. Shape into small balls to make about 30 to 36 balls. In ungreased skillet, brown balls slowly on all sides, about 15 minutes. Pour off excess fat. Combine remaining ingredients; pour over meat. Cover and simmer 30 minutes, stirring occasionally to coat meat balls.

MARINATED BEEF

Yield: 24 servings

½ pound cooked rare roast beef, thinly sliced and cut in strips
1 onion, sliced very thin and separated into rings

¾ teaspoon salt
Pepper, to taste
1½ tablespoon lemon juice
1 cup sour cream

Combine all ingredients together; mix and chill. Serve with toothpicks or cocktail forks.

NOTE: May buy beef in a supermarket deli. Serve with crackers or party bread slices.

CHIPPED BEEF DIP

Preheat oven to 350°

Yield: 10-12 servings

1 (8-ounce) package cream cheese
2 tablespoons milk
3 ounces coarsely chopped chipped beef
1 green onion, chopped
½ cup sour cream

Pepper, to taste
¼ teaspoon minced garlic
⅓ cup slivered almonds or chopped pecans
2 tablespoons butter
Corn chips or fresh raw vegetables for dipping

Soften cream cheese, and mix with milk. Add chipped beef, onion, sour cream, pepper and garlic. May be frozen at this point. Thaw. Sauté slivered almonds or pecans in butter. Add these to the top. Bake at 350° for 20 minutes or until heated through and browned on top. Serve with fresh raw vegetables or corn chips.

MUSHROOM FILLED TOASTS

Yield: 2 cups

Mushroom Filling:

1 medium onion, finely
  chopped or grated
4 tablespoons butter
½ pound fresh mushrooms,
  cleaned and finely chopped

½ teaspoon thyme
½ teaspoon salt
¼ teaspoon pepper
3 tablespoons flour
1 cup sour cream

Sauté onions in butter until tender. Add mushrooms and spices; cook for 6 minutes over medium heat, stirring frequently. Sprinkle in flour, and stir to mix well. Reduce heat, and add sour cream. Stir until thickened. Cool, then chill.

Mushroom Toasts

Preheat oven to 350°.
Spread mushroom filling on white bread slices or decorative bread shapes for canapés. Bake at 350° for 15 minutes or until brown and bubbly. Serve hot.

MUSHROOM LOGS

Preheat oven to 375°

Yield: 4 dozen

2 (8-ounce) cans refrigerated
  crescent dinner rolls
1 (8-ounce) package cream
  cheese, softened
2 (4-ounce) cans mushroom
  stems and pieces, drained
  and chopped

1 teaspoon seasoned salt
2 to 3 tablespoons bacon bits
1 egg, beaten
1 to 2 tablespoons poppy
  seeds

Separate crescent dough into 8 rectangles; press perforations to seal. Combine cream cheese, mushrooms, salt and bacon bits, and mix well. Spread mixture in equal portions over each rectangle. Starting at long sides, roll up each rectangle, jelly-roll fashion. Pinch seams to seal. Slice logs into 1-inch pieces; place seam side down on an ungreased baking sheet. Brush each log with beaten egg, and sprinkle with poppy seeds. Bake at 375° for 12 to 15 minutes.

NOTE: This dish should be prepared and served same day.

MUSHROOM STRUDEL

Preheat oven to 375°   Yield: 2 luncheon servings or
                                                      4 appetizers

1 pound fresh mushrooms,
  cleaned and dried
½ cup chopped green onion
¼ cup butter or margarine
½ teaspoon salt
¼ teaspoon pepper
½ teaspoon leaf tarragon,
  crumbled

2 tablespoons white dry
  sherry
¼ cup sour cream
7 strudel or phyllo leaves (½
  pound)
½ cup butter or margarine,
  melted
½ cup fresh bread crumbs

Reserve 2 small mushrooms for garnish; chop remainder finely. Sauté mushrooms with onions in ¼ cup butter in a large skillet about 5 minutes. Stir in salt, pepper and tarragon. Add sherry, and cook over moderately high heat until liquid evaporates and mixture is almost dry, stirring occasionally. Remove from heat; cool, and stir in sour cream.

Working quickly, put strudel leaf on clean towel. (Keep the rest of the strudel leaves covered with damp towel to prevent pastry from drying out.) Brush all over with melted butter; sprinkle with 1 tablespoon bread crumbs. Repeat with remaining strudel leaves, butter and crumbs, stacking prepared leaves evenly on top of each other.

Leaving 2-inch margins on sides, pile mushroom mixture on top of strudel leaves at the bottom edge. Fold in margins. Holding the lower corners of the towel tautly, flip the strudel over and over again until you are almost at the end. Brush end of strudel with butter, then complete the rolling. Gently lift strudel onto buttered jelly roll pan; brush surface with remaining butter. Bake at 375° for 30 minutes or until strudel is golden brown. Serve warm.

MUSHROOM AND SPINACH CRESCENTS

Preheat oven to 350°   Yield: 32 appetizers

2 tablespoons butter
½ pound fresh mushrooms,
  cleaned and chopped
1 medium onion, finely
  chopped
2 (10-ounce) packages frozen
  spinach

2 (3-ounce) packages cream
  cheese, softened
2 cans refrigerated crescent
  rolls

Melt butter in skillet, and sauté mushrooms and onion until tender and mushrooms are brown. Drain off juice. Cook spinach according to package directions. Drain and cool. Squeeze out all moisture from spinach. When cool, combine spinach, mushrooms, onions and cream cheese.

Unroll crescent rolls, and on large end of each triangle place a heaping teaspoon of the spinach mixture. Fold crescent roll over, and seal completely. Place on cookie sheet, and bake at 350° for 15 minutes or until browned. Remove from oven, and slice in half. Serve immediately.

PHYLLO-WRAPPED SPINACH ROLLS

Preheat oven to 350°   Yield: 72 servings

1 tablespoon olive oil
½ cup chopped onion
1 (10-ounce) package frozen
  chopped spinach, thawed,
  squeezed dry
8 ounces cottage cheese

4 ounces cream cheese
4 ounces crumbled Feta
  cheese
1 small egg, beaten
12 phyllo pastry sheets
1 cup (2 sticks) butter, melted

Heat oil in large skillet over medium high heat. Add onion, and sauté until translucent, about 3 minutes. Reduce heat to low, and add spinach. Slowly stir in cheeses until well blended. Cook 5 minutes. Remove from heat. Add egg, and mix well.

Butter a 13x18-inch baking sheet. Stack 3 phyllo sheets on damp towel. Brush each sheet with melted butter. Spoon about ½ cup filling into 1½-inch wide strip down long edge of phyllo. Roll up as for jelly roll, starting at long edge with filling and using towel as aid. Transfer to prepared baking sheet, arranging seam side down. Brush with melted butter. Repeat with remaining phyllo for 3 more rolls. Freeze 15 minutes. Cut rolls into 1-inch pieces. Bake at 350° until golden brown, about 15 minutes.

ARTICHOKE NIBBLES

Preheat oven to 325°   Yield: 36 pieces

2 (6-ounce) jars marinated
  artichoke hearts
1 small onion, grated
1 clove garlic, minced
4 tablespoons butter
4 eggs
¼ cup fine dry bread crumbs

¼ teaspoon salt
Pepper and oregano, to taste
½ pound sharp cheddar
  cheese
2 tablespoons minced
  parsley

Drain marinade from artichokes. Chop artichokes. Add onion, garlic and artichokes to frying pan, and sauté. Place eggs in a medium mixing bowl and beat with fork. Add crumbs, salt, pepper and oregano to taste. Stir in cheese and parsley, and add artichokes and onion mixture. Stir well. Turn into greased 7x11-inch baking pan. Bake at 325° for 30 minutes. Let cool in pan, and cut into 1-inch squares. Serve warm or cold.

ZUCCHINI SQUARES

Preheat oven to 350°   Yield: 9-12 servings

1 cup Bisquick Mix
½ teaspoon salt
½ cup chopped onion
2 teaspoons parsley
½ cup grated Parmesan
  cheese
½ teaspoon oregano

Dash pepper
½ cup vegetable oil
1 clove garlic, mashed
  (optional)
4 eggs, slightly beaten
3 cups zucchini, thinly sliced
  (about 4 zucchini)

Combine all ingredients, adding zucchini last after the other ingredients are thoroughly mixed. Spread in a greased 8-inch square pan. Bake at 350° for 35 to 40 minutes until brown. Cut into small squares for appetizers or large ones for a side dish.

SALMON MOUSSE

Yield: 6 cups

1 (10¾-ounce) can tomato
  soup, undiluted
1 (8-ounce) package cream
  cheese
1 tablespoon onion juice
1 tablespoon butter
1 envelope unflavored
  gelatin
¼ cup cold water

½ cup mayonnaise
½ cup whipped cream
½ cup chopped olives
Salt, to taste
1 tablespoon Worcestershire
  sauce
1 cup chopped green pepper
½ cup chopped celery
1 (15½-ounce) can salmon

Heat soup in double boiler. Add cheese, onion juice and butter. While cheese is heating, mix gelatin in cold water. When heated and mixture is smooth, add gelatin and cool. Add mayonnaise, whipped cream, olives and other ingredients. Turn into wet mold. Refrigerate at least 2 hours. May be frozen.

CRAB MOUSSE

Yield: 3 cups

1 (10¾-ounce) can cream of
  mushroom soup (undiluted)
1 envelope unflavored
  gelatin
3 tablespoons water
2 (6-ounce) cans crabmeat

1 cup mayonnaise
2 (3-ounce) packages cream
  cheese, softened
8 scallions, finely chopped
1 cup celery, finely chopped
Crackers

Heat mushroom soup — don't boil. Dissolve gelatin in water, and stir into soup. Stir in remaining ingredients. Pour into 3-quart mold, and refrigerate overnight or at least 5 hours. Unmold, and serve with crackers.

HOT CRAB APPETIZERS

Yield: 24 appetizers

1 (6-ounce) can crabmeat
6 ounces grated Swiss
 cheese
1 heaping tablespoon
 mayonnaise

Garlic powder, to taste
Cayenne pepper, to taste
Paprika, to taste
3 English muffins, split
 and toasted

Mix all together, and heap mixture on muffins. Broil until cheese melts. Cut each muffin into fourths to serve as appetizers. Serve whole as a luncheon main dish. Goes well with fresh fruit salad.

CRABMEAT AND BACON BALLS

Preheat oven to 375°   Yield: 24 balls

1 pound fresh crabmeat
¼ teaspoon dry mustard
¼ cup dry white sherry wine

⅛ teaspoon salt or less
1 cup dry bread crumbs
12 slices lean bacon

In a large mixing bowl, place crabmeat, dry mustard, wine, salt, and crumbs. Mix well. Form into 24 walnut-sized balls. Wrap each ball with ½ slice of lean bacon, and secure with a wooden toothpick. Place on cookie sheet, and bake at 375° for 15 minutes. Drain off fat, and transfer to a platter. Keep warm in a 200° oven until ready to serve.

Dipping Sauce:
3 tablespoons prepared
 mustard

1 cup mayonnaise

Mix the prepared mustard and mayonnaise together ahead of time, and chill until ready for use.

CRAB-STUFFED MUSHROOMS

Preheat oven to 350°   Yield: 12-16 servings

3 dozen large whole fresh
  mushrooms
1 (6-ounce) can crabmeat,
  drained, rinsed and flaked
1 tablespoon snipped fresh
  parsley

1 tablespoon chopped
  pimento
1 teaspoon chopped capers
¼ teaspoon dry mustard
½ cup mayonnaise

Wash and dry mushrooms. With a sharp knife, remove stems from mushrooms. Combine crabmeat, parsley, pimento and capers. Blend dry mustard into mayonnaise; toss with crab mixture. Fill each mushroom crown with about 2 tablespoons crab mixture. Bake at 350° for 8 to 10 minutes.

CRAB-STUFFED CHERRY TOMATOES

Yield: 36 appetizers

2 (6-ounce) packages frozen
  crabmeat
1 (3-ounce) package cream
  cheese, softened
1 (2-ounce) package Bleu
  cheese, crumbled

2 tablespoons minced green
  onion
18 cherry tomatoes
Parsley for garnish

Drain defrosted crabmeat. Mix well with next three ingredients. Cut tomatoes in half, and scoop out seeds and core. Drain, inverted, about 20 minutes. Stuff each half with crab/cheese mixture. Arrange on platter with parsley garnish.

CRAB STRUDEL

Preheat oven to 350°   Yield: 24 servings

½ cup chopped shallots or
green onions
½ cup butter
1 cup dry vermouth
1 (12-ounce) can crabmeat,
flaked
1 (4-ounce) package cream
cheese, cubed
4 anchovy fillets, finely
chopped (optional)

¼ cup snipped parsley
4 egg yolks
1 teaspoon salt
½ teaspoon pepper
8 frozen fillo strudel leaves,
thawed
Melted butter
1 egg, beaten
Parsley sprigs and lemon
wedges

1. Cook and stir shallots in ½ cup butter in 10-inch skillet until golden, about 3 minutes. Add vermouth; heat to boiling. Boil until liquid is reduced by half, 3 to 5 minutes. Remove from heat.

2. Stir crabmeat, cheese, anchovies, snipped parsley, egg yolks, salt and pepper into shallot mixture until cheese is melted. Cool.

3. Place 1 fillo leaf on kitchen towel; brush with melted butter. Place another leaf on top; brush with butter. Repeat, using 2 more fillo leaves.

4. Mound half the crab mixture lengthwise on fillo leaves, keeping mixture 2 inches from 1 long side. Lift towel, using it to roll leaves over filling jelly roll fashion, starting from long side nearest filling. Roll leaves into cylinder, 2 inches in diameter.

5. Place strudel on buttered jelly roll pan (15½x10½x1-inch). Repeat from step 3 for second strudel. Brush tops of strudel with melted butter, then with beaten egg. Bake 15 minutes. Increase oven temperature to 450°. Bake until strudels are brown and crisp, 5 to 10 minutes.

6. To serve, cut each strudel crosswise into 12 slices, about 1¼ inches wide. Serve warm, garnished with parsley sprigs and lemon wedges.

NOTE: Crab strudels can be made up to 1 week in advance. Cool completely. Wrap securely in plastic wrap, then in aluminum foil; freeze. Bake, uncovered, at 350° until heated through, 10 to 15 minutes.

CRABBIES

Preheat oven to 350°   Yield: 32 appetizers

½ cup margarine
1 (5-ounce) jar sharp cheese
  spread
1½ teaspoons mayonnaise

¼ teaspoon garlic powder
½ teaspoon seasoned salt
1 (6½-ounce) can crabmeat
6 to 8 English muffins, split

Let margarine and cheese soften. Mix together with mayonnaise, garlic powder and seasoned salt. Add crabmeat. Spread on split English muffin. Cut into quarters. Freeze on cookie sheet, and then store in plastic bags. Bake at 350° for 15 to 20 minutes or until lightly browned. Serve hot.

CRAB OR SHRIMP BREAD

Preheat oven to 350°   Yield: 20 appetizers

1 (6½-ounce) can white
  crabmeat, drained or
1 (4¼-ounce) can shrimp,
  drained
½ to 1 cup mayonnaise, to
  taste
½ teaspoon lemon juice

1 tablespoon grated onion
½ cup grated cheddar cheese
1 teaspoon Worcestershire
  sauce
1 loaf party pumpernickel
  bread

Combine the above ingredients, and spread on the slices of pumpernickel bread. Bake at 350° for 10 to 15 minutes or until cheese melts.

CRAB CURRY

Preheat oven to 300°   Yield: 6 cups

2 (8-ounce) packages cream
  cheese
1 (10¾-ounce) can cream of
  celery soup, undiluted
1 (3.5-ounce) can ripe olives,
  pitted
2 (6-ounce) cans white
  crabmeat, drained

1 to 1½ teaspoons curry
  powder
Dash Tabasco sauce
1 tablespoon lemon juice
French bread

Cut cream cheese in chunks, and mix with remaining ingredients in food processor or blender. Blend well. Place in 1½-quart ovenproof dish. Heat at 300° until cheese is melted and mixture can be thoroughly blended, about 20 minutes. Serve warm with chunks of French Bread.

CRAB SPREAD

Yield: 2 cups

1 (8-ounce) package cream
  cheese
Garlic salt, to taste
¾ cup chili sauce

1 (6½-ounce) can crabmeat,
  drained
½ pint chopped chives
Crackers

Layer first five ingredients on serving platter in order given. Serve with your favorite thin crackers. Chill well.

CRAB (FIX YOUR OWN) CANAPÉ

Yield: 2½cups

1 (8-ounce) package cream
  cheese
2 tablespoons horseradish
1 (6-ounce) bottle seafood
  cocktail sauce

1 (6½-ounce) can lump
  crabmeat, membrane or
  shell fragments removed
Crackers

Spread cream cheese on a platter about ⅜ inch thick, leaving room around the platter on all sides for crackers to be overlapped. Spread horseradish on cream cheese, then gently pour cocktail sauce over this. Sprinkle crabmeat on top. Lay crackers around edge of mixture. Serve with small spatula or cheese knife.

CRAB ALMOND DIP

Preheat oven to 350°   Yield: 2 cups

1 (6-ounce) can crabmeat
1 (8-ounce) package cream
  cheese
1 tablespoon milk
2 teaspoons Worcestershire
  sauce

2 tablespoons chopped green
  onion
¼ cup slivered almonds,
  toasted
Crackers or potato chips

Drain and flake crabmeat. Mix together cheese, milk and Worcestershire. Add green onion and crabmeat. Place in bake-and-serve dish, and bake at 350° for 15 to 20 minutes or until bubbly. Garnish with toasted almonds. Serve with crackers or potato chips.

SHRIMP SPREAD

Yield: 1½ cups

2 (3-ounce) packages cream
  cheese, softened
½ cup sour cream
¼ teaspoon garlic salt
1 cup shrimp, cooked and
  chopped

1 teaspoon chutney
1 rounded teaspoon curry
  powder
Crackers

Blend first 6 ingredients together. Chill, and serve on crackers.

SHRIMP DIP

Preheat oven to 350°   Yield: 4 cups

1 (8-ounce) package cream
  cheese
2 tablespoons chopped onion
1 teaspoon horseradish
2 to 6 tablespoons milk
1 pound shrimp, cooked and
  diced

Salt, to taste
1½ ounces toasted slivered
  almonds
Crackers

Let cream cheese soften to room temperature. Add onions and horseradish; mix. Add milk until desired consistency. Fold shrimp into the cream cheese. Salt to taste. Top with toasted almonds. Bake at 350° for 20 to 30 minutes. Serve with crackers.

SHRIMP MOUSSE

Yield: 12 servings

1 (10¾-ounce) can mushroom soup, undiluted
1 cup mayonnaise
2 (3-ounce) packages cream cheese
1 medium onion, grated
1 cup thinly sliced celery
2 envelopes unflavored gelatin, combined with ¼ cup water

3 (4-ounce) cans shrimp, drained, rinsed and mashed
1 tablespoon Worcestershire sauce
2 teaspoons salt
Crackers

In a double boiler, heat and beat the soup, mayonnaise and cream cheese until smooth. Add grated onion and celery. Cook until tender, but still green. Add remaining ingredients. Place in greased gelatin mold. Chill until set. Unmold on serving platter, and serve with crackers.

DILLY SHRIMP DIP

Yield: 2 cups

1 (8-ounce) package cream cheese
3 green onions, chopped
2 tablespoons mayonnaise
2 tablespoons sour cream
1 heaping teaspoon dill weed

Salt and pepper, to taste
A few drops Tabasco sauce
1 cup coarsely chopped cooked shrimp
Crackers or corn chips

Mix first eight ingredients together, adding shrimp last. Chill several hours. Serve with crackers or corn chips.

NOTE: Also makes great tea sandwiches.

TUNA MOUSSE COCKTAIL SPREAD

Yield: 2 quarts

1 (10¾-ounce) can zesty
tomato soup
2 (3-ounce) packages cream
cheese
2 envelopes unflavored
gelatin
¼ cup boiling water
1 cup mayonnaise
Juice of 1 lemon
1 teaspoon Worcestershire
sauce

⅛ teaspoon Tabasco sauce
⅛ teaspoon black pepper
⅛ teaspoon paprika
2 (6½-ounce) cans tuna,
flaked fine
¾ cup finely chopped onion
2 sticks celery, finely
chopped
Curly lettuce leaves

Grease a 2-quart mold (fish-shaped, if available) with mayonnaise. Melt cream cheese and soup over low heat. Dissolve gelatin in ¼ cup boiling water. Blend soup and cheese mixture with gelatin, mayonnaise, lemon juice and seasonings. Add tuna, onions and celery. Mix thoroughly. Place in mold and refrigerate. Unmold on lettuce greens.

CEVICHE

Yield: 16 servings

1 pound fish fillet (firm fish
such as grouper)
1 cup fresh lime juice
¼ cup chopped onion
2 fresh tomatoes, peeled and
chopped

1 (4-ounce) can green chilies
1 teaspoon salt
1 tablespoon coriander

Cut raw fish into 1-inch squares. Pour lime juice over it, and marinate at least 4 hours or overnight. Drain fish; don't rinse. Mix with onion, tomato, chopped green chilies and seasonings. Top with more lime juice.

CONCH FRITTERS

Yield: 72 fritters

2 packages yeast
2 cups warm milk
4 conch, skinned and
　cleaned
4 medium onions
2 large green peppers
2½ cups flour
2 eggs

2 teaspoons dried thyme
1 cup fresh parsley
½ teaspoon red pepper flakes
½ teaspoon cayenne pepper
2 teaspoons salt
1 teaspoon fresh ground
　pepper
Vegetable oil for frying

Dissolve yeast in warm milk (105 to 115°). Chop conch, onions and green peppers into 1-inch pieces. Place conch in workbowl of food processor fitted with steel blade. Process for 10 seconds. Add onions, green pepper, milk/yeast mixture, flour, eggs, thyme, parsley, red pepper flakes, cayenne, salt and freshly ground pepper to workbowl. Process for 1 minute, stopping when necessary to scrape down sides of bowl. Mixture should be well combined, without large lumps, and of uniform texture. If necessary, process for a longer period of time, but do not over process. Cover batter, and allow to rest for 1 hour. Drop the batter by teaspoonfuls into 2 inches of very hot oil. Deep fry for 3 to 5 minutes or until very brown. Keep warm, uncovered, in the oven. Serve the fritters with tartar sauce or red cocktail sauce.

NOTE: The conch (pronounced "konk") lives on the sea floor near the coast, often near coral reefs. It is native to tropical waters of the western North Atlantic, from the equator north to the Florida Keys. If you are not in a geological position to pluck your fresh conch from the sea, you can buy the meat fresh from a good seafood market. The conch fritter batter can be made several days in advance and fried when needed. Conch fritters can be fried several hours in advance and reheated.

CONCH FRITTERS II

Yield: 24 fritters

1 cup sifted all purpose flour
3 teaspoons baking powder
½ teaspoon salt
4 conch (enough to make 1
  cup ground)
¼ teaspoon pepper
Few drops Tabasco sauce
1 egg

½ cup milk
1 teaspoon lime juice
1 small grated onion
3 cloves garlic, finely
  chopped
½ green pepper, finely
  chopped

Sift together flour, baking powder and salt. Add remaining ingredients. Heat oil in deep fryer. Drop batter by tablespoons, and fry until golden on both sides, turning once.

SMOKED OYSTER DIP

Yield: 1⅔ cups

1 (8-ounce) package cream
  cheese, softened
1 teaspoon grated onion
1 tablespoon chopped
  parsley
2 tablespoons white dry
  sherry
2 tablespoons milk

1 (3.6 ounce) can smoked
  oysters, drained and
  chopped
¼ teaspoon salt
Pepper, to taste
Specialty crackers or
  saltines

Combine cream cheese, onion, parsley and sherry. Stir in oysters, salt and pepper. Chill. Serve with crackers.

INFLATION FIGHTER'S CAVIAR MOLD

Yield: 2½ cups

1 cup mayonnaise
½ cup sour cream
5 eggs, hard cooked and
   grated (reserve 1
   tablespoon for garnish)
3 tablespoons finely minced
   onion
1½ tablespoons
   Worcestershire sauce

2 tablespoons lemon juice
⅛ teaspoon cayenne pepper
1 (4-ounce) jar black
   Icelandic lumpfish caviar
   (reserve 1 tablespoon)
1 envelope unflavored
   gelatin
¼ cup cold water

Combine mayonnaise, sour cream, eggs and seasonings. Gently fold in caviar. Sprinkle gelatin on cold water in sauce pan. Heat to dissolve. Cool slightly, and then fold into caviar mixture thoroughly. Pour into lightly oiled 3½-cup mold. Chill at least 4 hours. Unmold, and garnish top with reserved caviar and grated egg.

CAVIAR PIE

Yield: 1 caviar pie

8 hard-cooked eggs
¼ cup finely chopped onions
1 stick melted butter or
   margarine

1½ pints sour cream
8 ounces caviar (black)
1 (9-inch) glass pie plate
Specialty crackers

Chop hard-cooked eggs well. Mix with onions and melted butter. Press into pie plate. Frost egg mixture with heavy coat of sour cream. Put in refrigerator to chill. Just before serving, spread or dot caviar on top. Serve immediately with specialty crackers.

SALMON BALL

Yield: 3½ cups

1 (8-ounce) package cream
  cheese
2 tablespoons lemon juice
3 teaspoons grated onion
2 teaspoons horseradish
½ teaspoon salt
⅛ teaspoon Worcestershire
  sauce

Cayenne pepper, to taste
¼ teaspoon liquid smoke
1 (1-pound) can red salmon
½ cup chopped pecans
  (optional)
3 tablespoons minced
  fresh parsley

In a small bowl, using an electric mixer, blend together cream cheese, lemon juice, onion, horseradish and salt. Add Worcestershire, cayenne and liquid smoke. When well blended, stir in flaked salmon. Check seasonings — may need more salt. Combine pecans and parsley, and spread on sheet of waxed paper. Turn salmon mixture several times on wax paper until sides are coated. Wrap in wax paper, and chill thoroughly.

PATÉ OF SMOKED SALMON
WITH CHIVES AND DILL

Yield: 3 cups

2 (8-ounce) packages cream
  cheese
⅓ cup sour cream
¼ pound smoked salmon, cut
  into 1-inch pieces
1 or 2 tablespoons lemon
  juice

⅛ cup chopped chives or 1
  tablespoon dried chives
¼ teaspoon dried dill weed
Fresh parsley
Cherry tomatoes
Lemon slices
French bread or crackers

In a mixer or food processor, beat cream cheese and sour cream until light and fluffy. Add salmon and lemon juice, and beat until salmon is nicely blended. DO NOT purée the salmon, but leave mixture flaked. Beat in chives and dill weed.

Lay a piece of plastic wrap (twice the length of the mold) into a 1-quart mold (one without a hole in the center). Place salmon in lined mold, and press it down to conform to the shape of the design. Cover mold with the overlapping plastic wrap, and refrigerate until serving time.

To serve, remove overlapping plastic wrap, and invert mold on a serving platter. Carefully peel off the plastic wrap. Decorate with fresh parsley, cherry tomatoes and lemon slices. Serve with French bread or crackers.

NOTE: May be prepared the day before serving and stored in the refrigerator. Do not freeze.

DEVILED HAM BALL

Yield: 1¼ cups

1 (5-ounce) can deviled ham, chilled
1 tablespoon minced onion
1 (3-ounce) package cream cheese, softened

2 to 3 teaspoons sour cream
1½ teaspoons brown mustard
Crackers

Combine chilled ham with onion. Roll into a ball. Combine cream cheese, sour cream and mustard. Frost the ham ball with mixture. Chill. Serve with crackers.

CHICKEN POLYNESIAN WITH CHUTNEY DIP

Yield: 48 appetizers

1 pound boneless skinned chicken breast
½ cup all purpose flour
3 eggs, beaten
2 cups grated coconut

1½ cups mango chutney, undrained
½ cup butter
Vegetable oil
Parsley sprigs

Cut chicken into ¾-inch cubes; dust lightly with flour. Dip cubes into beaten eggs; roll in coconut until lightly coated. Place on waxed paper-lined baking sheet. (Recipe can be prepared to this point up to 24 hours in advance. Cover securely with plastic wrap and refrigerate.) Heat chutney and butter in small sauce pan over low heat, stirring occasionally, until hot. Keep warm.

Heat oil (3 to 4 inches) in heavy pan to 375°. Fry chicken cubes, a few at a time, until golden, about 1 minute on each side. Drain on paper toweling. Garnish with parsley sprigs. Serve warm with wooden picks and chutney dip on the side.

GOLDEN CHICKEN NUGGETS

Preheat oven to 400°   Yield: 60 pieces

4 whole chicken breasts,
  boned
½ cup dry bread crumbs
¼ cup grated Parmesan
  cheese
½ to ¾ teaspoon salt

1 teaspoon dried leaf thyme
  (¼ teaspoon powdered)
1 teaspoon dried dill
½ cup margarine or butter,
  melted

Cut chicken breasts into approximately 1½-inch cubes. Combine crumbs, cheese, salt and herbs. Dip chicken nuggets in melted butter, then in crumb mixture. Place on foil-lined baking sheets. Bake at 400° for 10 minutes.

CHOPPED CHICKEN LIVER

Yield: 2 cups

1 pound chicken livers
3 tablespoons margarine
1 medium white onion,
  minced
5 hard-cooked eggs,
  separated

1 teaspoon salt
½ teaspoon pepper
4 tablespoons chicken fat,
  melted

Sauté livers in margarine for 6 to 8 minutes. DO NOT BROWN. Combine minced onion and 3 hard-cooked, minced, egg whites. Add salt, pepper, livers and all 5 egg yolks to wooden chopping bowl. Hand chop thoroughly. Add chicken fat gradually until desired spreading consistency is reached. Place in airtight container, and refrigerate until ready to use.

CHICKEN LIVER PATÉ

Yield: 3 cups

3 medium onions, chopped
3 cloves garlic, minced
½ cup butter
1 pound fresh chicken livers
¼ cup butter
1 tablespoon flour
¼ teaspoon tarragon
¼ teaspoon oregano

1 bay leaf
1 teaspoon salt
½ teaspoon pepper
¼ teaspoon thyme
4 tablespoons brandy
Crackers or thin rye bread

Sauté onions and garlic in the ½ cup butter until tender. Remove from skillet. Sauté livers in the ¼ cup butter until almost tender. Sprinkle with flour and spices. Cover, and simmer for 3 minutes or until livers are cooked. Remove bay leaf. Combine with onions and garlic. Using about ¼ of the mixture at a time, purée in blender. Add 1 tablespoon brandy each time. Refrigerate in airtight containers. Freezes beautifully but must be well wrapped. Serve with crackers or thin rye bread.

CHICKEN DRUMMETTES

Yield: About 48

3 pounds chicken wings
½ cup brown sugar
1 teaspoon dry mustard
1 cup soy sauce

1 cup sherry
⅓ cup Worcestershire
   sauce

Remove tips from wings, and cut in half at joints. Combine, and heat in a sauce pan the sugar, mustard, soy sauce, sherry and Worcestershire sauce. Place drummettes in a large (10x13x2-inch) baking pan. Pour heated mixture over drummettes. Bake at 325° for 2 to 2½ hours, turning drummettes 3 times during baking.

NOTE: These can be made ahead of time and frozen. (Be sure to freeze sauce with them, and just reheat when ready to use.)

CHICKEN TEA SANDWICHES

Yield: 2 dozen

½ cup finely chopped cooked chicken
¼ cup chopped walnuts
2 tablespoons finely chopped water chestnuts
1 tablespoon mayonnaise
1 teaspoon soy sauce

1½ teaspoons chopped green onion
1 to 2 tablespoons sour cream
1 loaf party Pumpernickel bread, sliced

Combine first 7 ingredients, using enough sour cream to make desired spreading consistency. Spread on bread. Cover, and chill until ready to serve.

CHUTNEY FINGERS

Yield: 48 appetizers

16 slices white bread
½ cup (1 stick) margarine or butter
1 tablespoon Dijon mustard
16 slices Muenster or Monterrey Jack cheese

2 (10-ounce) bottles mango chutney
1 pound bacon, fried crispy, well drained and crumbled

Remove crusts from bread. Cut each bread slice into 3 pieces lengthwise. Combine butter and mustard. Spread bread with mustard mixture. Slice cheese into same size as fingers. Save odd pieces. Place cheese slices on top of bread. Blend chutney so that it is a fairly even consistency. There will be some chunks of fruit. Combine chutney with bacon. Top cheese with pureed chutney and bacon mixture. Sprinkle with grated leftover cheese. (Can be made to this point a day ahead.) Brown under broiler until cheese is melted.

HOT JEZEBEL

Yield: 16 servings

1 cup pineapple preserves
1 cup apricot preserves
¼ cup horseradish, drained
1 teaspoon fresh ground
   black pepper

3 teaspoons dry mustard
1 (8-ounce) package cream
   cheese
Crackers

Mix preserves, horseradish, black pepper and mustard. Place in jar, and refrigerate. Can be kept one month.

To serve, pour over block of cream cheese. Serve with crackers.

BOURBON FRANKS

Yield: 3 cups

¾ cup bourbon or rum
1 cup ketchup
½ teaspoon crushed oregano
   or rosemary

½ cup brown sugar
1 teaspoon grated onion
1 pound frankfurters, cut in
   bite-size pieces

Mix together first 5 ingredients in a sauce pan. Simmer one hour, then add franks and cook over low heat for 15 minutes. Serve in chafing dish with toothpicks. May be reheated next day.

HORS D'OEUVRE SPREAD

Yield: 20-24 servings

½ cup bacon bits or 1 pound
   bacon, cooked, drained
   well and crumbled
8 ounces grated cheddar
   cheese
1 small bunch green onions,
   chopped

2 to 3 tablespoons
   mayonnaise or enough to
   hold mixture together
   to spread
1 loaf party rye bread, sliced

Combine bacon, cheese, onion and mayonnaise. Spread on rye bread slices. Place on ungreased cookie sheet, and place under broiler until cheese bubbles. Serve hot.

PARTY TAPATIA

Yield: 10-12 servings

1 (16-ounce) can refried
beans
2 mashed avocados
½ teaspoon chili powder
½ teaspoon cumin
1 tablespoon lemon juice
1 cup sour cream

1 (4-ounce) can green chilies,
chopped
1 medium onion, chopped
1 tomato, chopped
½ cup chopped black olives
1 cup grated cheddar cheese
Corn chips

Spread refried beans in a 10-inch pie plate. Mix mashed avocados with chili powder, cumin and lemon juice. Spread mixture over beans. Layer next with sour cream, followed by green chilies and onion, then tomato. Add chopped olives and grated cheese. Serve with corn chips.

CHILI CON QUESO

Yield: 12 servings

4 (4-ounce) cans whole green
chilies
1 medium onion, chopped
2 cloves garlic, minced
2 tablespoons cooking oil

1 (20-ounce) can tomatoes
1 pound cheddar cheese
1 pound Monterrey Jack
cheese
Tostados

Drain chilies, and reserve liquid. Sauté onion and garlic in oil until transparent. Slice chilies into narrow strips; add to onion and garlic, and simmer for 10 minutes. Mash tomatoes, and add juice and reserved juice from green chilies. Simmer for ½ hour.

Melt cheeses in a double boiler, and when melted, add chili/tomato mixture gradually, stirring until smooth. Serve warm with tostados.

NOTE: Freezes well.

LATINO SPREAD

Yield: 8 servings

½ pound ground beef
¼ cup chopped onion
¼ cup extra hot ketchup
1½ teaspoons chili powder
½ teaspoon salt
1 (15-ounce) can red kidney
   beans, drained

¼ cup chopped green olives
¼ cup chopped green onions,
   tops too
½ cup shredded cheddar
   cheese
Corn chips

Brown meat and onion in skillet. Drain off fat. Stir in ketchup, chili powder and salt. Mash beans, and add to meat mixture. Stir and heat through. Place in pie plate. Garnish with chopped olives and onions in center. Place cheddar cheese around edge of plate. Serve with corn chips.

NORWEGIAN STUFFED CUCUMBERS

Yield: 24-36 pieces

6 small cucumbers
12 anchovies
1 tablespoon chopped fresh
   dill
2 (3-ounce) packages cream
   cheese

Sour cream
Salt and pepper, to taste
Caviar
Lemon wedges and fresh
   parsley sprigs for garnish

Scrape 6 small, unpeeled, cucumbers lengthwise with fork tines to make long grooves. Cut into 1-inch sections, and hollow out seeds in center, leaving firm cucumber rings. Mash 12 anchovies, and mix well with 1 tablespoon chopped fresh dill and cream cheese softened with 2 tablespoons sour cream. Season to taste with salt and freshly ground pepper. Fill cucumber rings, and chill in refrigerator for several hours.

Serve with 1 teaspoon sour cream on top of each stuffed cucumber ring. Top with a little caviar. Serve chilled the same day as prepared. Garnish platter with lemon wedges and fresh parsley.

PICKLED MUSHROOMS

Yield: 1 quart

1 pound fresh mushrooms, cleaned	White vinegar Hot water

Place mushrooms in a sauce pan, and cover with equal amounts of white vinegar and hot water. Boil for 5 minutes. Drain. Pack hot mushrooms in a jar, and cover with the following:

¼ cup olive oil	2 cloves garlic, minced
2 teaspoons salt	1 teaspoon mace
2 teaspoons peppercorns	White vinegar to cover

Cover, and shake to mix well. Store in refrigerator for 2 days before serving.

NOTE: May be used as an hors d'oeuvre on toothpicks; in salads or as part of an Italian antipasto. Save the vinegar mixture for making salad dressings. Canned mushrooms may be used — they need no preliminary cooking, but drain them before adding oil and vinegar mixture.

SEASONED SNACK CRACKERS

Preheat oven to 300°

Yield: 1 quart

1 (31-ounce) box plain tiny fish-shaped crackers	1 (0.07-ounce) package ranch dressing mix, dry
⅓ cup vegetable oil	1½ teaspoons dill weed

Pour oil over crackers in a large mixing bowl. Mix to coat well. Combine dressing mix and dill weed together, and sprinkle over oiled crackers. Stir thoroughly. Place crackers on a 10x15-inch jelly roll pan, and bake at 300° for 20 minutes. Stir occasionally. When cooled, store in sealed plastic container or bags.

Beverages

QUEEN PALM

Hints for Beverages

To prevent glassware from cracking, hot liquids should be poured over a spoon placed in the container.

To prevent ice tea from clouding when refrigerated, stir in less than ⅛ teaspoon baking soda into a pitcher full of tea. Also, sun tea never clouds.

Store tea in an airtight container, and it will keep approximately one year.

The best way to store ground coffee is in the refrigerator. Keep the can upside down so the aroma rises and will not be lost so fast when turned right side up. Store coffee beans in the freezer.

Always start coffee with fresh cold water.

When heating liquids in your microwave, always stir them first. If you do not, they may erupt. Allow room for thicker liquids to expand when microwaving.

One 13-ounce can of all-method grind coffee makes 60 cups of coffee.

To defrost frozen juice, put the juice in a container and microwave 40 seconds, then just add water.

Five quarts of punch will serve 20 people, giving each person two four-ounce drinks.

Punch juices should be allowed to blend for an hour before serving to mix all the flavors. Add carbonated drinks to the punch just before serving.

Use large pieces of ice in punch bowls; they melt slower. You can use muffin tins, juice cans or an ice mold to freeze ice.

To prevent dilution, freeze some of the punch and use it instead of ice.

Champagne served in a tulip-shaped glass will not lose its bubbles as fast because of the narrow rim. Always chill the glasses before serving; it keeps the champagne more bubbly.

A wine glass should be filled half way to allow the aroma to be released.

At dinner, wine is served after the first course has been served. Any other wines are served upon completion of the previous course.

A wine bottle with a cork should be stored on its side to keep the cork moist.

To stock a bar for a party:
    A fifth will serve seventeen 1½-ounce drinks.
    A liter will serve twenty-one 1½-ounce drinks.
    A standard bottle of wine will serve four.
    Allow two drinks per person for a two-hour cocktail party.

Beer should never be served in a dry glass. Run cold water over the glass before pouring the beer. Glasses, when washed, should be allowed to drip dry. Any grease on a beer glass will kill the foam.

FLORIDA SUMMER PUNCH

Yield: 12-14 servings

1 (12-ounce) can frozen
  orange juice concentrate
3 orange juice cans water
1 (6-ounce) can frozen
  limeade
4 limeade cans water
1 quart cranberry juice

2 cups apple juice
1 (10-ounce) package frozen
  strawberries
1 (20-ounce) can pineapple
  tidbits, in its own juice
1 decorative ice ring
  (optional)

Mix above ingredients in order given, except ice ring. Pour into punch bowl and float the decorative ice ring.

ICED TEA DRINK

Yield: 8-10 servings

4 teaspoons instant tea
  (powder)
1 quart water

1 (6-ounce) can frozen
  lemonade, undiluted
1 quart ginger ale

Combine the above ingredients, and serve over ice.

CALYPSO CUP

Yield: 1 gallon

1 (12-ounce) can mango juice
1 (46-ounce) can pineapple
  juice
1 (12-ounce) can apricot
  nectar
1 (12-ounce) can frozen
  orange juice concentrate
36 ounces water

2 tablespoons grenadine
  syrup
2 dashes bitters
Juice of 2 limes
Juice of 4 oranges

Combine all of the above ingredients; chill and serve over ice.

NOTE: 2 (10-ounce) bottles ginger ale may be added to above, or 1 ounce rum may be added to each glass.

WINDSURFER'S PASSION FRUIT QUENCHER

Yield: 1¾ gallons

1 (46-ounce) can
  unsweetened pineapple
  juice
1 (12-ounce) can frozen
  orange juice concentrate

4 (12-ounce) juice cans water
1 (46-ounce) jar passion fruit
  and guava juice cocktail

Chill all of the above ingredients, and mix in very large mixing bowl. Serve over ice.

POOL-PARTY MINT TEA PUNCH
(A teen crowd refresher!)

Yield: 20 (5-ounce) servings

8 cups boiling water
2 large handfuls fresh mint
½ cup loose tea or 8
  regular tea bags
2 cups sugar

1 cup lemon juice
1 (46-ounce) can
  unsweetened pineapple
  juice

Pour boiling water over mint and tea and steep for 30 minutes. Strain and add sugar; stir and cool. Add juices just before serving. Serve over ice in glass garnished with a sprig of fresh mint.

JUICY GINGER ALE PUNCH

Yield: 12 servings

1 (6-ounce) can frozen
  orange juice
1 (6-ounce) can frozen
  lemonade
1 (6-ounce) can frozen
  limeade

4 cups cold water
1 quart ginger ale
1 ice block

Combine all ingredients, except ginger ale. Pour into punch bowl. Add ginger ale and ice block just before serving.

NOTE: May be easily doubled or tripled.

CHRISTMAS PUNCH

Yield: 60-70 servings

4 cups sugar
4 cups water
2 cups strong black tea (3
heaping tablespoons
instant tea to 2 cups
boiling water)
6 (6-ounce) cans frozen
lemonade, undiluted
2 (6-ounce) cans frozen
orange juice, undiluted

5 cups pineapple juice
2 cups fresh strawberries,
cut up or 1 (16-ounce)
package frozen
strawberries, thawed
1 gallon water
2 quarts chilled ginger ale

Combine all of the above ingredients, except ginger ale. Pour into punch bowl, adding chilled ginger ale just before serving.

MIMI'S COFFEE PUNCH

Yield: 40 servings

8 tablespoons instant coffee
granules
2 cups sugar
3 quarts hot water
2 quarts milk

1 tablespoon vanilla
1 (3.5-ounce) can chocolate
syrup
1 gallon vanilla ice cream

Combine instant coffee, sugar and hot water; mix well and cool; add milk, vanilla and chocolate syrup. Refrigerate overnight. Thirty minutes before serving, pour punch mixture into a punch bowl; cut the ice cream into chunks and place in punch bowl.

NOTE: Can be reduced by half successfully.

ELEGANT COFFEE PUNCH

Yield: 35 servings

½ gallon fresh brewed coffee
½ cup sugar
2 quarts Coffee Rich
½ gallon vanilla ice cream
  with vanilla beans

2 cups whipping cream
Nutmeg

Make coffee and add sugar; cool and refrigerate overnight. Next day, pour coffee into punch bowl; stir in half and half. Float the ice cream on top in one piece. Whip cream, and add, in mounds, around the edge of the ice cream. Sprinkle with nutmeg.

NOTE: Great to serve at showers, church socials, luncheons and other special occasions.

LIME SHERBET PUNCH

Yield: 27 (½-cup) servings

1 quart lime sherbet,
  softened
2 (6-ounce) cans frozen lime
  juice concentrate

4 cups water
1 (32-ounce) bottle ginger ale

Combine first three ingredients; add ginger ale just before serving. Serve in punch bowl.

NOTE: Use distilled water in gelatin mold to assure crystal clear ice ring. Fresh lime slices and mint leaves added to water make a pretty presentation in the ice ring.

FROZEN BANANA FRUIT PUNCH

Yield: 50 servings

2 cups sugar
4 cups water
2 quarts pineapple juice
1 (12-ounce) can frozen
   orange juice, mixed

1 (12-ounce) can frozen
   lemonade, mixed
5 large sized bananas,
   puréed
2 quarts gingerale

Combine sugar and water; bring to boil and stir until sugar dissolves. Cool. Combine with remaining ingredients except ginger ale. Freeze. Before serving, remove from freezer, thaw slightly and add ginger ale. Stir and serve.

ORANGE COW

Yield: 4 servings

1 (6-ounce) can frozen orange
   juice concentrate
1 cup milk
1 cup water

½ cup sugar
1 teaspoon vanilla
10 to 12 ice cubes

Combine all ingredients in blender. Cover and blend until smooth, about 1 minute. Serve immediately.

TOMATO JUICE COCKTAIL

Yield: 8 servings

1 (46-ounce) can tomato juice
Juice of ½ lemon
2 teaspoons sugar

1 teaspoon horseradish
½ teaspoon salt

Combine all ingredients. Chill and serve.

NOTE: A great weekend "waker-upper."

BLOODY MARYS FOR A CROWD

Yield: 15 servings

1 (32-ounce) bottle vodka
2 (46-ounce) cans tomato
  juice, chilled
10 teaspoons Worcestershire
  sauce

2 tablespoons lemon juice
1 tablespoon sugar
Salt, celery salt and Tabasco
  sauce, to taste

Combine first five ingredients; stir and mix well. Pour into individual glasses and sprinkle each with salt, celery salt and two or three drops Tabasco sauce before serving.

YELLOW BIRDS

Yield: 12 servings

1 pint rum
1 pint crème de banana

1½ quarts orange juice
1½ quarts pineapple juice

Combine all of the above ingredients and serve over ice.

MIAMI "VISE"

Yield: 6 servings

1 quart vanilla ice cream,
  softened
1½ ounces crème de cacao

1½ ounces crème de banana
1½ ounces white crème de
  menthe

Combine all ingredients in a blender; blend well. Serve in wine or champagne glasses. This is an after-dinner drink.

CHAMPAGNE PUNCH

Yield: 50 (½ cup) servings

3 (12-ounce) cans frozen
orange juice, undiluted
1½ cups light corn syrup
½ cup lime juice

5 quarts champagne or 3
quarts champagne and 2
(24-ounce) bottles ginger
ale

Combine in order given; stir to mix well and serve in punch bowl. Add champagne and ginger ale when serving.

CHAMPAGNE-BRANDY PUNCH

Yield: 60 (½ cup) servings

4 quarts champagne
1 fifth (750 milliliters)
brandy
1 quart orange juice
1 quart pineapple juice

1 quart club soda
1 quart ginger ale
1 lime, sliced
Orange or pineapple slices
Ice ring

Chill all ingredients. Combine first 3 ingredients; pour into punch bowl and add ice ring. Float orange and lime slices on top. Add soda and ginger ale when ready to serve.

FROSTY SOURS

Yield: 6 servings

⅓ cup bourbon
1 (6-ounce) can frozen
lemonade concentrate,
undiluted

1 tablespoon frozen orange
juice concentrate,
undiluted
Cracked ice

Combine first 3 ingredients in a blender; blend until smooth. Gradually add ice, blending until mixture reaches desired consistency.

IRISH CREAM
(Rich and expensive, but worth it)

Yield: 38 ounces

1¾ cups Irish whiskey
1 (14-ounce) can sweetened
 condensed milk
1 cup whipping cream
4 eggs
2 tablespoons chocolate
 syrup

2 teaspoons instant coffee
 granules
1 teaspoon vanilla
½ teaspoon almond extract

Combine all ingredients in blender; blend well. Divide equally into 2 1-quart containers. Cover and refrigerate. Keeps up to one month.

CRANBERRY EGGNOG

Yield: 12 servings

6 eggs, beaten
2 cups heavy cream, whipped

¾ cup sugar
4 cups cranberry juice

Combine eggs and whipped cream; fold in sugar. Add and stir in cranberry juice. Chill until ready to serve.

FROZEN EGGNOG SUPREME

Yield: 1½ gallons

½ gallon eggnog ice cream
½ liter rum
½ gallon commercial eggnog

1 cup brandy
Freshly ground nutmeg

Soften ice cream in large mixing bowl, and add rum, eggnog and brandy. Pour into punch cups or footed sherbet glasses. Garnish each cup with nutmeg.

GLÖGG

(This 300-year-old recipe is from Sweden)

Yield: 1½ gallons

1 gallon port wine
⅕ (750 milliliters) claret
  wine
⅕ (750 milliliters) brandy
20 cloves
3 whole sticks cinnamon
10 whole cardamom seeds
  (split the peel and remove
  the seeds)

2 whole nutmegs
1 orange peel
1 lemon peel
½ cup sugar
2 cups raisins
1 cup whole blanched
  almonds
Maraschino cherries, for
  garnish

In a large pot, pour in the port and claret wines; place all spices, including the orange and lemon peels, into cheese cloth and tie securely. Add raisins and spice bag to wine, and simmer for ½ hour. Add sugar; remove pot from heat and cool to about 140°. Add brandy. Remove cheese cloth bag and discard. It is now ready to serve, or you may cool further and return mixture to wine bottles. Serve with raisins and almonds.

NOTE: This is a great holiday drink. The aroma fills the house so wonderfully while brewing.

JABBA'S JUICE

Yield: 24 servings

½ gallon Gallo hearty
  burgundy wine
1 (16-ounce) can fruit
  cocktail
1 (12-ounce) can frozen Fruit
  Punch (red)

4 (12-ounce) juice cans of
  water
Juice of two limes
1 (48-ounce) bottle cranberry
  juice cocktail
¼ cup sugar

Combine all of the above ingredients. Chill. Serve over ice.

JIM'S SANGRIA

Yield: 4-6 servings

1 fifth (750 milliliters) red
   wine
1 cup orange juice
1 cup pineapple juice

Juice of 2 limes
¼ cup sugar
4 (1½-ounce) jiggers brandy
1 (10-ounce) bottle club soda

Combine first 6 ingredients together; chill. Just before serving, add the club soda.

MIAMI MOONLIGHT COCKTAIL

Yield: 1¾ gallons

6 cups water
2 cups sugar
1 (48-ounce) can pineapple
   juice
1 (48-ounce) can grapefruit
   juice

1 (8-ounce) jar maraschino
   cherries, undrained
2 cups gin
1 (33.8-ounce) bottle ginger
   ale, chilled

Combine water and sugar in a large saucepan; bring to a boil. Stir until dissolved. Cool.

Combine sugar mixture, juices and cherries; chill. Add gin and ginger ale just before serving.

SHARK'S MILK

Yield: 6 servings

⅔ cup vodka
1 cup cold coffee
1 pint vanilla ice cream

1 cup crushed ice
2 ounces crème de cacao

Combine all ingredients in a blender, and mix until well blended.

NOTE: Very rich but good. Best as a drink before brunch.

TROPICAL FRUIT COOLER

Yield: 8 servings

1 (46-ounce) can Very Berry
 juice
¼ cup sugar
½ cup brandy

1 fifth (750 milliliters)
 chilled champagne
1 orange, sliced in rings
1 ice ring

Mix all ingredients together, except orange slices and ice ring. Float orange slices and ice ring in punch bowl.

NOTE: This recipe can be doubled successfully.

TRINIDAD RUM PUNCH

Yield: 6 servings

12 ounces dark rum
6 ounces fresh lime juice
6 ounces simple syrup

Crushed ice
12 dashes bitters
6 maraschino cherries

Mix rum, lime juice and simple syrup. Pour over crushed ice in 6 highball glasses; add 2 dashes bitters to each drink and garnish with a maraschino cherry.

PEACH BRANDY

Yield: 1 gallon

2 pounds dried peaches   **2 quarts vodka**
2 pounds rock candy

Place all ingredients into a 1 gallon jar. Cover and set in a cool closet or pantry for at least 6 weeks. Strain and bottle.

NOTE: Makes great hostess gifts during the holidays.

EMERALD COOLER

Yield: 1 serving

1 ounce extra dry gin   **Club soda**
½ ounce green Crème de   **Lemon twist**
**   Menthe**
1 ounce sweetened lemon juice

Pour ingredients in order given over ice cubes in a high-ball glass. Stir. Garnish with lemon twist.

Breads

DATE PALM

Hints for Breads

To thaw bread or rolls, wrap in aluminum foil and heat in oven at 325° for 10 minutes or wrap in a paper towel and place in a microwave for 1½ minutes.

Use leftover hotdog buns or halved hamburger buns to serve at dinner. Spread them with butter or a little garlic butter and parsley.

Do not over knead biscuit dough; it will become tough.

Yeast that is bought in packets is dated with an expiration date. Be sure to discard the yeast after that date as the yeast becomes less effective and the bread will not rise.

You can tell if bread dough has risen enough by poking it with your finger. If the dent you make springs back, the dough needs to rise more. It usually takes about two hours in a humid climate.

Bread dough made with baking powder or baking soda should not be beaten. Stir only enough to mix it. Overmixing toughens and may produce large holes in the bread.

Bread will brown better, last longer, and taste fresher if you use potato water or milk instead of plain water.

French bread is great heated on the grill. Just cut it in half, spread with garlic butter, and wrap in heavy duty aluminum foil. Place it on the grill for 10 to 12 minutes.

When using muffin pans, do not grease the unused cups as the grease will burn. Put a small amount of water in the unused cups to prevent the pan from warping and to keep the muffins moist.

Use bread that is going stale for breadcrumbs, croutons, bread pudding or French toast.

After making bread, keep it away from drafts to prevent shrinkage.

Do not overcook cornstarch as it will lose its thickening power.

When using nuts, candied fruit, or dried fruit in batters, first sprinkle flour on them to prevent them from sinking to the bottom of the pan.

Only freeze whole loaves of bread. Single pieces tend to get soggy.

Always use clean baking pans when baking bread. Pans that are burnt and brown absorb more heat and can cause baked goods to overbrown or burn.

Flour should be kept in an airtight container in the refrigerator or freezer. Before using the flour for cooking, allow it to return to room temperature.

If wrapped tightly, bread will last two to three months in the freezer.

Bread is done when it has shrunk from the sides of the pan and sounds hollow when you tap it. Place the bread on a wire rack to cool.

Allow bread sufficient time to cool after baking and before wrapping to prevent it from becoming soggy.

TOASTED FINGERS

Preheat oven to 375°   Yield: 12 servings

2 loaves frozen Pepperidge
  Farm Sandwich Bread
2 jars Old English cheese
  spread
2 sticks butter or margarine
½ teaspoon Tabasco sauce

½ teaspoon onion powder
1 teaspoon Worcestershire
  sauce
1½ teaspoons dill weed
1 teaspoon Beau Monde
  seasoning

Thaw bread and cut crusts off. Combine cheese, butter or margarine, Tabasco, onion powder, Worcestershire, dill weed and Beau Monde. On waxed paper, spread bread slices with mixture, and stack 3 slices. Slice into finger sizes. Spread the mixture over all stacked slices like icing a cake, and freeze. When ready for use, bake at 375° for 12 to 15 minutes.

BUBBLE BREAD

Yield: 12-14 servings

1 cup scalded milk
½ cup shortening
½ cup sugar
1 teaspoon salt
1 package dry yeast
2 eggs, beaten
3½ cups all purpose flour

1 cup sugar
2 teaspoons ground
  cinnamon
1 cup raisins
1 cup finely chopped nuts
½ cup melted butter or
  margarine

Combine milk, shortening, ½ cup sugar and salt. Cool to lukewarm (105° to 115°F). Add yeast, and stir until dissolved. Stir in eggs and flour; mix well. Knead for 10 minutes on lightly floured surface. Place in greased mixing bowl, and turn to grease the top. Cover with clean cloth, and let rise in a warm place (85°F) until doubled in bulk — about 1½ hours.

Combine 1 cup sugar, cinnamon, raisins and nuts. Set aside.

Punch down dough, and roll with hands into 1½-inch balls. Dip in melted butter or margarine, and roll in sugar mixture. Place rolls in staggered rows and layers in well-greased 10-inch tube pan. Sprinkle the additional sugar mixture between each roll while arranging, and pour remaining butter or margarine over top. Let rise approximately 1 hour. Bake at 350° for 45 to 50 minutes.

REFRIGERATOR ROLLS

(Makes great cinnamon pecan rolls also)

Yield: 6 dozen

1 cup boiling water
½ cup sugar
½ cup shortening
1 package active dry yeast

1 cup lukewarm water
2 eggs, well beaten
1½ teaspoons salt
6 cups flour

Pour boiling water over sugar and shortening in very large mixing bowl. Dissolve yeast in lukewarm water in small bowl. When sugar and shortening mixture is lukewarm, add yeast mixture. Stir well. Add beaten eggs and salt. Stir in 6 cups flour, a little at a time, stirring thoroughly, and knead well at least 10 minutes.

Place in greased bowl, and grease top of dough by turning in bowl once. Heat oven to 200° for one minute, and turn off. Cover bowl with towel that has been dipped in hot water. Place in oven, and let rise until double in size. Punch down. Dough can now be placed in refrigerator, covered. Check occasionally, and punch down until it is thoroughly cooled (at which time it will no longer rise). It may be kept up to 10 days and used whenever wanted in that time period. Shape into rolls, and brush with melted butter. Again, place in 200° oven as before to rise. When doubled in size, bake at 350° for 25 to 30 minutes.

NOTE: To make cinnamon pecan rolls: Roll dough into oblong shape approximately ⅛ to ¼ inches thick. Spread with melted butter or margarine, and shake cinnamon over the top. Roll dough lengthwise, and cut into ¾- to 1-inch pieces. In the bottom of an ovenproof pan, pour melted butter, and add enough brown sugar to make a paste. Add chopped pecans; place dough over this and let rise in a warm oven (as above) until double in bulk. Bake at 350° for 35 minutes.

RUN-AROUND JENNY LYNNS

Yield: 5-6 servings

¾ cup flour
1½ cups milk
2 tablespoons sugar

6 eggs
6 tablespoons vegetable oil
⅛ teaspoon salt

Mix above ingredients together. Put large spoonful on hot griddle, and let run around until bottom of pan is covered. (Must be very thin.) Turn over until brown on both sides. Butter and sugar, and roll up. May be eaten with jam or jelly.

PARMESAN PUFF RING

Preheat oven to 400°   Yield: 5-6 servings

½ cup water   2 eggs
¼ cup butter   2 tablespoons grated
⅛ teaspoon salt   Parmesan cheese
½ cup flour

In sauce pan over high heat, add water, butter and salt; until butter melts and mixture boils. Reduce to low heat; add flour, and stir vigorously with wooden spoon until mixture forms a ball and leaves the side of pan. Remove from heat. Add eggs, one at a time, beating hard after each addition. Dough will be shiny. Grease cookie sheet, and arrange 5 rounds of dough in a circle side by side. Sprinkle with Parmesan cheese. Bake at 400° for 35 to 40 minutes. Cool on rack.

POPOVERS

Yield: 12 muffins

2 eggs   1 cup milk
1 cup flour   2 tablespoons melted butter
1 teaspoon salt   or margarine

Mix all ingredients together. Butter the inside of the muffin tins. Stir ingredients again before pouring. Pour muffin tins ⅔ full of batter. Place in cold oven. Bake at 425° for 30 to 35 minutes.

CHEDDAR CHEESE POPOVERS

Preheat oven to 400°   Yield: 6 servings

3 eggs   ¼ teaspoon salt
1¼ cups milk   3 tablespoons melted butter
1¼ cups sifted flour   ¾ cup grated cheddar cheese

Generously butter 6 (6-ounce) custard cups or 6 cups in a popover pan. In a large bowl, beat eggs well. Beat in milk. Add flour and salt, and beat until just smooth. Fill cups halfway with the batter. Top with cheese, dividing it equally among cups. Pour in remaining batter. Bake at 400° for 50 minutes or until puffed and brown. Let cool in pan a minute or two before removing.

HERB DRESSED ITALIAN BREAD

Preheat oven to 350°   Yield: 1 loaf

½ cup soft butter or
  margarine
1 teaspoon parsley flakes
¼ teaspoon oregano
¼ teaspoon dill seed

1 clove garlic, minced
1 tablespoon grated
  Parmesan cheese
1 loaf Italian bread, sliced

Combine first 6 ingredients together. Slice bread, and place on foil sheet. Spread each slice with herb butter mixture. Pull foil up to sides and ends of bread, leaving top exposed. Brush top with mixture. Bake at 350° until hot and browned, about 12 minutes.

CHEESE-CURRY MUFFINS
(Great for a brunch)

Preheat oven to 450°   Yield: 12 muffins

1 cup mayonnaise
1 (8-ounce) can ripe olives or
  mushrooms, chopped
½ cup chopped green onions
2 ounces cheddar cheese,
  grated

½ teaspoon curry powder
Dash of Tabasco sauce
Salt and pepper, to taste
6 whole English Muffins,
  split

Mix all ingredients together, and spread on muffins. Bake on ungreased cookie sheet at 450° for 8 to 10 minutes. May be frozen before baking.

SOUR CREAM MUFFINS

Preheat oven to 350°   Yield: 24 muffins

2 packages dry yeast
½ cup warm water
4⅔ cups flour
½ teaspoon baking soda

2 teaspoons salt
4 tablespoons sugar
2 cups sour cream
2 eggs

In a large mixing bowl, mix yeast and warm water. Add 2⅔ cups of the flour, baking soda, salt, sugar, sour cream and eggs. Mix 30 seconds on low speed of electric mixer, then 2 minutes on high speed. Stir in other 2 cups of flour. Fill greased muffin tins ⅔ full. Let rise 50 minutes. Bake at 350° for 30 minutes or until golden brown. Remove immediately from pan and brush with butter. Serve warm.

CORNY SOUR CREAM MUFFINS

Preheat oven to 375°   Yield: 12 muffins

1 cup self-rising corn meal
1 (8¾-ounce) can cream style
   corn
1 cup sour cream

½ cup vegetable oil
2 eggs
1 teaspoon baking powder

Combine all of the above ingredients. Mix well, and pour into well-greased and hot muffin tins. Bake at 375° for 35 minutes.

MAGIC MUFFINS

Preheat oven to 375°   Yield: About 30 muffins

1 cup boiling water
1 cup 100% bran flakes
1½ cups sugar
1 cup butter or margarine
2 eggs
1½ cups flour

2½ teaspoons baking soda
1 teaspoon salt
2 cups buttermilk
2 cups All-Bran or Bran
   Buds

Pour boiling water over bran flakes; let cool. Cream together sugar and butter or margarine; add eggs. Mix together flour, soda and salt. Add alternately with buttermilk to creamed mixture. Stir in cooled bran mixture, then add All-Bran or Bran Buds. Fill greased muffin tins ½ full. Bake at 375° for 20 minutes.

NOTE: To keep dough in refrigerator to use as needed, place in jars and cover tightly. Will keep 6 weeks.

CHERRY SURPRISES

Preheat oven to 350°   Yield: 48 miniature muffins

1 (10-ounce) jar maraschino
  cherries, well drained
1½ cups finely chopped
  pecans
½ cup brown sugar
¼ cup granulated sugar
½ cup butter

2 egg yolks, beaten
1 teaspoon vanilla
1 cup cake flour
¼ teaspoon baking powder
2 egg whites, beaten stiff
Confectioners sugar

Grease miniature muffin tins, and sprinkle with nuts. Cream butter and sugar together. Add egg yolks and vanilla. Sift dry ingredients together; add to butter mixture. Fold in beaten egg whites. Place 1 teaspoon batter on nuts. Press a cherry in center. Bake at 350° for 15 minutes. Remove from tins and, while warm, sprinkle with confectioners sugar.

NOTE: This recipe may also be made with 1 (20-ounce) can pineapple tidbits, drained, instead of cherries.

CITRUS LIME MUFFINS

Preheat oven to 400°   Yield: 12 muffins

2 cups sifted flour
1 cup sugar
3 teaspoons baking powder
½ teaspoon salt
¼ cup milk

2 eggs, lightly beaten
¼ cup vegetable oil
1 teaspoon grated lime rind
¼ cup lime juice

Sift together flour, sugar, baking powder and salt into a large bowl. Mix milk, eggs, oil, lime rind and lime juice in a 2 cup measure. Add all at once to flour mixture; stir lightly with fork just until moist. Batter will be lumpy. Spoon into 12 greased muffin tins, filling each tin ¾ full. Bake at 400° for 20 minutes or until golden.

MUFFINS A LA TROPICS

Preheat oven to 375°   Yield: 12 muffins

1¾ cups all-purpose flour
2 teaspoons baking powder
¼ teaspoon baking soda
½ cup sugar
½ cup flaked coconut
1 cup mashed ripe bananas

⅓ cup orange juice
1 teaspoon grated orange
  rind
⅓ cup vegetable oil
1 egg, beaten
1 teaspoon vanilla

Combine flour, baking powder, baking soda and sugar in large mixing bowl. Stir in coconut. Combine remaining ingredients together in separate bowl. Add to dry ingredients, and stir until moistened. Spoon into lightly greased muffin tins, filling two-thirds full. Bake at 375° for 25 minutes or until golden brown.

NOTE: Better the second day. Will moisten and flavors will blend more.

ORANGE DONUTS

Yield: 36 donuts

1 orange, unpeeled and cut
  in wedges
2 eggs
½ cup sugar
2 cups flour
2 teaspoons baking powder

½ teaspoon salt
1 teaspoon cinnamon
Vegetable oil for deep frying
Confectioners sugar for
  dusting

Place orange in blender, and liquify. Drop in eggs, and blend until mixed. Mix together ½ cup sugar, flour, baking powder, salt and cinnamon, and add orange-egg mixture. Stir until thoroughly mixed. Heat oil in deep pan, and drop batter by teaspoons into hot oil. Cook until done. Drain donuts on paper towels. Pour confectioners sugar into paper bag, and place drained donuts, a few at a time, into bag, shaking to coat.

OATMEAL RAISIN MUFFINS
(Easy)

Preheat oven to 400°   Yield: 1 dozen

1 cup instant oats   1 cup sifted flour
½ cup raisins   3 teaspoons baking powder
¾ cup milk   1 teaspoon salt
½ cup vegetable oil   ½ teaspoon cinnamon
⅓ cup brown sugar   ¼ teaspoon nutmeg
1 egg, beaten

Combine oats, raisins, milk, oil, brown sugar and egg. Mix thoroughly. Sift together flour, baking powder, salt, cinnamon and nutmeg. Add to oat mixture until moistened. Spoon into greased muffin tins.

Topping:
6 tablespoons flour   1½ teaspoons cinnamon
3 tablespoons brown sugar   3 tablespoons butter

Combine flour, brown sugar and cinnamon. Cut in butter. Sprinkle 1 tablespoon mixture on each muffin. Bake at 400° for 20 minutes.

CARROT-APPLE-RAISIN BREAD

Preheat oven to 350°   Yield: 2 loaves

1¾ cup sugar   1 teaspoon salt
⅓ cup brown sugar   2 teaspoons cinnamon
1½ cups vegetable oil   2 cups grated carrots
3 eggs   2 cups peeled and diced
2 teaspoons vanilla   apples
3 cups flour   ¾ cup raisins
1 teaspoon baking soda   1 cup chopped pecans or
1 teaspoon baking powder   walnuts

In large mixing bowl combine sugars, oil, eggs and vanilla, and mix on medium speed of electric mixer. Sift together dry ingredients and add to mixture ½ cup at a time, beating after each addition. With spoon, gently stir in carrots, apples, raisins and nuts. Divide batter evenly between 2 greased and floured 5x9-inch loaf pans. Bake at 350° or until top of bread springs back when lightly touched.

KEY LIME BREAD

Preheat oven to 350°   Yield: 2 loaves

⅔ cup butter or margarine, melted	3 cups flour
1¾ cups sugar	¾ teaspoon salt
4 eggs	2½ teaspoons baking powder
½ teaspoon vanilla	1 cup milk
2 medium key lime rinds, grated	1 cup chopped nuts

Blend butter and sugar. Add eggs, and stir in vanilla and grated rinds. Combine dry ingredients and add alternately with milk. Fold in chopped nuts. Pour mixture into two 5x9-inch greased loaf pans. Bake at 350° for 50 to 60 minutes.

Glaze:
Juice of 2 medium key limes   ½ cup sugar

Combine key lime juice and sugar. Spoon over hot bread while still in pans. Cool 10 minutes. Remove bread from pans. DO NOT slice for 18 to 20 hours.

APPLESAUCE NUT BREAD

Preheat oven to 350°   Yield: 1 loaf

1 cup sugar	1 teaspoon baking soda
1 cup applesauce	1 teaspoon baking powder
¼ cup vegetable oil	½ teaspoon salt
3 egg whites	½ teaspoon cinnamon
3 tablespoons milk	¼ teaspoon nutmeg
2 cups sifted flour	½ cup chopped pecans

Combine first five ingredients, and mix well. Add remaining ingredients (except nuts), and mix well. Stir in nuts. Bake in greased and floured loaf pan at 350° for 55 to 60 minutes.

TOP BANANA BREAD
(Easy)

Preheat oven to 350°   Yield: 1 loaf

1 stick (¼ pound) margarine
1 cup sugar
2 eggs
3 or 4 large ripe bananas

2 cups all purpose flour
1 teaspoon baking soda
½ teaspoon salt
½ cup chopped pecans

Cream butter, sugar, eggs and mashed bananas. Add sifted flour, soda and salt. Mix in nuts. Bake in a lightly greased loaf pan at 350° for 1 hour.

HONEY-WHEAT BANANA BREAD

Preheat oven to 350°   Yield: 1 loaf

¼ pound margarine or butter
½ cup honey
2 eggs
1½ cups whole wheat flour
½ cup bran

1 teaspoon baking soda
3 tablespoons buttermilk or
   whole milk
1 cup finely mashed bananas

Cream margarine and honey together. Add eggs, and mix well. Add flour and bran. Dissolve soda in milk, and add to flour mixture. Add mashed bananas. Mix well. Place in greased loaf pan, and bake at 350° for 40 to 50 minutes.

BEST EVER MANGO BREAD

Preheat oven to 350°   Yield: 2 loaves

2 cups flour
2 teaspoons cinnamon
2 teaspoons baking soda
½ teaspoon salt
¾ cup sugar
¾ cup dark brown sugar

3 slightly beaten eggs
¾ cup vegetable oil
½ cup raisins
½ cup chopped nuts
2 cups mashed mangoes

Sift, then measure flour. Add cinnamon, soda and salt. Sift dry ingredients together. Make a well in the flour, and add sugars, slightly beaten eggs and oil. Beat until well mixed. Fold in raisins, chopped nuts and mashed mangoes. Bake in 2 regular loaf pans at 350° for 50 minutes to 1 hour.

STRAWBERRY BREAD

Preheat oven to 350°   Yield: 1 large loaf

4 eggs, beaten
2 cups sugar
2 cups frozen, unsweetened,
   strawberries, thawed and
   drained
1¼ cups chopped pecans

½ cup vegetable oil
3 cups flour
1 teaspoon salt
¾ teaspoon baking powder
1 teaspoon cinnamon

Combine eggs, sugar, berries, nuts and oil in a medium bowl. Mix dry ingredients together, and add to egg mixture. Mix well. Pour into greased 9x5x3-inch loaf pan. Bake 1 hour and 15 minutes at 350°. Cool in pan 10 minutes before removing.

PUMPKIN BREAD

Preheat oven to 350°   Yield: 2 loaves

3½ cups flour
2 teaspoons baking soda
1 teaspoon cinnamon
1 teaspoon nutmeg
2 cups canned pumpkin

3 cups sugar
4 eggs
1 cup vegetable oil
⅔ cup water

Sift together first 4 ingredients. Put pumpkin into mixing bowl. Add sugar, then eggs, one at a time, while beating slowly. Add oil and water alternately with dry ingredients into pumpkin mixture.

Pour into greased and floured loaf pans. Bake at 350° for one hour or until tester comes out clean.

ZUCCHINI BREAD

Preheat oven to 350°   Yield: 2 loaves

1½ cups flour
½ teaspoon baking soda
½ teaspoon salt
1½ cups sugar
¾ cup wheat germ

3 eggs
¾ cup vegetable oil
3 cups shredded zucchini
¾ cup raisins (optional)

Sift dry ingredients together. Beat eggs. Add eggs, oil, zucchini and raisins to dry ingredients, mixing well. Pour into greased loaf pans. Bake at 350° for 1 hour.

SPICY PINEAPPLE ZUCCHINI BREAD

Preheat oven to 350°   Yield: 2 loaves

3 eggs, beaten
1 cup vegetable oil
2 cups sugar
2 teaspoons vanilla
2 cups coarsely shredded
   zucchini
1 can (8¼-ounce) crushed
   pineapple, undrained

3 cups all purpose flour
2 teaspoons baking soda
½ teaspoon baking powder
1 teaspoon salt
1½ teaspoons cinnamon
¾ teaspoon nutmeg
1 cup finely chopped walnuts
1 cup chopped white raisins

Place beaten eggs in bowl; add oil and blend. Add sugar and vanilla. Beat until thick and foamy. Add zucchini and pineapple, and stir until blended. Add remaining ingredients, and blend well. Place into 2 greased and floured loaf pans. Bake at 350° for 35 to 40 minutes.

RUTTI-TOOT FRUIT BREAD
(Easy)

Preheat oven to 350°   Yield: 1 loaf

2 cups sifted flour
1½ teaspoons baking powder
½ teaspoon baking soda
1 cup sugar
¼ cup butter
¾ cup orange juice
1 egg

1 tablespoon orange rind,
   grated
1 cup chopped pecans
1 cup raw cranberries
1 cup dried apricots, halved
1 (8-ounce) package cream
   cheese

Combine flour, baking powder, soda and sugar. Melt ¼ cup butter, and mix with orange juice. Add well-beaten egg and grated rind. Stir into sifted dry ingredients. Stir fruit and nuts into batter. Turn into well-greased loaf pan. Bake 1 hour at 350°. Cool, and serve with softened cream cheese.

BEER BREAD
(Quick and easy)

Preheat oven to 350°   Yield: 1 loaf

3 cups self-rising flour   1 teaspoon dill weed
3 tablespoons sugar   (optional)
1 (12-ounce) can beer (not
   light beer)

   Mix all ingredients together, and pour into a greased loaf pan. Bake at 350° for 40 to 45 minutes.

AVOCADO BREAD

Preheat oven to 350°   Yield: 2 loaves

2 cups sugar   1 teaspoon baking soda
3 eggs   1 teaspoon baking powder
1 teaspoon vanilla   ¼ teaspoon cinnamon
1 cup mashed avocados   1 teaspoon salt
¾ cup vegetable oil   ½ cup water
3 cups sifted all purpose   1½ cups chopped walnuts
   flour

   Combine sugar, eggs and vanilla. Beat well. Add avocado and oil, and blend until smooth. Gradually add sifted dry ingredients, and beat at medium speed until smooth. Add water, and beat until smooth. Stir in chopped nuts.
   Spoon into 2 greased and floured loaf pans, and bake at 350° for 50 to 55 minutes. Bread is done when toothpick inserted in center comes out clean.

NOTE: Best if made day before serving.

CUBAN BUNUELOS
(Cuban Fried Bread)

Yield: 15-18 pieces

1 pound yucca
1 pound malanga
1 egg
1 teaspoon ground anise

1 teaspoon salt
½ cup flour
Vegetable oil for deep frying

Syrup:
2 cups sugar
1 cup water
¼ teaspoon lemon juice

1 stick cinnamon
1 teaspoon vanilla

Peel the yucca and malanga; cut into small pieces. Place in large sauce pan, and cook in enough boiling water to cover, until tender but not too soft. Drain. Put through a food grinder or use a food processor. Add egg, anise, salt and flour. Mix well to make soft dough. Pull off small pieces, and roll into small strips with hands. Twist into figure 8's. Drop into hot (375°) oil, and cook until light brown in color.

Syrup:
Place all ingredients (except vanilla) in a sauce pan, and boil for five minutes over medium heat; add vanilla. Serve hot over the warm breads.

MEXICAN CORNBREAD

Preheat oven to 400°

Yield: 6-8 servings

1½ cups cornmeal
3 eggs
⅓ cup vegetable oil
1 teaspoon salt
3 teaspoons baking powder
1 tablespoon sugar
1 (8½-ounce) can creamed
  corn

½ cup milk
1 or 2 jalapeño peppers,
  chopped fine
3 or 4 green onions, chopped
½ chopped bell pepper
  (optional)
1 cup grated cheddar cheese

Combine ingredients in order given. Pour into greased 2-quart oblong pyrex baking dish. Bake at 400° for 25 to 30 minutes.

MEXICAN CORNBREAD STUFFING

Preheat oven to 350°   Yield: 2½-3 quarts

1 recipe Mexican Cornbread
1 (8-ounce) package herb
  stuffing mix
2 stalks celery, chopped and
  sautéed in 2 tablespoons
  margarine

1½ teaspoons poultry
  seasoning
1 (14½-ounce) can chicken
  broth
Hot water

Mix first 4 ingredients together. Heat broth in sauce pan. Add to bread mixture. Add hot water if needed, a little at a time, until moistened. Bake in greased pan or use to stuff hen or turkey. When baking alone in pan, bake at 350° for 30 minutes.

CORN SPOON BREAD

Preheat oven to 350°   Yield: 8-10 servings

2 large eggs, beaten
1 (8-ounce) box corn muffin
  mix
1 (8-ounce) can drained
  whole kernel corn

1 (8-ounce) can cream corn
1 cup sour cream
½ cup butter, melted
1 cup grated Swiss cheese

Combine all ingredients, except cheese. Spread into an 11x7-inch pan. Top with cheese, and bake at 350° for 50 minutes.

TRIDENT CORN BREAD

Preheat oven to 350°   Yield: 8-10 servings

⅔ cup vegetable oil
2 eggs, lightly beaten
8 ounces sour cream
1 (16-ounce) can cream corn
1 medium onion, grated

1½ cups yellow corn meal
2 teaspoons baking powder
1 teaspoon salt
1 cup grated sharp cheddar
  cheese

Oil a 9-inch round iron skillet. Mix together oil, eggs, sour cream, and corn. Stir in onion. Combine dry ingredients in a separate bowl. Then add liquid mixture to dry ingredients. Mix quickly. Batter will be a bit lumpy. Pour ½ of batter into pan. Sprinkle with ¾ cup cheese. Slowly pour on remaining batter. Top with remaining ¼ cup cheese. Bake at 350° for 45 minutes. Let stand in pan for 10 minutes. Cut into wedges.

SESAME BREAD

Yield: 8 servings

1 package yeast	3½ cups flour
1¼ cups warm water	1 stick (¼ pound) butter or
1 tablespoon sugar	margarine
1 teaspoon salt	2 tablespoons sesame seeds
2 eggs	

Dissolve yeast in warm water. Mix sugar, salt, eggs and flour together. Add yeast and water. Mix well. Place in greased bowl, and let rise until double in size, about one hour. Stir down, and knead for 5 minutes; place in 9x12-inch greased pan. Melt and spread butter or margarine and sesame seeds on top of dough. Let rise until double in size again, and bake at 400° for 25 minutes.

DILL BREAD

Yield: 2 small loaves or
1 regular loaf

1 package dry yeast	2 teaspoons dill seed
¼ cup warm water	1 teaspoon salt
1 cup small curd cottage	1 egg, well beaten
cheese	2¼ cups flour
2 tablespoons sugar	1 teaspoon baking soda
1 tablespoon minced onion	
1 tablespoon butter or	
margarine	

Dissolve yeast in warm water. In a small sauce pan, heat cheese, sugar, onion, butter or margarine, dill seed and salt. Do not bring to a boil. Let cool, then add yeast, water and beaten egg. Add flour and baking soda. Mix well. Place in greased bowl, turn once, cover and set aside in warm place until doubled in size. Turn out on floured surface. Knead 5 minutes, or until dough feels elastic. Place in greased and floured loaf pan. Let rise again until double in size. Bake at 350° for 25 minutes for 2 small loaves or 40 minutes for one loaf.

NOTE: Freezes well.

Eggs and Cheeses

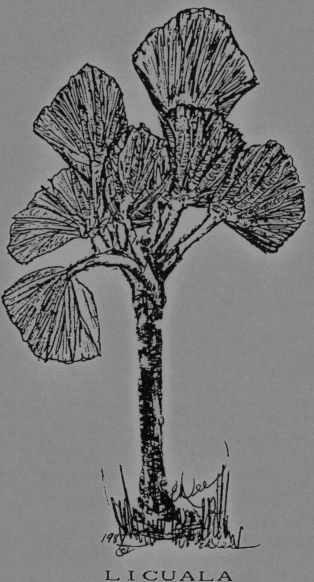

LICUALA

Hints for Eggs and Cheese

If cracks develop when boiling eggs, just add a pinch of salt or a few drops of vinegar to the water. This will prevent the white from coming out of the shell.

It is better to use eggs that are more than three days old for hard-cooked, baking or beating. Fresher eggs are more difficult to peel, may not beat up to as great a volume, and may turn greenish when hard-cooked.

Do not use an aluminum bowl to beat eggs as it will turn them gray. Plastic bowls may deteriorate the volume because of the chemicals contained in them.

Eggs may be wiped in preparation for storage, but do not wash them as they have a protective film on the shell which prevents bacteria from entering the egg.

Old eggs are shiny and smooth; fresh eggs are chalky and rough in appearance.

Store egg whites, covered tightly, in the refrigerator. To store egg yolks, first cover them with water and then cover the storage dish before putting them in the refrigerator. Egg whites or yolks can be kept up to four days.

Egg whites can be frozen for up to a year. Freeze them in ice trays and use when needed.

When making deviled eggs, use a pastry tube to stuff the yolks into the white halves to give them a more decorative look.

Do not hard-cook eggs in the microwave because the shell traps heat and will burst from the pressure. You may fry, poach, bake, or scramble eggs with good results. It is better to use medium or medium high heat when cooking due to the delicate nature of eggs.

To prevent curdling when combining eggs with a hot mixture, first add a small portion of the hot mixture, then add the balance.

To prevent a quiche crust from becoming soggy, brush the uncooked pie shell lightly with a beaten egg white.

Containerized cottage cheese that is stored upside down in the refrigerator will stay fresh for a longer period of time.

When serving cheese, do not crowd too many cheeses together. Place mild and strong cheeses on separate serving trays.

Use low heat to melt cheese. High heat makes cheese stringy.

Hard cheeses have more calcium than soft cheeses, but soft cheeses have more water-soluble vitamins.

To store large pices of hard cheeses such as Cheddar or Edam, butter the cut edges, wrap in foil and refrigerate.

Brush a small amount of oil on your grater for an easier clean-up.

Use the low setting on your microwave oven to soften cheeses for spreading or cutting.

Swiss, Cheddar and American cheese may be stored in the freezer for as many as three months when wrapped correctly.

If you are adding grated cheese to a hot mixture, do it as the last step. Remove the pan immediately from the heat to prevent the cheese from hardening on the bottom of the pan.

EGG, BACON AND BEEF BRUNCH

Preheat oven to 250°   Yield: 8-10 servings

Sauce:

4 slices bacon, diced
½ pound fresh mushrooms or
    4 ounces, canned
4 tablespoons butter

2 packages dried beef,
    shredded
½ cup flour
1 quart milk

Sauté bacon; drain and push to side of pan. Sauté mushrooms in butter. Add dried beef. Sprinkle flour over bacon, mushrooms and chipped beef. Add milk; stir until thickened; bring to a boil. Set aside.

Egg Mixture:

1 cup evaporated milk
16 eggs, beaten
¼ teaspoon salt

Dash of pepper
4 tablespoons butter

Stir evaporated milk into beaten eggs; add salt and pepper. Soft-scramble eggs in butter.

Use a 3-quart oblong oven dish. Layer the egg mixture, followed by the sauce, ending with sauce.

Bake at 250° for 1 hour.

NOTE: May be made the day before, refrigerated and cooked later.

HUEVOS PICANTE

(Men love this dish!)

Yield: 6-8 servings

1 tablespoon vegetable oil
1 small onion, chopped
1 or 2 cloves garlic, minced
1 (4-ounce) can green chilies,
    well-drained and chopped
    or 1 jalapeño pepper,
    chopped fine

2 fresh tomatoes, chopped
8 eggs
1 tablespoon milk
⅓ cup broken regular-size
    corn chips
½ to 1 teaspoon salt
¼ teaspoon black pepper

Using a 10-inch skillet, sauté onion, garlic, chilies and tomatoes until onions are soft and transparent. Scramble eggs with milk and add to sautéed vegetables; add broken corn chips, salt and pepper; continue to cook and stir until eggs are barely moist. Serve immediately.

NOTE: These are great for camping, boating or after-party fare.

BREAKFAST SOUFFLÉ

Preheat oven to 350°   Yield: 8-10 servings

1½ pounds bulk pork sausage
   cooked, crumbled and
   drained
9 eggs, beaten
3 cups milk
1½ teaspoons dry mustard

1 teaspoon salt
3 slices bread, cut into ¼-inch
   cubes
1½ cups shredded cheddar
   cheese

Combine all ingredients.
Mix and pour into well-greased 9x13-inch flat pyrex dish. Refrigerate, covered, overnight. Bake at 350° for 1 hour, uncovered.

CURRIED EGGS

Preheat oven to 370°   Yield: 4-6 servings

8 hard-boiled eggs
1 cup milk, scalded
1 cup cheddar cheese, grated
2 tablespoons flour
2 tablespoons margarine

¼ teaspoon paprika
1 teaspoon curry powder
¾ teaspoon salt
Bread crumbs

Slice eggs in half; place in buttered glass baking dish. Combine next 7 ingredients in blender. Cover and blend 10 to 15 seconds. Pour over eggs. Sprinkle bread crumbs, and dot with butter or margarine. Bake at 375° for 15 minutes or until brown.

EGGS ELEGANT

Yield: 2 cups

1 (8-ounce) package cream
   cheese, softened to room
   temperature
¼ cup sour cream
¼ cup grated Parmesan or
   Romano cheese

1 teaspoon chives
¼ teaspoon dill weed
3 chopped hard-boiled eggs
¼ teaspoon salt
¼ teaspoon pepper

Combine cream cheese, sour cream, Parmesan and seasonings. Stir in eggs. Chill and serve with melba rounds, etc. Can also be used as a sandwich spread.

SCRAMBLED EGGS

Preheat oven to 350°   Yield: 6 servings

10 eggs
1 (10¾-ounce) can cream of
mushroom soup, undiluted
¼ cup milk
1 teaspoon margarine,
melted in skillet
¼ pound dried beef, chopped
or ¼ pound cooked pork
sausage, chopped

Salt and pepper to taste
¼ pound cheddar cheese,
shredded
4 green onions, chopped or
chives

Combine eggs, soup and milk. Scramble in pan with melted margarine. When eggs are firm, fold in chopped beef or sausage and seasonings. Place half the mixture in buttered casserole dish. Sprinkle with grated cheese and onions or chives; repeat. Refrigerate until ready to use. Bake in 350° oven for 20 minutes or until heated throughout.

NOTE: May be prepared the day before serving.

CHILI-EGG PUFF

Preheat oven to 350°   Yield: 10 servings

10 eggs
½ cup flour
1 teaspoon baking powder
½ teaspoon salt
1 (16-ounce) carton creamed,
small curd cottage cheese
1 pound Monterrey Jack
cheese, shredded

½ cup butter or margarine
melted
2 cans (4 ounces each) diced
green chilies
1 pound bacon (optional),
cooked and crumbled

In a large bowl, beat eggs until light and lemon-colored. Add flour, baking powder, salt, cottage cheese, Jack cheese and melted butter. Blend until smooth. Add chilies; add bacon, if used.

Pour mixture into well-buttered 9x13-inch baking dish. Bake at 350° for 40 minutes or until top is browned and the center firm. Serve hot. This holds well in oven. If serving is delayed, turn oven to 200° and cover.

NOTE: Good with barbecued meats.

CHEESE FONDUE

Yield: 16 servings

1 tablespoon butter or
    margarine
2 pounds Velveeta cheese
2 (10-ounce) cans tomatoes
    with green chilies
2 (3-ounce) cans deviled ham
    or corned beef
2 (4-ounce) packages of Bel
    Paese or Bierkaise cheese

1 tablespoon Worcestershire
    sauce
½ teaspoon onion salt or
    garlic salt
1 loaf Pumpernickel bread
    (round type) from bakery,
    broken up into dipping
    pieces

Coat bottom of large Dutch oven with butter. Melt the Velveeta cheese using a plastic or wooden spoon to stir. Gradually add tomatoes so as not to get too much juice from can. Add Bel Paese or Bierkaise and melt; add deviled ham or corned beef. Season with Worcestershire and onion salt or garlic salt. Serve in chafing dish, with bread pieces.

NOTE: Always good at any party.

BLENDER QUICHE

Preheat oven to 350°   Yield: 6 servings

3 eggs
1 cup sour cream
¼ teaspoon salt
½ teaspoon Worcestershire
    sauce
1 cup Swiss cheese, grated
1 (6-ounce) can onion rings

¼ pound bacon, cooked and
    crumbled or 1 (6-ounce) can
    crabmeat, drained and
    rinsed or 1 (4-ounce) can
    shrimp, drained and rinsed
9-inch unbaked pie shell

Combine all ingredients in a blender, except the meat of your choice; blend well. Place meat of choice in the pie shell and pour mixture into shell. Bake at 350° for 30 minutes.

CONTINENTAL QUICHE

Preheat oven to 400°   Yield: 5 dozen

Pastry:

6 ounces cream cheese   ½ pound butter or margarine
2 cups flour

Combine cheese, flour and butter or margarine; mix well; refrigerate. When chilled, press small amount into 1-inch muffin tins. Bake at 400° for 6 minutes. Cool.

Filling:

1 pound mild Italian sausage   ½ cup sliced mushrooms
½ cup chopped onion   1½ cup shredded Swiss cheese
2 eggs, beaten   ¼ teaspoon oregano
1¼ cup milk   1 clove garlic, minced
1 (10-ounce) package frozen,   ¼ teaspoon nutmeg, freshly
   chopped spinach (thawed   ground
   and drained)   Grated Parmesan cheese

Reduce oven temperature to 350°. Brown sausage and onion in skillet and drain. Combine with remaining ingredients, except Parmesan. Pour into miniature muffin tins. Sprinkle with Parmesan cheese and bake at 350° for 30 minutes. Serve hot or at room temperature.

NOTE: Filling will also make two 9-inch size pies. Bake 40 minutes if using the 9-inch sizes.

QUICHE LORRAINE

Preheat oven to 325°   Yield: 4-6 servings

1 cup fresh mushrooms,   10 slices cooked bacon,
   chopped   chopped
½ cup green onions, chopped   ⅛ teaspoon salt
4 eggs   ⅛ teaspoon pepper
1 cup whipping cream   ⅛ teaspoon garlic powder
½ cup milk   9-inch pastry shell
1¼ cups grated Swiss cheese

Sauté mushrooms and onions together. Beat eggs until blended; mix well with cream and milk. Fold in cheese and remaining ingredients. Bake at 325° for 40 minutes or until custard appears firm.

CRAB AND SHRIMP QUICHE

Preheat oven to 425°   Yield: 6-8 servings

1 unbaked deep 9-inch pastry
  shell
8 ounces Swiss cheese, diced
2 tablespoons flour
1 cup milk
3 eggs, beaten
½ teaspoon salt

⅛ teaspoon ground pepper
Dash of ground nutmeg
1 (6-ounce) package frozen
  crabmeat
1 (4½-ounce) can shrimp,
  drained

Bake unpricked pie crust on preheated cookie sheet in 425° oven for 6 minutes or until slightly brown; set aside.

Reduce oven temperature to 350°.

Combine cheese and flour; set aside. Combine milk, eggs, salt, pepper and nutmeg; mix well. Stir in crabmeat, shrimp and cheese mixture. Pour into partially baked pastry shell. Bake at 350° for 50 to 60 minutes. Cool slightly before serving.

NOTE: To freeze, bake only 40 minutes; wrap tightly in aluminum foil and freeze. To serve, thaw quiche and bake 15 to 20 minutes.

It is just as easy to make two and freeze one for later use.

Good for a light supper. Cut it into quarters, and serve with a tossed salad and some fruit for dessert.

DEVILICIOUS QUICHE

Preheat oven to 450°   Yield: 6 servings

1 deep dish pie crust
1 (4½-ounce) can deviled ham
4 hard-cooked eggs, chopped
1 cup shredded cheddar
  cheese

1 cup shredded Swiss cheese
3 eggs, beaten
1 cup light cream
⅛ teaspoon pepper

Bake unpricked pie crust on preheated cookie sheet in 450° oven for 6 minutes. Remove pie crust from oven. Reduce oven temperature to 350°. Combine remaining ingredients and pour into prepared pie shell. Bake on cookie sheet for 35 to 40 minutes or until knife inserted in center comes out clean. Let stand 10 minutes before serving.

CHEESE AND MUSHROOM RAMEQUIN

Preheat oven to 400°   Yield: 4-6 servings

Filling:

1 cup fresh mushrooms,
  finely chopped
1 tablespoon butter or
  margarine
1 teaspoon vegetable oil

1 tablespoon green onions,
  chopped
1 tablespoon flour
4 tablespoons heavy cream
Salt and pepper, to taste

Sauté mushrooms and green onions in butter and oil for about 5 minutes, stirring frequently, until mushroom pieces begin to separate from each other and turn brown. Lower heat to medium; sprinkle in the flour. Stir and cook the flour. Remove from heat; pour in the cream and stir over medium heat until cream has thickened. Season with salt and pepper and set aside.

NOTE: You may substitute a 10-ounce package frozen spinach, thawed and drained or 1 cup cooked shrimp instead of mushrooms in the filling.

Ramequin Mixture:

½ cup granular all-purpose
  flour
2 tablespoons cold milk
3½ tablespoons butter or
  margarine
½ teaspoon salt
⅛ teaspoon pepper

⅛ teaspoon nutmeg or less
4 eggs
1½ cups coarsely grated
  Swiss cheese
9x9-inch baking dish,
  buttered
1 tablespoon butter

Place the flour in a heavy 2½-quart saucepan and gradually beat in the milk with a wire whip. Stir slowly and constantly over medium heat until mixture comes to a boil and thickens. Remove from heat; beat in butter, seasonings and eggs, one by one. Then beat in 1 cup cheese. Turn half the mixture into buttered dish; spread mushrooms on top, and cover with rest of the mixture. Sprinkle on remaining ⅓ cup of cheese and distribute the tablespoon of butter over cheese. (Set aside or refrigerate until you are ready to bake.)

Baking and Serving:

Bake in upper third of preheated 400° oven for about 25 minutes. (Five to ten minutes longer if it has been refrigerated.) The ramequin is done when it has puffed to double in height and is beautifully browned. Serve immediately.

NOTE: It will gradually sink as it cools.
Great with a green or mixed salad, French bread and a dry white wine.

GRITS SOUFFLÉ

Preheat oven to 400°   Yield: 6-8 servings

3 cups water
1½ cups milk
¼ teaspoon salt
1 cup grits
½ stick margarine

¾ cup sharp cheddar cheese,
  grated
½ stick margarine
1 clove garlic, minced
2 eggs, separated

Bring the water, milk and salt to a boil. Gradually add grits to boiling mixture. Stir often until thick and smooth. Add margarine, cheese and garlic; blend until melted. Remove from heat. Let cool slightly, and stir in beaten egg yolks. Mix well. Beat egg whites until stiff, and fold into grits mixture. Spoon into buttered 1½-quart casserole, and bake in 400° oven for 30 minutes or until puffed and slightly browned.

CHEESE GRITS

Preheat oven to 350°   Yield: 12 servings

8 cups boiling water
2 medium onions, chopped
1 teaspoon salt
2 cups grits, coarse grind
3 sticks margarine or butter,
  divided

4 cloves garlic, minced
1¼ pound Velveeta cheese
8 eggs, beaten well
4 individual packages corn
  flakes, crushed

Add onions, salt and grits gradually to the boiling water. Cook until thick. In a separate pan, melt 2 sticks margarine and add garlic and cheese over medium heat. Add butter and cheese mixture slowly and gradually to beaten eggs, stirring constantly. Add cheese mixture to grits, and pour into a 2-quart casserole which has been lightly buttered. Mix crushed cornflakes with remaining stick (melted) margarine, and spread on top. Bake at 350° for 30 minutes.

Soups

CABBAGE PALM

Hints for Soups

Soups can be garnished in many attractive ways by topping with parsley, chives, crisp croutons, a dab of sour cream, crumbled bacon, or almond slivers.

If soup is too highly seasoned with salt, cut up a peeled potato and cook it in the soup for five minutes, then remove.

Keep leftover meats and vegetables and freeze them for future use in soups.

Wine makes soup taste saltier, so be careful when adding salt so as not to overdo it.

A quick and nutritious lunch may be had by mixing two canned soups together (such as black bean and tomato or fish chowder and vegetable).

To remove grease from the top of soup, use a lettuce leaf, baster, paper towel, or skim the surface of the soup with a piece of ice.

Always remember to save bones from meats such as turkey or ham; they make great soups.

Tomato soup tends to separate when frozen.

Use milk cartons of all sizes to freeze soup in. They can be stacked to save space.

When you have a large quantity of soup, only heat as much as you will eat. If you heat all the soup each time, the soup ingredients will become overcooked.

Hot soups should be kept hot by using tureens or well-heated cups or bowls. Cold soup should be kept cold by chilling the bowls.

Add wine to soup sparingly, using only ¼ to ½ cup per quart of soup. Do not boil a soup with wine in it.

For an added touch, add fresh vegetables to canned vegetable soup just before serving it.

Certain spices such as pepper, cloves, garlic and celery intensify in flavor when frozen. Salt tends to lose flavor when frozen. When preparing soup to freeze, season with a light touch.

Never boil soup. Soup should be simmered.

AVGOLEMONO SOUP
(Greek Lemon Soup)

Yield: 8 servings

6 cups chicken broth or 3
  (10¾-ounce) cans
  condensed chicken broth
  and 2 soup cans water
¼ cup long grain white rice

1 teaspoon salt
3 eggs
¼ cup fresh lemon juice
8 thin slices lemon

Bring broth, rice and salt to a boil in a large sauce pan. Cover and reduce heat; simmer for 15 minutes (or until rice is tender). Set pan aside.

In a large mixing bowl, beat eggs until fluffy. Beat in the lemon juice gradually. Slowly add about 3 cups of the broth to the egg mixture. Pour this mixture back into sauce pan. Whisk vigorously until the soup begins to thicken. Cool to room temperature, and then refrigerate until very cold. Before serving, stir, and garnish with lemon slices. (The soup will have separated a little.)

NOTE: If you omit the rice, this soup becomes an excellent sauce for chicken or fish.

For Sauce:
Use only 3 (10¾-ounce) cans condensed chicken broth and other ingredients listed, except rice. Follow the same procedure listed above. The sauce may be used hot or cold.

SUMMERTIME CHERRY SOUP

Yield: 6-8 servings

1 (16-ounce) can pitted sweet
  red cherries, drained
  with syrup reserved
1 cup water
¼ cup sugar
1 (2-inch) stick cinnamon
⅛ teaspoon nutmeg

⅛ teaspoon cloves
1 tablespoon water
1 tablespoon corn starch
2 tablespoons lemon juice
½ cup dry red wine
1 cup sour cream

Combine drained cherry syrup, water, sugar and spices. Bring to a boil, and simmer uncovered for 5 minutes. Remove cinnamon stick. In a small pan, mix water and cornstarch together. Cook until thick. Add lemon juice and wine. Cool to room temperature. Blend in sour cream and cherries. Chill for several hours.

CITRUS AND STRAWBERRY SOUP

Yield: 4-6 servings

2 pints fresh strawberries
1 tablespoon cornstarch
1 cup orange juice

1 cup red wine
¼ to ½ cup sugar
1 cup sour cream

Purée berries. Blend cornstarch with ¼ cup orange juice in a 2-quart sauce pan; add remaining orange juice, wine, sugar, and berries. Heat to boiling point; stir and remove from heat. Stir in sour cream with a whisk. Cover and refrigerate until thoroughly chilled. Serve cold.

COLD PEACH SOUP

Yield: 8 servings

5 ripe peaches, peeled and
**   quartered**
¼ cup sugar
1 cup sour cream
¼ cup fresh lemon juice

¼ cup sweet sherry
2 tablespoons thawed
**   orange juice concentrate**
Lemon slices

Purée 5 peaches with sugar in blender or food processor. Mix in sour cream. Add lemon juice, sherry and orange juice concentrate; blend until smooth. Transfer to bowl. Cover and refrigerate until well chilled. Ladle soup into bowls. Garnish each bowl with sliced lemon and serve.

MICROWAVE STRAWBERRY SOUP SUPREME

Yield: 6 servings

2 pints fresh strawberries
1 cup orange juice
1½ teaspoons quick cooking
 tapioca
⅛ teaspoon ground
 cinnamon

⅛ teaspoon ground allspice
1 cup buttermilk
½ cup sugar
1 tablespoon lemon juice
1 teaspoon grated lemon
 rind

Wash strawberries, and reserve 6 berries for garnish. Hull remaining strawberries. Place strawberries in blender or food processor. Pureé strawberries. Add orange juice, tapioca, cinnamon, and allspice; process 10 seconds.

Pour strawberry mixture into a 2½-quart casserole. Microwave at High for 5 to 6 minutes or until tapioca is transparent. Stir in buttermilk, sugar, lemon juice and lemon rind. Cover and chill several hours or overnight.

GAZPACHO-COLD SPANISH SOUP

Yield: 8 servings

1 (46-ounce) can spicy
 tomato juice
2 tablespoons olive oil
1 tablespoon wine vinegar
½ cup white vinegar
¼ cup dry sherry
3 dashes Tabasco sauce
1 tablespoon Worcestershire
 sauce
2 large cucumbers, cubed
2 large tomatoes, cubed

1 large green pepper, cubed
½ package onion soup mix or
 1 medium onion, chopped
2 tablespoons chopped
 parsley
½ teaspoon Accent
½ teaspoon garlic powder
½ teaspoon celery powder
½ teaspoon salt
10 turns of freshly ground
 pepper (pepper mill)

Mix all liquids. Stir well. Add cucumbers, tomatoes, green peppers and onion soup mix (or chopped onions). Add remaining seasonings. Chill 4 hours.

GAZPACHO
(Andalusian Soup)

Yield: 10-12 servings

1 large tomato, peeled and diced
1 large cucumber, peeled and diced
1 bunch green onions, chopped
1 small green pepper, chopped
1 (46-ounce) can V-8 juice
½ cup chopped celery

1 clove garlic, minced
¼ cup vegetable oil
¼ teaspoon Tabasco
1½ teaspoons salt
¼ teaspoon fresh ground black pepper
1 teaspoon Worcestershire sauce
⅓ cup vinegar
Croutons and fresh parsley

In blender combine ½ tomato, ½ cucumber, ¼ green pepper, garlic, and ½ cup V-8 juice. Blend (purée) for 30 seconds. In very large bowl or pitcher, combine puréed vegetables, remaining vegetables and tomato juice with vinegar, oil and seasonings. Cover and chill in refrigerator overnight. Serve chilled in individual bowls garnished with parsley sprigs and croutons.

COLD AVOCADO SOUP

Yield: 4 servings

2 ripe avocados
2 cups chicken broth
1 cup whipping cream
2 tablespoons white rum
1 teaspoon curry powder

½ teaspoon salt
Freshly ground pepper, to taste
1 lemon or lime
Chopped parsley

Put all ingredients, except lemon or lime and parsley, in blender and blend until smooth. Serve with lemon or lime wedges. Sprinkle top with chopped parsley. Prepare in advance and keep in refrigerator. Blend again before serving.

ASPARAGUS CHOWDER

Yield: 6-8 servings

3 cups fresh mushrooms,
  sliced
1 bunch scallions, sliced
1 package frozen cut
  asparagus or 1 pound
  fresh asparagus
4 tablespoons margarine
2 tablespoons flour
½ teaspoon salt
⅛ teaspoon pepper

2 cups chicken broth
2 cups light cream or half
  and half
1 (12-ounce) can white whole
  kernel corn
1 tablespoon chopped
  pimento
⅛ teaspoon saffron, or to
  taste

In large sauce pan, cook mushrooms, scallions and asparagus in margarine until tender but not brown — about 15 minutes. Stir in flour, salt and pepper. Add chicken broth and cream. Cook and stir until thick and bubbly. Stir in drained corn, pimento and saffron. Serve hot, but do not boil.

CHEESY CHICKEN CORN CHOWDER

Yield: 4-6 servings

1 whole chicken breast,
  cooked
¼ cup chopped onion
¼ cup chopped celery
2 baking potatoes, peeled
  and diced
½ cup water

1 can cream of chicken soup,
  undiluted
½ cup milk
½ cup shredded American
  cheese
1 (8¾-ounce) can corn

Combine chicken, onion, celery, potatoes and ½ cup water. Cook for 20 minutes. Chop chicken and stir in remaining ingredients. Cook uncovered on low heat for 10 minutes.

BISCAYNE BAY FISH CHOWDER

Yield: 4-6 servings

1 bunch celery, chopped
2 large onions, chopped fine
½ stick (2 ounces) butter
¾ pound fresh flounder
  fillets or 1 (12-ounce) box
  frozen flounder fillets
1 (12-ounce) can white corn
  with liquid

2 (10¾-ounce) cans cream of
  potato soup, undiluted
3 soup cans skim milk or 2
  soup cans whole milk and
  1 can water

Sauté celery and onions in butter in large soup pot over medium heat until clear and soft. Lay fish fillets on top of mixture, and cook for about 10 minutes. (Fish should break up easily with fork.) Add remaining ingredients, stir occasionally until heated through.

NOTE: Great for galley cooking while cruising!

GROUPER CHOWDER

Yield: 4-5 servings

2 pounds grouper fillet (save
  head and bones)
¼ pound salt pork, cut into
  ¼-inch cubes
1 (6-ounce) can tomato paste
1 green pepper, diced
5 to 6 medium potatoes,
  pared and cut into
  bite-sized pieces

5 or 6 drops Tabasco sauce
1 teaspoon paprika
1 teaspoon salt, or more to
  taste
¼ teaspoon pepper
¼ teaspoon thyme
1 bay leaf

Cook bones in 2½ cups water. Strain. Set aside broth. Sauté salt pork and onion in 4-quart pot until pork is browned. Add tomato paste, green pepper, strained broth, potatoes and seasonings. Cover and simmer until potatoes are done.

Cut grouper in 2-inch squares and place gently on top of liquid. Cook about 10 minutes or until fish is done.

FLORIDA CLAM CHOWDER

Yield: 6 servings

2 cups clams, minced (fresh
  or canned)
¼ cup chopped bacon
½ cup chopped onion
2 cups chopped celery

1 cup diced potatoes
1 teaspoon salt
¼ teaspoon thyme
2 cups milk
Parsley for garnish

Drain clams; save liquid. Chop. Fry bacon until brown; remove and add onion and celery to bacon drippings. Cook until tender. Add clam liquid, potatoes, seasonings and clams. Cook 15 minutes or until potatoes are tender. Add milk. Heat. Garnish with chopped parsley.

CONCH CHOWDER

Yield: 8 servings

¼ pound salt pork, diced
3 to 4 medium onions,
  minced
4 cloves garlic, minced
1 large green pepper, minced
2 quarts boiling water
1 (20-ounce) can tomatoes
1 (6-ounce) can tomato paste

2 bay leaves
1 tablespoon oregano
½ teaspoon black pepper
1½ teaspoons salt
6 to 8 large conchs
3 to 4 medium potatoes,
  diced

In a large pot, fry salt pork to render fat. Add onion, garlic and green pepper. Cook slowly until tender. Drain excess fat. Add boiling water, tomatoes, tomato paste, bay leaves, oregano, pepper and salt. Pound conch with mallet, and cut into small pieces. May be put through coarse meat grinder. Add conch to mixture. Bring to boil, and then simmer for one hour. Add potatoes and cook until done.

NOTE: Adding ⅓ cup of dry sherry is a nice touch.

BABY CLAM SOUP

Yield: 6 servings

2 (28-ounce) cans peeled
   tomatoes with basil
2 dozen cherrystone clams
²/₃ cup light olive oil
2 cloves crushed garlic
½ cup chopped parsley

3 tablespoons chopped onion
1 tablespoon oregano
1 teaspoon salt, or to taste
⅛ teaspoon pepper, or to
   taste
1 loaf French bread

Drain tomatoes, reserving liquid; chop coarsely. Wash and scrub clams; soak for 30 minutes. Rinse thoroughly under running water. Heat oil in large, heavy pan. Sauté garlic, but do not brown. Add parsley and onion. Cook over low heat for 2 to 3 minutes; add tomatoes and oregano. Season with salt and pepper. Raise heat to moderate, cook 15 minutes. Add clams; cover pan; lower heat; cook for about 10 minutes or until shells open. Sprinkle with freshly ground pepper. Serve immediately, poured over slices of toasted French bread in individual bowls.

ALMOND SOUP

(Sopa Castilla La Vieja)

Yield: 12 servings

6 (10¾-ounce) cans beef
   consommé
6 consommé cans of water
1 cup ground, blanched
   almonds

2 tablespoons olive oil
²/₃ cup grated, fresh
   Parmesan cheese
Plain croutons
Toasted sliced almonds

Heat water and consommé in sauce pan. Mix ground almonds and oil. Add to soup. Stir until well blended. Heat. Pour into individual serving bowls, and sprinkle each with scant tablespoon Parmesan cheese, croutons and sliced toasted almonds. Serve hot.

NOTE: To grind almonds: Place in blender or food processor and grind dry for few seconds.

To toast almonds: Spread sliced almonds on cookie sheet and toast at 325° for 10 minutes. Watch to avoid burning.

CALLOLOO SOUP
(A Trinidad Recipe)

Yield: 6 servings

2 (10-ounce) packages frozen
  spinach
12 okra pods
1 large onion
1 large tomato
1 clove garlic, finely minced
2 green onions

2 teaspoons salt
1 teaspoon black pepper
3 strips bacon diced
Water to cover
1 (6-ounce) can crabmeat
1 teaspoon butter

Place all ingredients in a large pot, except crabmeat and butter. Cover with water and bring to a full boil. Lower heat, and cook for 30 minutes or until okra is soft. Place ingredients in blender, and pureé until well blended. Return to pot; add crabmeat and butter; adjust seasonings. If too thick, add water to bring to soup consistency.

GARBANZO BEAN SOUP

Yield: 6 servings

1 (8-ounce) package dry
  garbanzo beans
1 beef soup bone
1 ham hock
2 quarts water
2 tablespoons vegetable oil
1 medium onion, chopped

4 ounces salt pork, chopped
1 pound potatoes, peeled and
  cut into eighths
⅛ teaspoon saffron
2 tablespoons salt
2 to 3 chorizos (sausage)

Soak beans overnight in salted water. Next morning, drain beans and place in large pot with beef bone, ham hock and 2 quarts water. Bring to a boil, and simmer on low heat for 2 to 3 hours. In a medium size sauce pan, sauté onions and salt pork in oil, until onions are soft. Add to soup. Add potatoes, saffron, salt and chorizos. Cook over low heat for 2 to 3 more hours.

POTAJE de GARBANZO

Yield: 8 servings

2 pounds dry garbanzo beans
5 quarts water
½ pound salt pork, finely
   sliced
2 pounds stew beef
2 tablespoons vegetable oil
1 large onion, chopped
1 medium green pepper,
   chopped
2 cloves garlic, minced

1 bay leaf
⅛ teaspoon cumin
1 package bijol or saffron
½ pound boiled ham, diced
2 to 4 chorizos, sliced
2 pounds potatoes, peeled
   and sliced in eighths
1 large head cabbage,
   chopped

Soak beans overnight in slightly salted water. (Water level must be several inches above beans.) Drain the next day. In large stock pot filled with 5 quarts of water, cook beans with salt pork and stew meat until tender, about 3 hours. In a sauce pan, add vegetable oil; sauté onions, green pepper and garlic. Cook until soft, and then add to soup pot. Add remaining ingredients, except cabbage; cover and simmer for 30 minutes. Add cabbage and cook, uncovered, for 15 minutes.

CREAM OF BROCCOLI SOUP

Yield: 4 servings

2 cups chopped broccoli
   (fresh or frozen)
1 small onion, thinly sliced
1 green onion, thinly sliced
   (white part only)
1 small stick celery
1 tablespoon margarine or
   butter

½ cup water
2 teaspoons salt
⅛ teaspoon cayenne pepper
3 tablespoons uncooked rice
2 cups chicken broth, divided
½ cup half and half cream

Cook broccoli in a small amount of water. Drain, reserving liquid. Set aside. Combine onion, green onion, celery, butter and water in 2-quart sauce pan. Place on medium heat, and simmer slowly 2 minutes. Add salt, pepper, rice and cup of broth. Simmer for 15 minutes. DO NOT BOIL. Place broccoli, onion mixture and remaining 1 cup broth into blender, and blend until smooth. Combine half and half and soup mixture in sauce pan. Heat and serve. Use reserved broccoli liquid as thinner if necessary.

NOTE: Also good with ¼ pound Velveeta cheese added.

CREAM OF CAULIFLOWER SOUP

Yield: 6-8 servings

1 large head cauliflower
Juice of 1 lemon
1 cup water
2 tablespoons minced onion
2 celery sticks, minced
1 tablespoon butter

¼ cup flour
4 cups chicken broth
2 cups light cream
1 teaspoon salt
⅛ teaspoon nutmeg
Grated Parmesan cheese

Wash cauliflower, and break into flowerets. Cook with lemon juice and small amount of boiling water until tender. Drain and whirl in blender or food processor until puréed. Sauté onion and celery in butter for 2 minutes; blend in flour and stir in the broth. Cook, stirring until thickened. Stir in cauliflower, cream, salt and nutmeg. Garnish with Parmesan cheese.

FRESH MUSHROOM SOUP

Yield: 4 servings

¼ cup butter or margarine
4 cups sliced fresh
    mushrooms
1 cup sliced onion
2 tablespoons flour

⅛ teaspoon pepper
5 cups chicken broth (2 cans)
2 tablespoons chopped
    parsley

Sauté mushrooms and onions lightly in butter. Add flour and pepper. Add chicken broth; gradually bring to a boil, stirring constantly. Reduce heat and simmer 5 minutes. Serve warm with chopped parsley.

ONION SOUP

Yield: 4-6 servings

½ pound butter
6 large onions, sliced and
    separated into rings
3 to 4 cloves of garlic,
    minced

2 (10¾-ounce) cans beef
    consommé
2 soup cans of water
Peppercorns
Salt to taste

Slowly sauté onions in butter. Add garlic and cook until onions turn a deep yellow color. Add consommé, water, several peppercorns and salt. Cover and simmer for 2 hours. Set aside for 1 hour. Reheat to serve.

NORWEGIAN SPLIT PEA SOUP

Yield: ¾ gallon

2 (12-ounce) packages yellow
  dry split peas
4 quarts water
1 ham hock

2 large onions, diced
1 teaspoon black pepper
1 teaspoon salt
3 tablespoons thyme

Wash and sort peas; place in large soup pot and cover with 4 quarts of cold water. Add ham hock, onion, salt, pepper and thyme. Bring to a boil; cover and reduce heat to simmer. Simmer for 2 hours, stirring occasionally.

NOTE: Yes, it is 3 "tablespoons" thyme. That's the secret to the success of the recipe.

SWISS POTATO SOUP
(Easy)

Yield: 8 servings

4 large white potatoes
1 teaspoon salt
½ teaspoon marjoram
2 tablespoons chopped
  celery leaves
5 green onions
2 tablespoons butter

2 tablespoons flour
3 cups milk
½ cup parsley, finely
  chopped
¼ teaspoon pepper
1¾ cups shredded Swiss
  cheese

Peel potatoes and slice. Place in large sauce pan and add water (enough to cover potatoes), salt, marjoram, celery leaves and the white part of 3 onions, finely chopped. Bring to a boil, and simmer 25 minutes, covered, or until tender. Remove from heat. Drain potatoes, reserving liquid. Mash potatoes with a potato masher. Melt butter and flour in reserved potato water, stirring; cook for two minutes. Add milk and cook until thickened, stirring constantly. Add the potatoes. Finely chop the remaining 2 onions, using the tops too, and add to soup along with the parsley and pepper. Cover and let stand a few minutes. Sprinkle grated cheese on each serving.

PUMPKIN MUSHROOM SOUP

Yield: 6 servings

½ pound fresh mushrooms,
  cleaned and sliced
½ cup onions, chopped
2 tablespoons butter or
  vegetable oil
2 tablespoons flour
1 tablespoon curry powder,
  or to taste

3 cups chicken broth
1 (1-pound) can pumpkin
1 tablespoon honey
⅛ teaspoon nutmeg
Salt and pepper, to taste
1 cup evaporated milk
Sour cream or plain yogurt,
  optional

Sauté mushrooms and onions in butter or oil. Add flour and curry, and stir. Gradually add broth. Add remaining ingredients except milk, and cook over medium heat, stirring, for 10 to 15 minutes. Add milk and heat through without boiling. May top each serving with sour cream or yogurt.

WILD RICE SOUP

Yield: 8 servings

½ cup wild rice
1½ cups water
4 tablespoons margarine
1 medium onion, chopped
3 large cloves garlic,
  chopped
2 carrots, peeled, finely
  diced
6 stalks fresh asparagus,
  finely diced

½ cup flour
5 cups chicken broth
1 bay leaf
½ teaspoon thyme
¼ teaspoon nutmeg
Salt and pepper, to taste
2 cups half and half cream
2 cups milk
1 cup cooked, chopped
  chicken

Cook wild rice in covered pan in the water until done (20 to 25 minutes). Melt margarine, and simmer garlic and onion. Add carrots and asparagus; cook until tender. Add flour slowly. Stir and cook over low heat for about 10 minutes. Pour in chicken stock, blending until smooth. Add spices, and simmer for 20 minutes. Remove bay leaf. Add half and half cream and milk. Heat to serving temperature. Stir in cooked rice and cooked chicken. Serve hot.

NEVER FAIL MATZO BALL SOUP

Yield: 4-6 servings

½ cup club soda
¼ cup melted chicken fat
1 teaspoon salt
1 teaspoon black pepper
4 eggs, beaten
1 cup Matzo meal

1½ quarts water
½ teaspoon salt
4 to 6 cups clear chicken
  broth
Fresh dill for garnish

Combine club soda, fat, salt and pepper to beaten eggs; mix well. Add matzo meal; stir until well mixed. Cover and refrigerate for 20 minutes. In a 2-quart sauce pan, bring water and salt to a boil. Remove matzo dough from refrigerator. Wet hands. Spoon small amount of dough into hands; shape into balls. Drop matzo balls into boiling water. Reduce heat and gently boil for 30 minutes. Remove and place in clear heated chicken broth. Garnish with fresh dill if available.

CHICKEN NOODLE SOUP

Yield: 6-8 servings

1 whole fryer
2 quarts water
1 stick celery, chopped
1 teaspoon salt
¼ teaspoon pepper
2 carrots, cleaned and diced

1 medium onion, chopped
½ teaspoon seasoned salt
⅛ teaspoon celery salt
1 cup water
1 cup fine, uncooked, egg
  noodles

Boil chicken in water with celery, salt and pepper until tender. (If pressure cooker is used, cook at highest pressure level 35 minutes.) Remove chicken from liquid. Skin, de-bone and chop chicken when cool enough to handle. Add one cup water to broth along with carrots, onions and rest of seasonings. Cook over medium heat until tender, about 12 minutes. Add egg noodles, and cook 6 more minutes.

INCREDIBLE STEAK SOUP

Yield: 1 gallon

½ pound butter or margarine
1 pound sirloin steak
1 large carrot, chopped fine
1 large onion, chopped fine
4 large celery stalks,
    chopped fine
1 cup flour
1 (29-ounce) can tomatoes,
    crushed

3 quarts beef stock or
    consommé
Salt and pepper, to taste
1 tablespoon Worcestershire
    sauce
1¼ tablespoon monosodium
    glutamate (optional)
1½ cups half and half cream

Braise meat, carrot, onion and celery in butter; add flour. Mix well, and cook over low heat 10 minutes. Add tomatoes, beef stock and spices; simmer 1 hour. Add cream during the last 5 minutes before serving.

NOTE: May be frozen. If too thick, add more stock and seasonings.

SUNDAY SUPPER SOUP

Yield: 6 servings

1½ pounds ground chuck
1 egg, slightly beaten
½ cup soft bread crumbs
¼ teaspoon salt
1 tablespoon chopped
    parsley
2 tablespoons butter or
    margarine
2 cups water
1 (10¾-ounce) can condensed
    beef broth

1 (1-pound) can whole
    tomatoes
1 envelope dry onion soup
    mix
2 cups sliced carrots
¼ cup chopped celery tops
¼ chopped parsley
¼ teaspoon pepper
¼ teaspoon dried oregano
¼ teaspoon basil leaves
1 bay leaf

In medium bowl, combine beef, egg, 3 tablespoons water, bread crumbs, salt and parsley. Mix lightly. Shape into 24 balls. In hot butter in 5-quart Dutch oven, sauté meatballs, a single layer at a time, until browned on all sides. Drain off fat. Set meatballs aside.

In same Dutch oven, combine 2 cups water and beef broth with remaining ingredients. Bring to boil, then reduce heat and simmer, covered, for 30 minutes, stirring occasionally to break up tomatoes. Add meatballs and simmer.

SAUSAGE BEAN CHOWDER

Yield: 8 servings

1 pound bulk pork sausage
2 (16-ounce) cans kidney
  beans
1 (29-ounce) can tomatoes,
  chopped
1 quart water
1 large onion, chopped

1 clove garlic, minced
1 bay leaf
1½ teaspoons seasoned salt
½ teaspoon thyme
⅛ teaspoon pepper
1 cup diced potatoes
½ green pepper, chopped

Brown and crumble sausage in medium skillet. Drain. In a large Dutch oven, combine beans, tomatoes, water, onion, garlic, bay leaf, salt, thyme and pepper. Add sausage. Cover and simmer for 1 hour. Add potatoes and green pepper. Cover and simmer 20 minutes or until potatoes are soft. Remove bay leaf before serving.

Salads and
Dressings

JELLY PALM

Hints for Salads and Dressings

When storing celery in the refrigerator, wrap in paper towel to keep fresh longer.

Substitute yogurt for mayonnaise in salad dressings to cut down on calories.

Never cut lettuce with a knife, always tear it apart. It will not turn brown as quickly.

Line the vegetable bin with paper towels to absorb moisture.

Keep in mind the rest of the menu when preparing your salad. Have a light salad with a heavy main course.

Be sure the lettuce that you use in a salad is perfectly dry or the dressing will not cling to the leaves.

To keep your salad fresh until guests arrive, cover it with a damp paper towel. Do not put the dressing on until the last minute.

Do not hull strawberries until you are ready to use them. They will become mushy.

Remember when buying greens, the darker salad vegetables offer larger amounts of vitamin A and C and are richer in iron than the paler ones.

Select chicory, endive and escarole that have a few dark outer leaves. The inner leaves are more likely to stay crisp longer and have a better flavor.

Celery cannot be frozen whole, but it can be frozen if cut into small pieces.

Do not freeze salads that have a large amount of mayonnaise or salad dressing; they tend to separate. Salads that have a base of cream cheese, whipped cream or cottage cheese freeze very well.

Sprinkle lemon juice on avocados to prevent the fruit from discoloring, or place seed in center and cover.

Dry greens gently so as not to bruise them. Roll them up in a paper towel and place in refrigerator until ready to use.

To get rid of bugs on your greens, add four tablespoons salt to a gallon of water. Wash off your greens; rinse well and then place them in refrigerator to crisp.

When making your fruit salads, keep these Florida fruits in mind:

a. Loquat: This fruit is available all year long. It is a yellowish, pear-shaped fruit about two inches long which can be eaten fresh, stewed or as a preserve.

b. Carambolas: The carambola is a five-inch long yellow fruit with a waxlike skin and five ribs, giving it the nickname "star-fruit." They are best eaten raw and make an attractive addition to salads and punches.

c. Mango: Mangoes are fruits that are yellow when ripe and slightly red. There are many different varieties. The flesh is yellow when riped. They can be eaten raw, used in a dessert or a salad.

d. Lychees: Lychees are bright red fruits about the size of plums. They have a rough rind but are delicious when peeled and the seeds taken out. They make an excellent addition to any salad.

e. Mamey: This fruit has a rough textured brown skin which surrounds a red sweet flesh. It can be eaten raw or sliced in a fruit salad.

f. Papayas: There are many different varieties of papayas ranging from nut size to over 20 pounds in all different shapes. They have a thin green or yellow skin with an orange flesh.

g. Avocado: This fruit is quite abundant in South Florida. The fruit is green or purple with a yellow flesh. It is great when used with a tuna fish salad or guacamole, also breads and soups.

h. Plantains: Very similar to bananas but larger. Contain more starch, but are not as sweet. They are usually fried.

MARINATED VEGETABLE SALAD

Yield: 6-8 servings

1 head cauliflower
1 bunch fresh broccoli
1 or 2 cucumbers
1 medium onion
2 tomatoes or several cherry
tomatoes

1 (12-ounce) bottle zesty
Italian dressing
1 (1-ounce) package ranch
dressing mix

Break up cauliflower into flowerets. Separate the broccoli into flowerets. Slice and chop remaining vegetables; mix with dressings, and let stand overnight in refrigerator. Stir occasionally.

NOTE: Keeps a long time in the refrigerator.

PARMESAN VEGETABLE BOWL

Yield: 8 servings

3 medium zucchini, bias
sliced ¼ inch thick (about
4 cups)
2 medium tomatoes, cut in
wedges and seeded
1 small head cauliflower,
broken into small buds

½ cup vegetable oil
⅓ cup vinegar
1 (1-ounce) envelope Italian
cheese salad dressing mix

In a large bowl, combine zucchini, tomatoes and cauliflower. In a screw-top jar, combine oil, vinegar and salad dressing mix. Cover, and shake vigorously to blend. Pour dressing over vegetables, stirring gently. Cover and refrigerate for several hours. Drain and serve.

BROCCOLI SALAD

Yield: 6 servings

2 bunches fresh broccoli in
  flowerets
1 cup chopped purple onion
1 cup chopped celery
1 cup golden raisins

1 (8-ounce) can water
  chestnuts, sliced and
  drained
½ pound bacon, fried,
  drained and crumbled

Rinse broccoli; drain and cut into flowerets. Combine with all of the remaining ingredients in a medium sized mixing bowl. Mix with salad dressing below.

Dressing:
1 cup mayonnaise
⅓ cup sugar

2 teaspoons white vinegar

Combine mayonnaise, sugar and vinegar. Mix together with salad. Serve chilled.

TOSSED CAULIFLOWER SALAD

Yield: 4-6 servings

2 cups thinly sliced
  cauliflower
½ cup chopped, pitted black
  olives

1 (2-ounce) jar chopped
  pimentos
3 tablespoons chopped onion
⅓ cup chopped green pepper

Slice cauliflower vertically to retain shape. Combine all vegetables.

Dressing:
½ tablespoon lemon juice
1½ tablespoons wine vinegar
4½ tablespoons vegetable oil

1 teaspoon salt
⅛ teaspoon black pepper
¼ teaspoon sugar

Blend dressing ingredients with beater. Pour over vegetables, and marinate several hours or overnight.

GREEK SALAD

Yield: 8 servings

8 cups torn mixed salad
  greens
2 cups halved cherry tomatoes
1 medium cucumber, pared
  and sliced
1 cup sliced radishes

½ cup sliced, pitted ripe
  olives
½ cup chopped green onion
¼ cup snipped parsley
8 ounces Feta cheese,
  crumbled

Place ingredients in order given in large salad bowl. Chill until serving time.

Dressing:
½ teaspoon black pepper
¼ cup lemon juice
1½ teaspoon dried oregano,
  crushed

2 cloves garlic, crushed
1 teaspoon salt
¼ cup olive oil

Mix ingredients; cover and chill.

NOTE: Salad dressing is best when made the day before. You may substitute Greek olives for ripe olives.

RAIN FOREST SUPREME SALAD

Yield: 4 servings

⅓ head shredded lettuce
⅛ head shredded red cabbage
2 stalks chopped celery
2 shredded carrots
5 slices cucumber
2 tomatoes, quartered
5 broccoli flowerets
5 cauliflower flowerets

5 slices green pepper
5 slices red pepper
5 slices gold pepper (if
  available)
4 thin slices raw mushroom
¼ cup frozen baby English
  peas
Alfalfa and radish sprouts

Combine lettuce, red cabbage, celery and carrots on a 10-inch flat plate. Arrange remaining vegetables on top of the above. Top with alfalfa and radish sprouts.

Garnish:
4 spears asparagus (canned
  or freshly cooked)
4 pieces hearts of palm

4 black olives
4 green olives
2 sprigs parsley

Serve with choice of dressing.

KOREAN SALAD

Yield: 8-10 servings

½ pound bacon, diced
1 pound fresh spinach
1 (16-ounce) can bean
  sprouts, drained or use
2 cups fresh sprouts

1 (8-ounce) can sliced water
  chestnuts, drained
4 hard-cooked eggs, sliced

Fry bacon until crisp; drain on paper towels. Wash spinach; dry thoroughly. Tear into small pieces. Chill. Chill remaining ingredients until serving time.

Dressing:
1 cup vegetable oil
¾ cup sugar
¼ cup vinegar
⅓ cup ketchup

1 small onion, chopped
1 tablespoon Worcestershire
  sauce
2 teaspoons salt

Place ingredients in blender until emulsified, about 1 to 2 minutes.

At serving time, toss spinach gently with well-drained bean sprouts, water chestnuts and eggs. Use enough dressing to coat leaves well (⅓ to ½ cup). Top with bacon.

GREEN BEAN SALAD PROVENCAL

Yield: 6 servings

1 pound fresh snap green
  beans
3 ripe tomatoes, cut into 6
  wedges each

½ cup jicama, sliced in thin
  julienne strips
½ cup sliced green olives

Garnish:
Lettuce leaves

3 hard-cooked eggs, sliced

Cut beans into thin julienne strips, and steam until BARELY tender. Rinse in cold water, and drain. Place beans and tomatoes in one bowl; olives and jicama in another.

Garlic Dressing:
½ cup vegetable oil
6 tablespoons wine vinegar
Salt and pepper, to taste

4 cloves garlic, minced
¼ teaspoon chervil

Combine dressing ingredients, and pour over green beans and tomatoes. Toss well, and refrigerate 3 to 4 hours.

To serve, place lettuce leaves on salad plates. Divide green beans and place (lined in one direction) on lettuce. Place olives on top of one end of the beans and jicama slices on the other end. Garnish with 3 tomato wedges and two egg slices on the side.

BEAN SPROUT AND SPINACH SALAD

Yield: 10-12 servings

2 cups fresh bean sprouts
1 package fresh spinach

½ cup thinly sliced water
  chestnuts

Steam fresh bean sprouts slightly, and cool to room temperature. Wash, drain and discard stems from fresh spinach.

Chill cleaned spinach, bean sprouts and water chestnuts.

Dressing:
½ cup sesame seed oil or
  peanut oil
¼ cup soy sauce
2 tablespoons lemon juice
1½ tablespoons minced onion

1½ tablespoons sesame
  seeds, toasted
½ teaspoon sugar
¼ teaspoon pepper

In a small mixing bowl, combine oil with remaining ingredients. Let stand at room temperature for 1 hour before serving.

To serve, arrange spinach in large salad bowl. Top with bean sprouts and water chestnuts. Pour enough dressing on salad to coat, and toss thoroughly.

MUSHROOM AND CELERY SALAD

Yield: 4 servings

½ pound mushrooms
2 tablespoons chopped
  scallions
2 tablespoons diced green or
  red bell peppers

½ cup thinly sliced celery
½ cup French dressing or ½
  cup Italian dressing
Lettuce

Clean, and pat mushrooms dry. Slice. Combine with vegetables. Marinate at least 30 minutes or more in French or Italian dressing. Serve on lettuce-lined plates.

SOUTHERN COLE SLAW

Yield: 6 servings

1 medium size cabbage
1 small onion

1 medium carrot
2 large dill pickles

Quarter cabbage. Wash and drain in colander. Peel and quarter onion and carrot. Grate cabbage, onion and carrot in food processor. Chop, and add dill pickles.

Dressing:
¾ cup mayonnaise
2 teaspoons salt
½ teaspoon pepper

2 tablespoons sugar
½ teaspoon prepared mustard
1 teaspoon lemon juice

To Serve: Mix dressing ingredients. Place vegetables in mixing bowl; combine with dressing, and stir until well-mixed.

GUATEMALAN STUFFED TOMATOES

Yield: 4 servings

3 hard-cooked eggs
1 tablespoon butter
2 medium onions, chopped
1 tablespoon flour
1 cup white wine
2 ounces capers
1 teaspoon chopped parsley

¾ teaspoon salt
⅛ teaspoon pepper
1 tablespoon vegetable oil
4 whole tomatoes
4 stuffed olives
Lettuce leaves

Separate hard-cooked egg yolks and whites. Chop each into separate bowls. Sauté onions in butter; add flour and chopped yolks from hard-cooked eggs; mix thoroughly. Add white wine, and cook over low heat until mixture thickens. Add capers, chopped egg whites, pepper, oil, chopped parsley, salt and pepper to taste. Scoop out the inside of the raw tomatoes, and fill with the cooked mixture. Top each tomato with one stuffed olive, and place on lettuce on individual plates.

POTPOURRI SALAD

Yield: 15 servings

1 (16-ounce) can French style
   green beans, drained
1 large onion, chopped
1 green pepper, chopped
1 (16-ounce) can bean
   sprouts, drained
1 (4-ounce) can mushroom
   pieces, drained
1 (2-ounce) jar chopped
   pimento

1 cup chopped celery
1 small head cauliflower, cut
   in small pieces
3 large carrots, grated
1 (8-ounce) can sliced water
   chestnuts, drained
1 (5-ounce) can garbanzo
   beans, drained

Combine all of the vegetables, and mix gently.

Dressing:
1½ cups white vinegar
1 cup vegetable oil
2 cups sugar

6 teaspoons salt
¼ teaspoon pepper

Combine vinegar, oil, sugar, salt and pepper in a sauce pan, and bring to a boil. Stir and cool.

To serve: Pour the cooled oil mixture over the vegetables. Cover and chill for 24 hours. Stir to coat vegetables once during the day. Stir again before serving.

TRICOLOR SALAD

Yield: 4-6 servings

6 teaspoons pignola (pine
  nuts)
1 bunch Belgian endive
1 bunch radicchio (Italian
  lettuce)

1 bunch watercress
½ pound bacon, cooked,
  well-drained and crumbled

Roast pine nuts in 350° oven until lightly browned. Cool. Arrange endive, watercress and radicchio in a pleasing pattern on individual salad plates. Chill.

Dressing:
2 tablespoons raspberry
  vinegar
3 tablespoons walnut oil

3 tablespoons Italian olive oil
½ teaspoon sugar
Salt and pepper, to taste

In a bowl, beat together raspberry vinegar, walnut and olive oils. Add salt and pepper to taste; add sugar.

To serve: Sprinkle salad greens with bacon bits and 1 teaspoon pine nuts per serving. Sprinkle dressing over salad. DO NOT TOSS.

SAUERKRAUT SALAD

Yield: 6-8 servings

1 quart sauerkraut
1 large green pepper,
  chopped
1 large onion, chopped

1 cup chopped celery
1 (2-ounce) jar pimentos,
  finely chopped

Drain and cut sauerkraut with knife or kitchen shears. Add chopped vegetables.

Dressing:
1 cup granulated sugar
¼ cup water
½ cup vegetable oil (not olive
  oil)

¾ cup vinegar
1 teaspoon celery seed

Mix dressing ingredients together, and combine thoroughly with sauerkraut. Refrigerate 24 hours before serving.

NOTE: Keeps indefinitely in the refrigerator.

EASY PATIO SALAD

Yield: 6-8 servings

1 large apple, cored and cut
    in bite-size pieces
1 tablespoon lemon juice
1 orange, peeled and
    sectioned (1 cup)
1 (16-ounce) can apricots,
    drained, or 1 cup fresh
    apricots

1 cup bite-size pieces fresh
    pineapple
½ cup diced celery
¼ cup slivered almonds
1 cup torn lettuce
½ cup sour cream
2 tablespoons apricot brandy

In a large salad bowl, toss the apple with the lemon juice. Add orange, apricots, pineapple, celery and almonds. Cover, and chill until serving time. Toss gently with lettuce, and make dressing of sour cream and brandy. Spoon on dressing. Toss again.

SALAD MANDARIN

Yield: 6 servings

1 medium head Bibb or
    Boston lettuce, torn
1 (11-ounce) can mandarin
    oranges, drained
½ medium avocado, peeled
    and thinly sliced
½ cup toasted, coarsely
    chopped, pecans

2 green onions, thinly sliced
Freshly ground pepper, to
    taste
⅓ cup Italian dressing

Combine first 6 ingredients in a medium bowl. Add Italian dressing and pepper. Toss gently. Serve chilled.

PINK FROZEN FRUIT SALAD

Yield: 6-8 servings

2 (3-ounce) packages cream
  cheese, softened
1 (8½-ounce) can crushed
  pineapple, undrained
1 cup finely chopped dates
¼ cup chopped maraschino
  cherries

3 tablespoons syrup from
  cherries
⅛ teaspoon salt
½ cup whipping cream,
  whipped
¼ cup chopped nuts

Blend cheese and undrained pineapple. Add remaining ingredients. Pour into individual molds or 8x8x2-inch square dish. Freeze overnight or until firm. Remove from freezer 20 to 30 minutes before serving. Unmold, and garnish with more cherries.

FROZEN CRANBERRY SALAD

Yield: 12-16 servings

1 (14-ounce) can sweetened
  condensed milk
¼ cup lemon juice
1 (16-ounce) can whole berry
  cranberry sauce
1 (20-ounce) can crushed
  pineapple, drained

½ cup chopped walnuts or
  pecans
1 (9-ounce) container frozen
  whipped topping, thawed

In a large bowl combine condensed milk and lemon juice. Stir in cranberry sauce, pineapple and nuts. Fold in whipped topping. Spread in 9x13-inch pan, and freeze until firm. Remove from freezer 10 minutes before cutting. Return leftovers to freezer.

CHICKEN CURRY SALAD

Yield: 6 servings

2 cups bite-size pieces
  cooked chicken
¼ cup sliced water chestnuts
½ pound green grapes,
  halved
½ cup chopped celery

1 (8-ounce) can pineapple
  chunks, drained
½ cup toasted, coarsely
  chopped almonds, pecans
  or walnuts

Combine the above ingredients together in a medium sized mixing bowl.

Dressing:

Yield: 1 cup

½ cup mayonnaise
½ cup lemon yogurt
1 teaspoon curry powder

2 teaspoons soy sauce
1 teaspoon lemon juice

Combine the above ingredients together in a small mixing bowl, and mix with salad. Chill until ready to use.

NOTE: May be served in a salad bowl or on a bed of lettuce on individual plates.

CONCH SALAD

Yield: 4 servings

6 large conchs
2 medium onions, sliced
¼ cup diced green pepper
¼ cup diced tomato
¼ cup diced celery

Lime juice
½ teaspoon salt
Tabasco sauce, to taste
Lettuce

Pound conch, and dice. Add onions, green pepper, tomato and celery. Add enough lime juice to cover; add salt and Tabasco. Chill several hours. Serve on crisp lettuce bed.

SEAFOOD SALAD

Yield: 8 servings

8 ounces small macaroni
(3½ to 4 cups)
1 to 2 cups cooked, chopped
shrimp or lobster
1 cup sliced celery
1 cup diced cucumber
½ cup mayonnaise

½ cup sour cream
3 tablespoons lemon juice
2 tablespoons capers
1 teaspoon salt
¼ teaspoon dry mustard
⅛ teaspoon Tabasco sauce
Greens

Cook macaroni as directed. Drain. Rinse with cold water. Mix with seafood and other ingredients. Serve on crisp greens.

NOTE: This is especially good with cantaloupe balls.

HOT SEAFOOD SALAD

Yield: 4-5 servings

1 cup fresh or frozen shrimp,
well drained
1 cup fresh or frozen
crabmeat, well drained
½ medium green pepper,
chopped

¼ cup minced onion
1 cup chopped celery
1 cup mayonnaise
½ teaspoon salt
¼ teaspoon pepper
2 hard-cooked eggs, chopped

Topping:
½ cup soft bread crumbs

1 tablespoon butter

Combine crab and shrimp; add green pepper, onion, celery, mayonnaise, salt, pepper and eggs. Mix well, and place in a 1-quart oven-proof casserole dish. Top with bread crumb mixture. Bake at 350° for 30 minutes.

NOTE: Can be used as a main dish or salad. May be served hot or cold.

ELEGANT SHRIMP BOATS

Yield: 4 servings

4 large ripe tomatoes
Lettuce leaves
2 pounds large shrimp,
  cooked and cleaned

1 can whole asparagus
4 hard-cooked eggs, sliced

Cut each tomato into 8 wedges. Place lettuce leaves on four salad plates. Arrange tomato wedges in a circle on lettuce bed, and pile shrimp in center of tomatoes.

Sauce:
Equal parts of:
Chili sauce
Mayonnaise

Durkee's sauce
Add chives, to taste

Serve on top of shrimp. Garnish with asparagus and egg slices. Serve with interesting type crackers.

NOTE: Great for ladies luncheon.

TACO SALAD

Yield: 6-8 servings

1 pound lean ground beef
1 (15-ounce) can kidney
  beans, drained
6 drops Tabasco sauce
1 onion, sliced or chopped
3 tomatoes, chopped
4 ounces grated cheddar
  cheese

1 head lettuce, shredded
1 (8-ounce) bottle Italian
  dressing
1 bag corn chips, crushed
1 to 2 avocados, sliced

Brown meat, and drain well. Add beans and Tabasco. Simmer for 10 minutes. Cool. Combine onion, tomatoes, cheese and lettuce; add beans and meat mixture. Pour on dressing, and toss. Add crushed corn chips. Serve immediately with avocado slices.

JULY 4th POTATO SALAD

Yield: 25 servings

10 pounds potatoes
1 tablespoon salt
1 tablespoon pepper
4 cups diced celery
2 cups diced onion
1 (12-ounce) jar pickle relish,
  drained

10 hard-cooked eggs,
  chopped
4 cups mayonnaise
1 (8-ounce) bottle Russian
  dressing
Celery seed, to taste

Boil potatoes in a large pot until fork tender. Do not overcook potatoes. Cool; peel and dice into very large mixing bowl. Sprinkle salt and pepper over potatoes. Add celery, onion, relish and eggs. Combine mayonnaise and Russian dressing in small mixing bowl, and stir until well blended. Pour dressing mixture over potatoes, and stir until well mixed. Stir in celery seed. Cover, and chill overnight.

NOTE: This is usually served directly from the mixing bowl at cookouts.

SUMMER PEACH AND HAM TOSS

Yield: 4 servings

2 cups cubed, fully cooked
  ham
2 cups peeled, sliced fresh
  peaches
½ cup diced celery
⅓ cup mayonnaise

1 tablespoon vinegar
1 teaspoon vegetable oil
¼ cup broken, toasted
  walnuts
Lettuce

In a large bowl, combine ham, peaches and celery. Blend together mayonnaise, vinegar and oil; toss with ham mixture. Cover and chill. Just before serving, fold in nuts. Serve fruit and ham in lettuce-lined bowls.

WILD RICE SALAD

Yield: 6-8 servings

Vinaigrette Dressing:

⅓ cup wine vinegar
2 sprigs parsley
2 teaspoons Dijon mustard
1 teaspoon salt

Pepper, to taste
1 cup plus 1 teaspoon
  vegetable oil

Purée vinegar, parsley, mustard and spices; blend in oil.

Salad:

2 cups wild rice
⅓ cup olive oil
4 cups chicken broth
⅔ cup sliced water chestnuts
½ cup sliced red bell pepper
¼ cup sliced green onion

Salt and pepper, to taste
¾ pound fresh snow peas
½ pound sliced fresh
  mushrooms
Vinaigrette dressing

Rinse 2 cups wild rice under cold water, and drain well. Sauté rice in olive oil, cooking 5 minutes or until lightly browned. Stir in chicken broth. Bake, covered, at 325° for 1½ hours. (If rice seems too moist, remove cover, and bake extra 5 to 10 minutes.) Transfer rice to bowl, and toss with ½ cup vinaigrette dressing. Add water chestnuts, red pepper, onion, salt and pepper to taste. Chill, preferably overnight.

String snow peas, and blanche 30 seconds in salted boiling water. Pat dry, and cut diagonally into 1-inch pieces. Marinate mushrooms and snow peas in vinaigrette dressing only 1 hour. (Color will fade if marinated longer.)

Put rice in serving dish. Make a well in center, and mound peas and mushrooms in well.

ARTICHOKE-RICE SALAD

Yield: 6 servings

1 (8-ounce) package chicken flavored rice vermicelli mixture
4 scallions, sliced
½ green pepper, chopped
12 stuffed green olives, sliced

2 (6-ounce) jars marinated artichoke hearts
¾ teaspoon curry powder
⅓ cup mayonnaise

Cook rice mixture according to package directions. Be careful not to overcook, or rice will be too soft for a salad. Cool. Combine in serving bowl with scallions, pepper and olives. Drain artichokes, and reserve marinade. Chop artichokes, and add to rice mixture. Combine marinade from artichoke hearts with curry powder and mayonnaise. Toss dressing with rice mixture, and chill.

HEARTY PASTA AND RED BEAN SALAD

Yield: 6-8 servings

2 cups uncooked medium sized pasta (rotelli, ziti, etc.)
2 cups cooked or canned kidney beans
1 cup diced raw zucchini (1 medium sized)
1 small green pepper, finely chopped
1 medium sized tomato, chopped
⅓ cup chopped green olives

⅓ cup grated Parmesan cheese
1 cup plain yogurt or 1 cup crumbled tofu
½ teaspoon chili powder, or more to taste
½ teaspoon ground coriander
½ teaspoon paprika
¼ teaspoon dried sage
Salt and pepper, to taste

Cook pasta according to package directions. Rinse and drain. Add remaining ingredients, and mix well. Chill and serve.

NOTE: If using dried kidney beans, cook ¾ cup in seasoned water, to your taste.

PASTA SALAD

Yield: 4-6 servings

½ pound pasta, cooked, drained and rinsed

2 tablespoons good vinegar (balsamic, wine or cider)

1 tablespoon oil (olive, walnut or hazelnut)

Combine cooked pasta, vinegar and oil. Mix well, and chill 3 to 4 hours, tossing mixture several times. If all vinegar and oil are absorbed right away, add equal portions of oil and vinegar to the pasta to moisten.

Dressing:

1 tablespoon diced sweet pickle

1 tablespoon diced dill pickle

1 tablespoon prepared mustard

½ teaspoon dry mustard

½ to 1 teaspoon capers

1 tablespoon chopped green onion

½ teaspoon ground black pepper, or to taste

¼ teaspoon well mashed green peppercorns

½ teaspoon favorite dried herbs (oregano, basil, parsley, etc.) or 1 teaspoon favorite fresh herbs

Using a blender, combine the above ingredients. Chill.

When ready to serve, mix pasta with one cup total of any of the items listed below:

Sliced black olives

Sliced green olives

Chopped sweet pickle

Marinated artichoke quarters

Marinated mushrooms

Almonds, sliced or slivered

Sliced celery

Diced red bell pepper or pimento

Chinese pea pods, steamed

Toss lightly with dressing.

BEET SALAD

Yield: 10-12 servings

2 (3-ounce) packages lemon
  gelatin
1¼ cup hot water
1 (16-ounce) can shoestring
  beets, drained, juice
  reserved

Water, if needed
1 teaspoon grated onion
1 teaspoon vinegar
½ teaspoon salt
2 tablespoons horseradish
½ cup diced celery

Dissolve gelatin in hot water. Drain beets; save juice. Add enough water to beet juice to make 1¾ cups. Add this to the gelatin mixture and cool. Combine remaining ingredients; add to gelatin mixture. Pour into large mold, and chill.

QUICK CONGEALED TOMATO ASPIC

Yield: 6 servings

2 (3-ounce) packages lemon
  gelatin
¾ cup boiling water
2 (16-ounce) cans stewed
  tomatoes

Lettuce leaves
6 teaspoons mayonnaise

Pour boiling water over lemon gelatin, and stir until completely dissolved. Pour stewed tomatoes over melted gelatin, and mix well. Chill several hours until firm. Serve squares of aspic on lettuce leaves with a teaspoon mayonnaise on top.

CUCUMBER GELATIN

Yield: 6-8 servings

1 (3-ounce) package lime
  gelatin
¾ cup boiling water
¼ cup lemon juice

1 cup sour cream
1 cup diced, unpared
  cucumber
1 teaspoon onion juice

Dissolve gelatin in boiling water; add lemon juice. Place in greased 4-cup mold. Chill until partially set. Add remaining ingredients, and chill until firm.

BLACK CHERRY-LEMON PEACH SALAD

Yield: 8 servings

1 (6-ounce) package black
  cherry gelatin
Mayonnaise
1 (16-ounce) can bing
  cherries, drained
1 (8-ounce) package cream
  cheese
1 (3-ounce) package cream
  cheese

½ cup chopped pecans
1 (6-ounce) package lemon
  gelatin
1 (16-ounce) can sliced
  peaches, drained
Lettuce leaves

Mix black cherry gelatin according to package directions. Place in mayonnaise greased 2-quart oblong pyrex dish. Chill until partially set, 30 to 45 minutes. Add drained bing cherries to gelatin. Chill until firmly set. Soften cream cheese, and mix with chopped nuts. Spread over gelatin. Chill until cheese and nut mixture is firm to touch. Make lemon gelatin according to package directions. Pour cooled lemon gelatin over cream cheese. Arrange drained peaches in the lemon gelatin. Chill until set. Slice in squares. Place on bed of lettuce.

NOTE: Worth the time it takes to make this.

CRANBERRY MOLD

Yield: 6 servings

Oil a 4-cup mold, and place in freezer for 1 to 2 hours before use.

2 (3-ounce) packages
  raspberry gelatin
2 cups boiling water
1 cup cold water
1 (8-ounce) can crushed
  pineapples, drained

1 (16-ounce) can whole berry
  cranberry sauce
½ cup chopped walnuts

Dissolve gelatin in hot water. Add cold water, and chill until partially thickened. Fold in pineapple, cranberry and nuts. Pour into the 4-cup chilled mold, and refrigerate until set.

PICKLED PEACH SALAD

Yield: 8 servings

2 (17-ounce) jars spiced
  peaches or 1 (29-ounce) jar
  pickled peaches
5 or 6 whole cloves
½ inch piece stick cinnamon
1 (3-ounce) package lemon
  gelatin

½ cup chopped pecans
6 to 8 lettuce leaves
1 or 2 tablespoons sour
  cream
6 to 8 pecan halves, for
  garnish

Drain juice from peaches into a pan, and set aside peaches. Add water, if needed, to make 2 cups juice. Add cloves and cinnamon stick to peach juice. Boil 3 to 4 minutes. Remove spices; add lemon gelatin, and dissolve well. Cut peaches into small pieces. Add nuts, and combine with gelatin mixture. Pour mixture into 9-inch square dish. Place in refrigerator until firm. Cut into squares, and place on lettuce leaves. Top with dollop of sour cream and pecan half.

ORANGE-MINCEMEAT CONGEALED SALAD

Yield: 30 servings

2 (6-ounce) packages orange
  gelatin
5 envelopes unflavored
  gelatin
2 (29-ounce) bottles
  mincemeat

1 cup miniature
  marshmallows
½ cup chopped walnuts
Mayonnaise

Prepare gelatin according to package instructions. Add unflavored gelatin; mix thoroughly until dissolved. Add mincemeat, marshmallows and nuts. Pour into 2 well-oiled (with mayonnaise) large ring molds.

To serve, mix the following and place in center of molds:

2 (8-ounce) packages cream
  cheese, softened

1 (12-ounce) jar sour orange
  marmalade

NOTE: Can be successfully divided using 2 envelopes unflavored gelatin in the above recipe and dividing remaining ingredients equally.

MANGO SALAD

Yield: 12 servings

3 (3-ounce) packages lemon
  gelatin
3 cups boiling water
2 cups mangoes, drained

1 (8-ounce) package cream
  cheese
Juice of 1 lime
Lettuce leaves

Dissolve gelatin in boiling water; set aside. Place mangoes and cream cheese into blender, and blend until creamy. Add to gelatin mixture, and stir in lime juice. Pour into 9x13-inch pan. Chill at least 4 to 6 hours. Cut into squares, and serve on lettuce.

PINEAPPLE AND CHEESE SALAD

Yield: 6-8 servings

2 cups crushed pineapple
Juice of 1 lemon
1 cup sugar
2 envelopes (2 tablespoons)
  gelatin

½ cup cold water
1 cup sharp grated cheese
½ cup chopped stuffed green
  olives
½ pint heavy cream, whipped

Heat crushed pineapple, lemon juice and sugar. Stir until sugar is dissolved. Soak gelatin in water. Then add to pineapple mixture. Cool until thickened but not set. Add cheese, olives, and whipped heavy cream. Mix well, and pour into 9-inch square glass dish. Chill.

WINE GELATIN RING

Yield: 8-10 servings

2 envelopes (2 tablespoons)
  unflavored gelatin
½ cup cold water
2 cups boiling water
1 cup sugar
½ cup sherry

½ cup port wine
3 tablespoons lemon juice
Pineapple slices
Sliced apple rings
Lettuce leaves

Add cold water to gelatin, and let stand 5 minutes to soften. Then add boiling water; stir until dissolved. Add sugar. When cool, add wines and lemon juice. Pour into 4-cup mold, and chill until firm. Serve with pineapple slices and spiced apple rings on lettuce.

NOTE: Good with roasts.

CUCUMBER AND CRAB MOUSSE

Yield: 8 servings

2 envelopes unflavored
  gelatin
½ cup cold water
2 cups boiling water
Green food coloring
1 (8-ounce) package cream
  cheese
½ cup mayonnaise
1 cup sour cream
¼ cup cider vinegar
2 tablespoons sugar
1 teaspoon grated lemon
  rind

2 tablespoons lemon juice
2 medium sized cucumbers,
  pared and diced
1 cup minced celery
1½ teaspoons salt
1 teaspoon dried thyme
⅓ cup thinly sliced green
  onions
2 (6-ounce) cans crabmeat,
  drained and flaked

Sprinkle gelatin over the cold water. Let stand 5 minutes. Add boiling water; stir until gelatin dissolves. Stir in a few drops food coloring. Chill just until mixture begins to thicken, about 30 minutes.

Combine cream cheese, mayonnaise, sour cream, vinegar, sugar, lemon rind and juice in medium sized bowl; beat until smooth. Blend gelatin mixture into cream cheese mixture; add rest of ingredients. Pour into 8-cup greased mold. Chill. Unmold onto chilled serving platter. Garnish with crisp greens, radish roses and/or carrot curls, if desired.

NOTE: This recipe can be halved successfully.

HONEY SPICE DRESSING

Yield: ½ cup

½ cup French dressing
1 tablespoon honey
½ teaspoon cinnamon

¼ teaspoon ground cloves
⅛ teaspoon ground ginger

Combine all ingredients, and mix well.

NOTE: Great on fruit salads.

CELERY SEED DRESSING

Yield: 1½ cups

1 teaspoon celery seed
½ cup sugar
1 teaspoon onion salt
1 teaspoon paprika

1 teaspoon dry mustard
¼ cup vinegar
1 cup vegetable oil

Combine celery seed, sugar, onion salt, paprika and dry mustard in small mixing bowl. Add alternately, 1 tablespoon vinegar and ¼ cup oil, until vinegar and oil are used up, beating after each addition. Continue beating for 5 minutes or until dressing thickens.

NOTE: Serve on avocado salad, fruit salad, sliced tomatoes or on Iceberg lettuce.

FRENCH DRESSING

Yield: 1 quart

2 tablespoons dry mustard
1 teaspoon salt
½ cup sugar
½ teaspoon black pepper
1 (10¾-ounce) can tomato
   soup
½ cup vinegar

3 teaspoons grated celery
3 teaspoons grated onion
¼ green pepper, grated
2 teaspoons lemon juice
½ teaspoon Tabasco sauce
1 cup vegetable oil

Combine mustard, salt, sugar and pepper. Add remaining ingredients. Beat well with mixer until thoroughly blended.

DIJON-HERB DRESSING

Yield: ⅔ cup

⅓ cup white wine vinegar
1 tablespoon Dijon-style
   mustard
1 teaspoon fresh oregano

⅛ teaspoon freshly ground
   black pepper
⅓ cup olive oil

Combine above ingredients. Mix well, and pour into dressing cruet. Store in refrigerator several hours before serving. Shake well before serving. Serve over favorite salad greens.

MEDITERRANEAN DRESSING

Yield: ⅔ cup

1 clove garlic, minced
½ teaspoon salt
½ teaspoon grated lemon
  rind
¼ teaspoon paprika

¼ teaspoon pepper
2 tablespoons tarragon
  vinegar
½ cup olive oil
2 tablespoons sour cream

Combine garlic, salt, lemon rind, paprika and pepper with tarragon vinegar in a blender. Gradually add oil, and blend well; add sour cream, and blend a few seconds more. Pour into a ½-pint container and chill.

NOTE: Great over spinach salad.

POPPY SEED DRESSING

Yield: 3½ cups

1½ cups sugar
2 teaspoons dry mustard
2 teaspoons salt
⅔ cup vinegar

3 tablespoons grated onion
2 cups vegetable oil
3 tablespoons poppy seed

Combine sugar, mustard, salt and vinegar; add onion. Stir thoroughly. Slowly add oil, beating constantly, and continue to beat until thick. When you think it is thick enough, beat 5 minutes longer. Add poppy seed, and beat a few more minutes. Refrigerate.

THOUSAND ISLAND DRESSING

Yield: about 3 cups

1 pint real mayonnaise
½ cup ketchup
¼ cup chopped purple onion
2 sticks celery, chopped
1 sprig fresh parsley,
  chopped

2 sweet pickles, chopped
2 teaspoons chopped
  pimentos
1 egg, hard-cooked and
  chopped

Blend mayonnaise and ketchup together by hand or at lowest speed on blender. Add remaining ingredients, and blend just enough to mix.

Sauces and Condiments

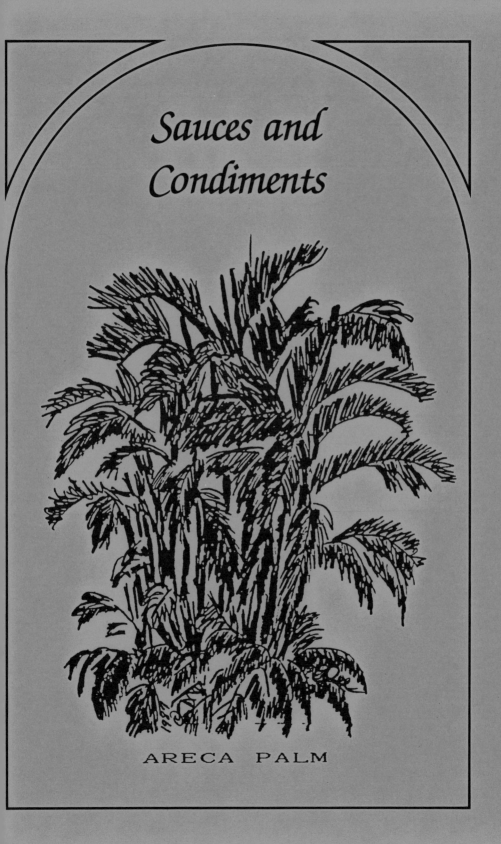

ARECA PALM

Hints for Sauces and Condiments

Garlic should have clean skins and firm bulbs. White is milder than rose colored garlics, but elephant garlic is the mildest.

Do not store garlic in the refrigerator. Keep it in a dry area with good ventilation. It will keep six to eight weeks.

To rid your hands of a garlic smell, rub them with salt, lemon juice or baking soda.

When adding oil to mayonnaise, do so very slowly. Continue to stir or else the ingredients will separate.

Microwaving enhances the natural flavor of food. Reduce your seasonings.

To help you find all the different spices on your shelf quickly, put them in alphabetical order.

Butter can be stored in the refrigerator for two weeks.

To keep salt loose in containers, insert a few grains of rice.

To get rid of a garlic taste in your mouth, eat parsley.

When preparing sauces in the microwave, use a glass container twice the size as the volume of sauce.

Use your leftover pickle juice to marinate fresh vegetables.

You will get more juice from a lemon or lime if you put it in warm water for ten minutes before juicing or microwave on high for 10 seconds.

Red spices should be stored in the refrigerator in order to retain their color and flavor.

Mushrooms stay fresher in the refrigerator when placed in a brown paper bag.

Onions peeled under cold water will keep you from crying.

Put sauce that has curdled in the blender and blend to remove curds.

To prevent gravy from lumping, first mix the flour with a small amount of water, and then add this to the pan juices.

Ground spices have only about a six month shelf life.

When substituting flour for cornstarch, use two tablespoons of flour to one tablespoon of cornstarch.

FAKE HOLLANDAISE
(Never-fail recipe)

Yield: 1 cup

¾ cup mayonnaise
⅓ cup milk

Salt and pepper, to taste
1 teaspoon lemon juice

Using a double boiler, cook mayonnaise and milk together over medium heat, for five minutes, stirring constantly. Add seasonings and lemon juice, stirring to blend flavors.

CREAMY MUSHROOM GARLIC SAUCE

Yield: 1½ cups

¼ pound fresh mushrooms
6 garlic cloves, minced
6 tablespoons butter
1 cup heavy cream

½ cup minced fresh parsley
1 cup grated fresh Parmesan
   cheese

Wash and drain mushrooms. Slice thin. Sauté mushrooms and garlic in butter for 15 minutes or until liquid has evaporated. Add cream and parsley, and simmer for 5 minutes. Add fresh Parmesan cheese, and stir until cheese is melted. Serve over pasta.

BASIC WHITE SAUCE

Yield: 4 cups

4 tablespoons butter or
   margarine
4 tablespoons flour

1 teaspoon salt
½ teaspoon pepper
4 cups milk

Melt butter in sauce pan. Remove from heat, and stir in flour, salt and pepper until smooth. Return to heat, and gradually stir in milk. Cook over medium heat until thickened.

NOTE: May be reduced successfully into fourths or halved.

CURRY SAUCE

Yield: 2¾ cups

1 medium onion, chopped
1 clove garlic, minced
2 tablespoons butter or
  margarine
3 tablespoons curry powder
1 large apple, chopped
2 tablespoons chopped
  cucumber

2 tablespoons chopped
  pimento
2 large carrots, chopped
2 cups chicken stock
½ cup coconut milk
2 tablespoons cornstarch

Sauté onion and garlic in butter until tender. Stir in curry powder. Cook until lightly browned. Add apples, cucumber, pimento and carrots. Add stock. Cook until vegetables are done. Puree in blender. Add coconut milk and cornstarch; heat and stir until thickened. Season to taste.

NOTE: Can be reduced by ½ successfully.

SAUCE DIABLO

Yield: 1½ cups

3 cloves garlic, finely
  chopped
1 medium onion, finely
  chopped
¼ cup vegetable oil
1 teaspoon cornstarch
¼ cup chopped dill pickle or
  pickle relish

2 tablespoons vinegar
½ cup ketchup
⅓ cup Worcestershire sauce
½ teaspoon salt
1 teaspoon dry mustard
1 teaspoon capers (optional)

Sauté chopped garlic and onion in the oil until soft. Add cornstarch, and cook for 10 minutes. Add chopped pickle, vinegar, ketchup and Worcestershire sauce. Bring to boil, and then add remaining ingredients.

NOTE: Great dipping sauce for fondue or sauce for meats.

BARBECUE SAUCE FOR CHICKEN OR TURKEY

Yield: 3 cups

1 pound margarine, melted
Juice of 6 lemons
1 (5-ounce) bottle
  horseradish
1 tablespoon Tabasco

½ cup white vinegar
2 tablespoons Worcestershire
  sauce
3 tablespoons salt

Mix all the ingredients together. Brush on chicken or turkey during last five minutes of cooking.

REMOULADE

Yield: 1⅓ cups

1 tablespoon each: chopped
  onion, chopped parsley,
  chopped celery
1 cup mayonnaise
2 tablespoons Dijon mustard
½ teaspoon Worcestershire
  sauce

1 tablespoon horseradish
½ teaspoon salt
1 teaspoon paprika
Dash Tabasco
1 tablespoon vinegar
¼ cup salad oil

Combine all ingredients. Mix well and chill. Serve with seafood.

COCKTAIL SAUCE FOR SEAFOOD

Yield: 1½ cups

1 cup chili sauce
½ cup horseradish
Dash of Tabasco sauce
2 tablespoons minced celery

Dash of Worcestershire
  sauce
1 teaspoon lime or lemon
  juice

Mix all ingredients together, and chill. Serve cold.

TARTAR SAUCE

Yield: 1½ cups

⅓ cup sour pickle, chopped fine

⅓ cup sweet pickle, chopped fine

⅓ cup chopped onion or shallots

1 tablespoon capers, well-drained

⅓ cup celery, minced

1 tablespoon green pepper, minced

¼ teaspoon dry chervil or several sprigs of chopped fresh chervil

⅛ teaspoon dry mustard

⅛ teaspoon white ground pepper

¼ cup mayonnaise

1 tablespoon horseradish

Drain all vegetables well. Mix all ingredients together, except mayonnaise and horseradish, and blend well. Add mayonnaise and horseradish; continue to blend. More mayonnaise may be added to achieve desired texture.

VARIATION: For a chicken spread, use 1 cup minced cooked chicken, and use the tartar sauce, omitting the mustard and horseradish. Add 6 to 8 drops Tabasco sauce and 6 to 8 drops Liquid Smoke.

HINTS: Use the tartar sauce recipe as the base for a smoked fish spread. Using your favorite smoked fish, flake with fork, and add enough tartar sauce to hold together. Good for open Danish sandwiches or crackers.

QUICK TARTAR SAUCE

Yield: ½ cup

½ cup mayonnaise

¼ teaspoon Worcestershire sauce

½ teaspoon grated onion

1 tablespoon each chopped pickle, chopped olives and lemon juice

Combine all ingredients. Stir just enough to mix well. Chill.

GO WITH ANYTHING SAUCE

Yield: 4 cups

1 small onion, chopped	⅛ teaspoon thyme
2 tablespoons butter	¼ cup water
1 (16-ounce) can peeled	½ cup heavy cream
tomatoes	Salt and pepper, to taste
⅔ cup white wine	¼ teaspoon garlic powder
1 teaspoon parsley	Fresh parsley to garnish

Brown onion in butter until tender; add can of chopped tomatoes. Add wine, parsley, and thyme; bring to a boil. Stir in water, and bring to boil again; turn down, and simmer for 5 minutes. Add cream and seasonings to mixture, reheat but do not boil. Serve hot.

NOTE: One pound of shrimp can be added and then poured over angel hair pasta. For an unusual flavor, ½ pound of sliced pepperoni can be used instead of the shrimp. Or use your imagination with fish or meats. This is a basic sauce.

DILL MUSTARD SAUCE

Yield: 1¼ cups

2 tablespoons butter or	¼ teaspoon dried dill weed
margarine	1 cup milk
2 tablespoons flour	1 tablespoon prepared
¼ teaspoon salt	mustard
⅛ teaspoon pepper	¼ cup sour cream

Melt butter in heavy pan. Blend in flour, salt, pepper and dill weed. Cook over low heat, stirring until smooth and bubbly. Remove from heat. Stir in milk and mustard. Bring to a boil, stirring constantly. Add small amount of sauce to the sour cream, and mix well until smooth. Put the two mixtures together and heat, but do not boil.

NOTE: This is delicious over vegetables, and the *Chicken Breasts in Ham* recipe.

GINGERED PLUM SAUCE

(Great basting sauce for chicken or a marinade for lamb kebabs!)

Yield: 1¼ cups

1 (16-ounce) can purple
  plums
1 medium onion, chopped
2 tablespoons margarine
⅓ cup brown sugar, firmly
  packed

¼ cup chili sauce
2 tablespoons soy sauce
1 teaspoon ground ginger
2 teaspoons lemon juice

Drain plums, saving liquid. Remove pits. Purée plums with liquid in blender. Cook onion in margarine until limp. Place all ingredients in pot, and simmer, uncovered, about 30 minutes, until slightly thickened. Stir occasionally. Cool, and pour into airtight container and refrigerate.

NOTE: Can be made a week before using.

BERKELEY MEAT SAUCE

Yield: about ½ cup

½ cup currant jelly
1 tablespoon lemon juice

1 tablespoon Worcestershire
  sauce

Combine all ingredients, and heat slightly in a sauce pan. Serve with any roasted meat. Good with cold meats, too.

MARINATING SAUCE FOR PORK ROAST

Yield: 1⅓ cups

½ cup soy sauce
⅓ cup honey
⅓ cup medium dry sherry

1 clove garlic, minced
¼ teaspoon ground ginger

In a sauce pan, combine all ingredients, and bring to a boil over moderate heat, stirring constantly. Reduce heat, and simmer for 5 minutes. Let cool. Marinate pork roast for at least 4 hours. Use to baste pork while cooking.

CHOCOLATE SAUCE

Yield: 1 pint

1 (14-ounce) can sweetened condensed milk
2 (1-ounce) squares unsweetened chocolate

½ stick butter or margarine

Melt chocolate in small amount of milk. Continue adding milk as chocolate melts. Add butter or margarine. Stir well. Store in pint jar. (Do not refrigerate.)

CARAMEL-RAISIN SAUCE

Yield: 1¼ cup

3 tablespoons butter
1 cup light brown sugar, packed firmly

½ cup cream or half and half
½ cup golden raisins
1 teaspoon vanilla extract

Heat butter in small sauce pan. Add brown sugar. Stir constantly over low heat for 10 minutes or until smooth. Remove from heat, and slowly add cream, stirring after each addition until blended. Heat 1 minute longer, and stir in raisins and vanilla. Serve either chilled or warmed.

NOTE: Good with vanilla or coffee ice cream pie or served over plain cake.

ORANGE SAUCE

Yield: 2 cups

½ cup sugar
2 tablespoons cornstarch
⅛ teaspoon salt
1 cup water
1 (11-ounce) can mandarin
    oranges

1 teaspoon grated orange
    rind
½ cup orange juice
3 tablespoons butter or
    margarine

In medium size sauce pan, combine sugar, cornstarch and salt. Add water slowly, and cook over medium heat, stirring constantly, until mixture thickens and boils about 3 minutes. Gently stir in remaining ingredients, and heat for 1 minute.

NOTE: May be made ahead and kept warm until serving time. Good over puddings or fruit cake.

ORANGE PANCAKE SAUCE

Yield: 1½ cups

1 (6-ounce) can frozen
    orange juice concentrate

1 cup sugar
½ cup butter or margarine

Combine ingredients in small sauce pan, and bring to boiling point only. Serve hot.

MARINATED CHICKPEAS (Garbanzos)

Serves 4 to 6 or more
if used as a salad garnishment

¼ cup olive oil
¼ cup wine vinegar
¼ teaspoon oregano
3 cloves garlic, minced
⅛ teaspoon red pepper flakes
⅛ teaspoon or less of sugar

3 to 4 capers
1 (16-ounce) can chickpeas
  or garbanzos, drained
6 sliced green olives
⅓ cup onion, coarsely
  chopped

In a blender, blend the first 7 ingredients together until thick and creamy. Add to the drained garbanzos, and mix well. Add sliced green olives and chopped onion. Mix well, cover and refrigerate. Chill at least 3 to 4 hours.

SQUASH PICKLES

Yield: 2 quarts

8 cups sliced squash (mix
  zucchini and yellow)
2 cups onions, sliced thin
¼ cup salt
4 green peppers, sliced

2 cups vinegar
3 cups sugar
1 teaspoon celery seed
1 teaspoon mustard seed

Sprinkle sliced squash, onions and peppers with salt. Stir to mix salt. Cover with ice. Let stand 1 hour. Drain. Bring vinegar, sugar and spices to a hard boil in a sauce pan. Remove from heat. Put squash mixture into syrup. Let stand one hour. Bring to a hard boil again. Put into sterilized jars, and seal.

NOTE: Good hostess gifts when put in ½ pint jars.

NUTTY MANGO CHUTNEY

Yield: 3 pints

1¼ cups vinegar
3½ cups sugar
6 cups chopped ripe mangoes
¼ cup crystalized ginger or 8
  small pieces ginger root
1 or 2 fresh chili peppers or
  1 teaspoon dried chili
  peppers

1 clove garlic, minced
1½ cups raisins
1 large onion, sliced thin
1 teaspoon salt
½ teaspoon nutmeg
½ teaspoon allspice
½ cup almonds, slivered
  and chopped

Boil and sterilize jars. In large sauce pan, bring to boil vinegar and sugar. Boil for 5 minutes. Stir in remaining ingredients, and cook over medium heat for 45 minutes, stirring occasionally. Pour into hot jars. Tighten lids lightly. Tighten after cooling.

CRANBERRY RELISH

Yield: 10-12 servings

4 cups fresh cranberries
1 cup water
2 oranges, quartered and
  seeds removed
½ lemon, juice and grated
  rind

1 teaspoon grated lemon
  rind
4 cups sugar
½ cup raisins
½ cup chopped nuts

Wash and remove stems of cranberries, and place in sauce pan. In a blender, grind the quartered oranges, and pour into sauce pan with cranberries. Add water, lemon juice, grated lemon rind and sugar. Bring to boiling point, stirring occasionally. Reduce heat to low for 5 to 10 minutes. Stir well, and turn off heat. Let stand for 30 minutes. Add raisins and nuts. Chill and use as needed.

SWEET PEPPER RELISH

(What to do with all those red bell peppers)

Yield: 1 quart

6 large red bell peppers   1 cup white vinegar
½ teaspoon salt   1 tablespoon butter
1½ cups sugar   1 sterilized quart jar

Grind peppers; sprinkle with salt and set aside for 2 hours. Drain well. Add sugar, vinegar and butter. Simmer 2 hours, stirring occasionally. Put into sterilized quart jar or 2 pint jars.

NOTE: Keeps in the refrigerator for months. It is great chilled and served over cream cheese with wheat crackers.

BRANDIED CRANBERRIES

Preheat oven to 300°   Yield: 10-12 servings

1 package fresh cranberries   ⅓ to ½ cup brandy
2 cups sugar

Wash berries, and put in a 9x13-inch pyrex baking dish. Pour sugar over berries. Cover with foil, and bake 1 hour or more at 300°. Let cool. Add brandy, and mix. Chill.

PEAR CONSERVE

Yield: 9 (6-ounce) jars

12 medium size pears, cored   8¼ cups sugar
1 (14-ounce) can pineapple   1 (3-ounce) bottle
  (1½ cups)   maraschino cherries
1 orange, juice and grated
  rind

Chop unpeeled pears and pineapple. Add orange juice, rind and sugar. Let stand overnight. Next morning, cook fruits slowly until thick, about 2½ hours. Add chopped maraschino cherries. Seal in hot, sterilized glasses.

FRESH FRUIT DIP

Yield: 1⅔ cups

**1 (9-ounce) container
whipped topping
½ cup sweet liqueur**

**½ (3-ounce) package instant
vanilla pudding**

Combine whipped topping and liqueur; sprinkle dry pudding mix over the top. Mix thoroughly, and chill. Use as dipping sauce for fresh fruit such as cantaloupe, pineapple, strawberries, etc.

STRAWBERRY BUTTER

Yield: 1¾ cups

**¾ cup frozen strawberries,
thawed and drained
1 cup butter, softened**

**3 tablespoons confectioners
sugar**

Combine all ingredients in a blender, and blend until smooth. Store in sealed container, and chill until ready to use.

NOTE: Delicious on hot homemade rolls or nut breads.

Vegetables

MEXICAN WASHINGTONIA

Hints for Vegetables and Side Dishes

Do not buy green-tinted or sprouted potatoes; their flavor will be decreased.

Use leftover mashed potatoes and make potato pancakes. (Mix with a beaten egg, salt and pepper. Saute in skillet until lightly browned.)

When microwaving potatoes, puncture each potato and wrap in a paper towel to get that oven flavor.

To remove sand from spinach, soak it in warm salt water for three minutes.

To prevent peppers from getting dry edges, wrap them in paper towels before putting in the refrigerator.

If you desire a different flavor when steaming vegetables, you can use beef bouillon or chicken stock instead of water.

Remember! Valuable vitamins are contained in the skin of the potato.

After peeling potatoes, place them in cool water to prevent them from turning brown before cooking.

Never add baking soda to green vegetables; it destroys their vitamin content.

Be sure you do not overcook cabbage. It will lose its vitamin content and its color. It will also smell bad!

To core lettuce, hit it once on its core. The core can then be removed easily.

After washing mushrooms, use immediately or they will turn brown. Save the stems for gravies, meat sauces, soups or stuffings.

Rice can be stored in a sealed container for years without deteriorating.

When steaming vegetables, use as little water as possible.

Frozen vegetables can be microwaved in their box by simply piercing the box several times before cooking.

Tofu are soybeans that have been made into a cheese-like substance. Tofu has no cholesterol and is very high in vitamins and minerals. It should be stored in the refrigerator in water which is changed daily. It will keep approximately a week. Tofu may be used as a substitute for cottage cheese and Ricotta cheese in recipes. It is also excellent for dips.

When using vegetables try some of these Florida favorites:

a. Cilantro: It is also known as Chinese parsley. It has a flat leaf and long stem. It will keep fresh for about a week if the roots are put in a glass of water and the leaves are covered with a plastic bag. Keep it in the refrigerator. It adds a unique flavor to guacamole.

b. Jicama: It is a root vegetable that is round and flattened on the top and bottom. It looks like a potato. It is great for a vegetable dipper when peeled and cut into strips. Mexicans use this vegetable in a variety of cold vegetable plates.

c. Malanga: Potato-sized growths are produced on underground stems of the Malanga plant. These underground portions are cooked and utilized the same way white potatoes are.

d. Boniatos: These are large red-skinned sweet potatoes. They have a white flesh and are usually baked or steamed.

e. Calabaza: It is also called West Indian Pumpkin. It is a hard-shelled squash. These squash are usually baked. They have a thick yellowish green rind and an orange-yellow flesh.

ARTICHOKE PIE

Preheat oven to 350°   Yield: 6 servings

1 (16-ounce) can artichoke
   hearts
3 tablespoons butter
¼ cup Parmesan cheese
4 ounces Mozzarella cheese,
   diced

Salt, to taste
Pepper, to taste
½ teaspoon garlic powder
Dash of Tabasco
4 eggs, beaten
2 (9-inch) pie crusts

Combine artichokes and butter in a skillet; sauté, mashing the artichokes. Combine the rest of the ingredients and pour into the 9-inch pie shell. Top with the other crust. Seal the edges and make a few slits in the top. Bake at 350° for 30 to 40 minutes or until golden brown.

BAKED ASPARAGUS

Preheat oven to 300°   Yield: 4 servings

1-1½ pounds fresh asparagus
3 tablespoons butter

Salt and pepper to taste

Rinse and trim asparagus; place 1 or 2 layers deep in flat baking dish. Dot with butter, salt and pepper. Cover tightly with foil and bake at 300° for 30 minutes. Asparagus will be bright green and still crunchy.

THOSE GOOD GREEN BEANS

Preheat oven to 350°   Yield: 6 servings

½ cup chopped onion
2 tablespoons butter
2 tablespoons flour
1 teaspoon salt
¼ teaspoon pepper
1 cup sour cream

2 (10-ounce) packages frozen
   French style green beans
   (cooked and drained)
1½ cups shredded sharp
   cheese

Cook onions in butter until tender. Blend in flour, salt and pepper; add sour cream. Cook, stirring constantly, until smooth and thick. Add beans and pour into buttered casserole. Top with cheese. Bake at 350° for 30 minutes.

STRING BEANS—NEW ORLEANS STYLE

Yield: 4 servings

2 slices bacon, cut in
  1-inch pieces
¼ cup chopped onion
1 (16-ounce) can string beans

½ cup stewed tomatoes
¼ teaspoon salt
Pepper, to taste

Fry bacon and onion together until golden brown; remove and drain bacon. Add green beans, tomatoes, salt and pepper. Heat 10 to 15 minutes. Crumble bacon over mixture just before serving.

SOUTHERN GREEN BEANS

Yield: 8 servings

2 pounds fresh green beans
3 to 4 strips thick-sliced
  bacon
2 teaspoons salt

1 quart water
1 tablespoon molasses
⅛ to ¼ teaspoon black pepper

Wash and drain beans. Remove ends and break into 2-inch lengths. Cut bacon in ½-inch pieces, and sauté over medium heat in large heavy pan. Add beans, salt and enough water to cover. Bring to boil; reduce heat; cover and cook 20 minutes. Stir in molasses; cover and simmer 1 hour. Beans will be firm and tender. Serve with freshly ground pepper.

GREEN BEANS IN SOUR CREAM SAUCE

Yield: 12 servings

¾ cup mayonnaise
⅓ cup finely chopped onion
1 teaspoon anchovy paste
½ teaspoon vinegar
2 teaspoons lemon juice
½ teaspoon Accent (optional)

1 teaspoon garlic juice or
  powder
4 (16-ounce) cans French
  style green beans
1 cup sour cream

Combine mayonnaise, onion, anchovy paste, vinegar, lemon juice, Accent and garlic in blender. Blend well. Drain green beans well. In large mixing bowl, combine sour cream and blended dressing mixture. Add beans and mix well. Place in 1½-quart casserole dish; cover and refrigerate for 24 hours.

NOTE: Garnish with sprigs of fresh parsley and cherry tomatoes to add color. Expect raves over this one!

BRAZILIAN BLACK BEANS

Yield: 6-8 servings

1½ pounds dried black beans, soaked overnight or 5 cans cooked black beans, undrained
1 (2½-ounce) jar dried beef, rinsed well in warm water
½ pound or 4 chorizos (Spanish style pork sausage)

2 smoked pork chops or 1 pound good smoked ham
1 pound pork spareribs or other pork
1 cup chopped onion
3 or 4 chopped jalapeño peppers
3 cloves garlic, minced

If using dried beans — Place in large pot; cover with 1½ quarts water. Cook 2 hours. Add all meat, cut into 1-inch pieces, except spareribs. Cut spareribs only to separate the ribs. Place in cookpot with beans, increasing liquid, if necessary. Lightly sauté vegetables, and add to beans and meat. Simmer until beans are tender or about 1 hour longer.

If using canned beans — Sauté spareribs until lightly browned, and add other meats and 2 cups of water. Simmer gently ½ hour, then add meats to large pot with lightly sautéed vegetables. Add beans, and cook gently for 10 minutes.

CUBAN BLACK BEANS

Yield: 4-6 servings

½ pound dried black beans
½ cup olive oil
1 large onion, chopped
2 green peppers, chopped
1 clove garlic, minced

1 tablespoon salt
1 quart water
½ pound ham, cubed
¼ cup vinegar (optional)

Soak beans overnight. Drain. Sauté onion, green pepper and garlic in olive oil. Combine remaining ingredients except vinegar. Cook over slow heat until beans are tender and liquid is thick (about 3 hours). If necessary, water may be added. Stir in vinegar just before serving.

NOTE: Great served over cooked rice.

CHEESY BROCCOLI BAKE

Preheat oven to 350°   Yield: 6-8 servings

2 (10-ounce) packages frozen
  broccoli
½ cup chopped onion
4 ounces chopped mushrooms
2 tablespoons butter
1 (8-ounce) can sliced water
  chestnuts, drained
½ pound Velveeta cheese,
  cubed

1 (10¾-ounce) can cream of
  mushroom soup
¼ teaspoon garlic salt
¼ teaspoon pepper
4 to 6 ounces shredded
  cheddar cheese

Prepare broccoli according to package directions, and drain thoroughly. Sauté onion and mushrooms in butter until tender and drain. Combine with broccoli and water chestnuts, stirring gently. Set aside. Combine Velveeta and soup; cook over low heat until cheese melts. Pour over broccoli, and stir in salt and pepper. Spoon into greased 2-quart casserole dish, and bake at 350° for 25 minutes. Sprinkle with cheddar cheese, and bake an additional 5 minutes. Let stand 10 to 15 minutes before serving.

SICILIAN BROCCOLI

Yield: 6-8 servings

1 bunch fresh broccoli
4 tablespoons butter
2 cloves garlic, minced
½ cup large black olives,
  pitted and sliced

Grated Parmesan cheese
Lemon wedges

Divide broccoli into flowerets, and steam until cooked but still crisp. Drain and place in warm serving dish. In a small pan, melt butter, and sauté garlic. Add sliced olives. Pour butter mixture over broccoli, and sprinkle Parmesan cheese on top. Serve with lemon wedges.

CHEESE BROCCOLI WITH SPAGHETTI

Preheat oven to 350°   Yield: 8 servings

1 (8-ounce) package fine   1 pound Velveeta cheese,
  spaghetti   cubed
1 large bunch fresh broccoli   Buttered bread crumbs
Diced onion, to taste   1 cup half and half

Cook and drain spaghetti according to package directions. Cook broccoli until almost done, and cut into bite-sized pieces. Brown onion slightly in margarine, and mix with broccoli.

Using a 2½-quart buttered casserole, layer the spaghetti, broccoli, onion and cheese. Repeat layers and top with buttered bread crumbs. At this point the mixture can be refrigerated.

To bake, pour half and half over top. Bake uncovered at 350° for 30 minutes (longer if refrigerated before baking).

NOTE: This is a good dish to serve with ham, pork, beef or chicken. Also good reheated with a little milk.

CARROT SOUFFLÉ

Preheat oven to 350°   Yield: 4-6 servings

1 pound cleaned, cooked   1 teaspoon vanilla
  carrots   ½ cup melted butter or
3 eggs   margarine
¾ cup sugar   ⅛ teaspoon each of nutmeg
3 tablespoons flour   and cinnamon
1 teaspoon baking powder

Combine cooked carrots and eggs in blender or food processor. Add sugar, flour, baking powder, vanilla, butter and spices; blend everything well. Pour into lightly greased 1½-quart dish.

Topping:
¼ cup cornflake crumbs   ¼ cup chopped walnuts
3 tablespoons brown sugar   ⅛ teaspoon each of nutmeg
2 tablespoons butter   and cinnamon

Mix above ingredients, and place on top of carrot mixture. Bake, uncovered, at 350° for 45 minutes or until center is set.

ITALIAN FLAVORED BAKED CARROTS

Preheat oven to 350°   Yield: 4-6 servings

4 cups (about 2 pounds)
  cooked carrots, mashed
Reserved carrot water
1 cup Italian flavored bread
  crumbs
1 small onion, chopped fine

3 tablespoons melted butter
¼ teaspoon pepper
1 teaspoon salt
¼ cup grated Provolone
  cheese

Combine cooked carrots, crumbs, onion, butter, pepper and salt. Add ¼ cup to ½ cup carrot water to moisten. Turn into a 1½-quart greased baking dish. Sprinkle with grated cheese. Bake uncovered at 350° for 15 to 20 minutes.

HONEY BUTTERED CARROTS
(Easy)

Yield: 8 servings

1 (16-ounce) bag frozen baby
  carrots
1 cup water
½ teaspoon salt

3 tablespoons honey
3 tablespoons butter
¼ teaspoon cinnamon
¼ teaspoon nutmeg

Cook carrots in water and salt for 15 minutes. Drain, and add honey, butter and spices. Heat for 5 minutes.

CARROTS LYONNAISE

Yield: 4-6 servings

1 pound carrots
½ cup boiling water
1 beef bouillon cube
¼ cup butter
3 medium onions, sliced

1 tablespoon flour
Dash of pepper
¼ teaspoon salt
¾ cup water
1 teaspoon sugar

Pare and julienne carrots. Dissolve bouillon cube in boiling water. Cook carrots in this water, covered, for 10 minutes. Melt butter in sauce pan; add onions; cover and cook slowly until limp. Mix flour with ¾ cup water. Pour into onion-butter mixture and stir. Add salt and pepper, and carrots with liquid; simmer, uncovered, 10 minutes. Sprinkle with 1 teaspoon sugar.

ZESTY CARROTS

Preheat oven to 375°   Yield: 4 servings

6 to 8 carrots, cleaned and cut   ½ cup mayonnaise
    in strips   ½ teaspoon salt
2 cups water   ¼ teaspoon pepper
¼ cup liquid from carrots   Dash paprika
2 tablespoons minced onion   ¼ cup cracker crumbs
2 tablespoons horseradish   1 tablespoon butter

Place carrot strips in sauce pan and cover with 2 cups water. Cook over medium heat until barely tender, 6 to 8 minutes. Drain, reserving ¼ cup liquid. Place carrots in shallow baking dish. Mix the reserved liquid, onion, horseradish, mayonnaise, salt, pepper and paprika. Pour over carrots, and sprinkle cracker crumbs on top. Dot with butter. Bake at 375° for 15 to 20 minutes.

CAULIFLOWER CASSEROLE

Preheat oven to 350°   Yield: 8 servings

1 head cauliflower, broken   1½ teaspoons salt
    into flowerets   1 cup boiling water
2 cups diced celery

Pour boiling water and salt over cauliflower and celery; cover and let set for 12 to 15 minutes. Drain. Set aside.

Sauce:
¼ cup butter   ¼ cup onion, chopped
⅛ teaspoon pepper   1 tablespoon green pepper,
¼ cup flour   diced
1½ cups milk   ½ cup cheddar cheese,
2 tablespoons diced pimento   shredded

Melt butter; add pepper and flour; stir to blend until smooth. Add milk slowly, stirring constantly. Add pimento, onion, green pepper and shredded cheese. Mix with cauliflower. Pour into greased casserole. Bake at 350° for 25 minutes.

BAKED CAULIFLOWER

Preheat oven to 350°   Yield: 4 servings

1 large whole cauliflower   **1 teaspoon Dijon mustard**
½ cup mayonnaise   **½ cup grated cheddar cheese**

Boil or steam cauliflower until tender. Place cauliflower in glass baking dish. Mix mayonnaise and mustard, and pour over cauliflower. Sprinkle with grated cheese, and bake at 350° for about 15 minutes. Serve whole.

MANDA'S BAKED CORN

Preheat oven to 350°   Yield: 6 servings

1 (15 or 16-ounce) can cream   **1 egg**
** style corn**   **½ cup cream or**
¼ cup flour   ** ¼ cup of milk**
1 large green pepper, diced   **2 tablespoons butter or**
1 tablespoon sugar   ** margarine, melted**

Combine ingredients in order. Pour into 1-quart casserole dish. Bake at 350° for 1 hour.

SOUTHERN STYLE CREAMED CORN

                                                        Yield: 8 servings

2 (10-ounce) packages frozen   **6 teaspoons sugar**
** corn**   **⅛ teaspoon white pepper**
8 ounces whipping cream   **2 tablespoons melted butter**
8 ounces whole milk   **2 tablespoons flour**
¼ teaspoon monosodium
** glutamate (optional)**

Combine all ingredients except butter and flour. Bring to a boil, and simmer for 5 minutes. Blend butter with the flour; add to corn. Mix well and simmer until thickened slightly.

CORN CASSEROLE

Preheat oven to 350°   Yield: 6 servings

½ cup butter
1 (16-ounce) can whole kernel
   corn, drained
1 (16-ounce) can cream style
   corn
1 cup sour cream

2 eggs
1 (8-ounce) package corn
   bread mix
1 small onion, grated
Grated cheddar cheese, for
   topping

Combine all ingredients except cheese. Place in greased 8x8-inch casserole dish. Top with grated cheese. Bake in greased 8x8-inch casserole at 350° for 45 minutes.

QUICK EGGPLANT PARMESAN

Preheat oven to 350°   Yield: 4-6 servings

1 large eggplant, peeled and
   cubed
¼ cup vegetable oil
1 can (8-ounce) tomato sauce

½ cup Parmesan cheese,
   grated
1 (4-ounce) package shredded
   Mozzarella cheese

Peel and cube eggplant. Sauté in oil until lightly browned. In greased baking dish, layer eggplant, tomato sauce, Parmesan and Mozzarella cheese until dish is filled, ending with cheese layer. Bake at 350° about 15 to 20 minutes, until cheese melts.

STUFFED EGGPLANT

Preheat oven to 300°   Yield: 4-6 servings

1 medium eggplant
Vegetable oil (for oiling
  inside and outside of
  eggplant)
Salt, to taste
Aluminum foil
1 medium apple, pared, cored
  and diced
1 medium onion, chopped

1 large tomato, seeded and
  chopped
1 clove garlic, crushed
1 teaspoon thyme
2 tablespoons butter or
  margarine
1/3 cup wheat germ
1/3 cup Parmesan cheese

Cut eggplant in half, lengthwise; scoop out pulp to within ½ inch of skin. Reserve pulp. Brush eggplant with oil inside and out. Sprinkle with salt, and cover with foil. Place on cookie sheet in 300° oven for 15 minutes. Remove foil from eggplant. Combine remaining ingredients (except butter, wheat germ and Parmesan cheese) with pulp from eggplant. Place mixture in warm eggplant shells.

In a sauce pan, melt butter, and add wheat germ and the Parmesan cheese. Stir until thoroughly mixed. Spoon over stuffed eggplant, and bake at 350°, uncovered, for 40 to 45 minutes or until heated through and brown on top.

CREAMED ONIONS

Yield: 6 servings

24 small (pearl or boiler)
  onions
1 tablespoon butter or
  margarine
1 bay leaf
1/8 teaspoon thyme
1/4 teaspoon black pepper

1/4 cup chicken broth
1/4 cup white wine
1 tablespoon cornstarch
1 teaspoon water or more
1 cup heavy cream
Chopped parsley for garnish

Peel onions. Pierce X in root end of onions. Arrange side by side in large sauce pan.

Mix butter, bay leaf, thyme and pepper with equal amounts of wine and chicken broth. Pour over onions. Cover the onions, and simmer until onions are tender. Mixture should evaporate. If not, boil quickly until the mixture evaporates. Add cornstarch with cold water to keep from lumping, and then mix with heavy cream. Pour over onions. Simmer to thicken.

Before serving, sprinkle with chopped parsley. Serve warm.

ONION CELESTE

Preheat oven to 350°   Yield: 6 servings

2 tablespoons butter, melted
2 large onions
2 cups grated Swiss cheese
¼ teaspoon pepper
1 (10¾-ounce) can cream of
  chicken soup

1 cup half and half
8 slices of slightly dry and
  buttered French bread

Cook onions in butter until soft. Spoon into a 6-cup baking dish, and spread cheese evenly on top. Sprinkle with pepper. Heat soup and half and half in a medium sauce pan for a few minutes. Stir until smooth. Pour over onion/cheese layer. Lift lightly with a knife to allow sauce to flow to bottom of dish. Overlap bread slices on top of dish. Bake at 350° for 30 minutes or until bread is toasted and sauce is bubbly.

CARIBBEAN PIGEON PEAS AND RICE

Yield: 8 servings

¼ pound salt pork or ham,
  diced
2 tablespoons vegetable oil
1 small onion, sliced
½ green pepper, chopped
1 stalk celery, chopped
2 teaspoons thyme
1 (6-ounce) can tomato paste,
  optional

¾ cup cooked pigeon peas
4 cups water
1½ tablespoons salt
Black pepper or cayenne
  pepper, to taste
2 cups uncooked rice

In a 2-quart sauce pan or pot, fry the salt pork to render out the fat. Add oil, and sauté onion until transparent. Add green pepper, celery, thyme and tomato paste; simmer 5 minutes. Add peas, and cook another 5 minutes. Add water, salt and the pepper to taste. Boil 10 minutes. Add rice and cook, covered, over medium heat until liquid is gone, about 25 minutes. Fluff rice.

NOTE: Pigeon peas are Caribbean peas found in the specialty or freezer section of your grocery store.

BLEU CHEESE POTATO CASSEROLE

Preheat oven to 300°   Yield: 6 servings

6 medium potatoes
1 pint sour cream
2 ounces grated Bleu cheese
2 cups grated cheddar cheese
8 green onions, chopped
⅓ cup milk
½ teaspoon Nature's Seasons
    seasoning blend

Pepper to taste
4 teaspoons butter or
    margarine
2 cups soft bread crumbs
¼ cup finely chopped nuts,
    preferably pecans

Peel potatoes and grate coarsely. Blend in sour cream, cheeses, onions, milk and spices. Mix and place in 9x13-inch pan. Melt 2 tablespoons butter, and add crumbs to butter. Scatter buttered crumbs and nuts over potato mixture. Bake at ° for 50 minutes or until golden.

POTATOES ELEGANTÉ

Preheat oven to 350°   Yield: 8 servings

4 cups hot mashed potatoes
1 (8-ounce) package cream
    cheese (room temperature)
1 egg, well beaten
⅓ cup finely chopped onion

¼ cup finely chopped
    pimento
1 teaspoon salt
Dash of pepper

Mix ingredients in order given. Place in 2-quart casserole dish, and bake at 350° for 45 minutes.

OVEN BAKED POTATOES

Preheat oven to 400°   Yield: 6 servings

4 large baking potatoes
¼ cup butter
¼ cup vegetable oil
2 garlic cloves, minced

½ teaspoon salt
½ teaspoon dried thyme
    leaves

Cut unpared potatoes in ¼-inch thick slices. Place overlapping slices in a buttered 9x13-inch baking dish. Dribble melted butter and oil over potatoes. Sprinkle with garlic, salt and thyme. Bake at 400° for 25 to 30 minutes or until potatoes are done and browned at edges. Serve at once.

COMPANY POTATOES

Preheat oven to 350°   Yield: 6 servings

6 medium potatoes
1 cup sour cream
1 can cream of chicken soup
1 teaspoon salt
¼ teaspoon pepper

¼ teaspoon curry powder
4 hard-cooked eggs, sliced
½ cup soft bread crumbs
½ cup sharp cheddar cheese,
  grated

Cook potatoes until tender, and slice to about ¼ inch thickness. Combine sour cream, soup, salt, pepper and curry powder. Cover bottom of 2-quart casserole with about ⅓ of the potatoes. Top with layer of egg slices, then layer of soup mixture, using about ⅓. Repeat layers, ending with soup mixture. Combine crumbs with cheese, and sprinkle over top. It may be necessary to add a small amount of milk if a creamy consistency is desired. Bake at 350° about 30 minutes.

SWEET POTATO CASSEROLE

Preheat oven to 350°   Yield: 8 servings

½ cup milk
2 eggs, slightly beaten
3 cups sweet potatoes,
  cooked and mashed

¼ cup sugar
½ teaspoon salt
1 teaspoon vanilla
1 stick (¼ pound) margarine

Mix all ingredients together, and pour into well-greased 2-quart casserole. Top with topping below.

Topping:
⅓ cup melted margarine
1 cup chopped pecans or
  walnuts

½ cup self-rising flour
1 cup firmly packed brown
  sugar

Mix all ingredients together, and spread evenly over potatoes. Bake at 350° for 35 minutes.

NOTE: This recipe may be made ahead and frozen before baking. Thaw before baking.

SWEET POTATO PATTIES

Yield: 2-4 servings

2 medium sweet potatoes,
  baked
2 tablespoons butter or
  margarine, divided

½ teaspoon ground ginger
1 teaspoon pumpkin pie
  seasoning spice
3 tablespoons chopped nuts

Scoop out baked potatoes. Mash. Beat in 1 tablespoon butter, ginger and seasoning spice. Shape into 4 patties. Roll patties in chopped nuts.

Heat remaining butter over low heat, and place patties in pan. Cook over medium heat until crisp.

EASY POTATOES AU GRATIN

Preheat oven to 350°

Yield: 8 servings

1 (2-pound) package frozen
  hash brown potatoes
½ cup butter or margarine,
  melted
1 (10¾-ounce) can cream of
  chicken soup
1 pint sour cream

2 cups Velveeta or American
  cheese, grated
2 tablespoons minced onion
1 teaspoon salt
½ teaspoon pepper
Cracker crumbs and butter
  pats (optional)

Thaw hash browns; mix with remaining ingredients, and place in 9x13-inch baking dish. Sprinkle top with cracker crumbs and pats of butter. Bake at 350° for 1 hour.

SPINACH POTATOES

Preheat oven to 350°

Yield: 6-8 servings

5 to 6 medium potatoes
1 cup sour cream
¼ cup milk
1 tablespoon butter
Salt and pepper to taste
1 (10-ounce) package frozen
  chopped spinach

1 teaspoon dill weed
2 tablespoons Parmesan
  cheese, grated
2 or 3 tablespoons butter

Peel, boil and mash potatoes. Add sour cream, milk, butter, salt and pepper. Cook spinach according to package instructions. Drain thoroughly. Fold into potato mixture; add dill weed and Parmesan cheese. Mix well. Place in 9x9-inch casserole dish, and cover with additional Parmesan cheese. Dot with butter. Bake at 350° for 20 to 30 minutes, covered. Should have a little crust when ready.

SPINACH CASSEROLE

Preheat oven to 350°   Yield: 6 servings

2 (10-ounce) packages frozen
  chopped spinach
1 envelope onion soup mix
1 cup sour cream

¼ cup herb stuffing mix
4 tablespoons butter or
  margarine

Cook spinach; drain and add soup mix and sour cream. Bake in greased 1½-quart casserole at 350° for 30 minutes. Add the ¼ cup of stuffing mix which has been moistened in melted butter to the top. Bake 10 minutes more.

SPINACH AND ARTICHOKE CASSEROLE

Preheat oven to 350°   Yield: 16 servings

7 (10-ounce) packages frozen
  chopped spinach
2 (8-ounce) cans artichoke
  hearts
1 (8-ounce) can water
  chestnuts, sliced
2 (8-ounce) packages cream
  cheese

½ pound butter or margarine
1 clove garlic, minced
2 tablespoons onion flakes
⅛ teaspoon salt
1 teaspoon freshly ground
  pepper
Bread crumbs for topping

Cook spinach according to package directions and drain. Butter a 9x13-inch casserole. Add layer of artichoke hearts, then a layer of water chestnuts. Melt cream cheese and butter in double boiler over low heat. Mix together with spinach. Add garlic, onion flakes, salt and pepper. Pour this mixture in the casserole over chestnuts and artichokes. Sprinkle with bread crumbs, and bake at 350° for 35 minutes.

SUPERB SPINACH PIE

Preheat oven to 350°   Yield: 6-8 servings

1 (10-ounce) package frozen
  chopped spinach
1 (3-ounce) package cream
  cheese, softened
5 eggs, slightly beaten
1 cup sharp cheddar cheese
  grated

½ teaspoon salt
¼ cup chopped green onion
2 teaspoons chopped parsley
1 tomato, thinly sliced
9-inch unbaked pie shell
¼ cup Parmesan cheese,
  grated

Squeeze cooked spinach and drain. Combine cream cheese, eggs, sharp cheddar cheese, salt, onion, parsley and spinach; pour into pie shell. Place tomato slices on top, and sprinkle with Parmesan cheese. Bake at 350° for 35 minutes.

SUMMER SQUASH BAKE

Preheat oven to 350°   Yield: 6 servings

2 cups yellow squash,
  cooked, drained and mashed
1 (10¾-ounce) can cream of
  chicken soup
2 carrots, grated (optional)
1 (2-ounce) jar chopped
  pimentos, drained

½ to 1 teaspoon salt
¼ teaspoon pepper
1 stick margarine or butter,
  melted
1 (8-ounce) package of
  cornbread stuffing mix

Mix together the squash, soup, carrots, pimentos, salt and pepper. Reserve ¾ cup stuffing mix for top of casserole. Mix remainder stuffing mix with melted butter. Line bottom of 2-quart casserole with stuffing mixture. Add squash mixture on top of stuffing mixture, and place reserved ¾ cup of crumbs on top. Bake at 350° for 30 to 40 minutes.

BAKED STUFFED TOMATOES

Preheat oven to 400°   Yield: 1 serving

1 medium tomato per person,
  slice off top

Place following on top of each tomato:

⅛ teaspoon dry mustard
1 teaspoon brown sugar
⅛ teaspoon seasoning salt
1 heaping tablespoon
  seasoned stuffing or
  cornflake crumbs

1 heaping tablespoon
  Parmesan cheese, grated
1 tablespoon butter or
  margarine
1 tablespoon brandy

Bake at 400° for 40 minutes, uncovered.

TOMATO CORN CASSEROLE

Preheat oven to 350°   Yield: 4 servings

2 cups herb stuffing mix
2 tablespoons melted
  margarine or butter
1 (17-ounce) can whole
  kernel corn, drained
1 (10½-ounce) can condensed
  tomato soup
½ soup can of light cream

1 tablespoon chopped onion
1 tablespoon brown sugar
1 teaspoon dried parsley
  flakes, crushed
½ teaspoon basil leaves,
  crushed

In a shallow (10x6x2-inch) baking dish, toss stuffing mix with butter. Top with corn. Blend remaining ingredients and pour over corn. Bake at 350° for 30 minutes or until hot and bubbly.

SPINACH-TOPPED TOMATOES

Preheat oven to 350°   Yield: 4-6 servings

2 tablespoons butter or
  margarine
1 small onion, minced
1 clove garlic, minced
1 (10-ounce) package frozen
  chopped spinach

½ cup dried bread crumbs
1 teaspoon salt
1 egg, beaten
⅛ teaspoon ground nutmeg
2 large or 3 small tomatoes,
  cut in half

Cook onion and garlic in butter until tender. Add spinach, and cook 8 minutes, stirring occasionally. Remove from heat; stir in bread crumbs, salt, nutmeg and egg. Set aside.

Place tomato halves, cut side up, in baking dish. Mound ½ cup mixture onto each half. Bake at 350° for 25 minutes or until heated through.

TOMATO PIE

Preheat oven to 425°   Yield: 6-8 servings

8- or 9-inch pie crust,
  unbaked
5 medium tomatoes, peeled
  and sliced

½ cup mayonnaise
½ cup Parmesan cheese
1 teaspoon garlic juice
½ teaspoon salt

Bake pie crust 5 minutes at 425°. Reduce heat to 300°. Remove and add tomatoes to shell. Mix remaining ingredients, and pour over tomatoes. Bake at 300° for 45 minutes.

TOMATOES IN CREAM SAUCE

Yield: 4 servings

2 (16-ounce) cans tomatoes
2 tablespoons minced onion
½ cup chopped celery
¾ teaspoon salt
¼ teaspoon paprika

2 teaspoons brown sugar
1 tablespoon flour
½ cup light cream or ½ cup milk plus 2 tablespoons butter

Simmer tomatoes, onion and celery for 10 minutes. Season with salt, paprika and sugar. Combine flour and cream in separate sauce pan, and bring to a boil, stirring until smooth. Add tomato mixture to cream slowly. Stir constantly to avoid curdling. (Be careful not to reverse the process.)

COLORFUL ZUCCHINI

Preheat oven to 350°

Yield: 4 servings

6 small zucchini, cut in ¼-inch slices
1 (16-ounce) can tomatoes, drained well
1 (4-ounce) package grated Mozzarella cheese

½ medium onion, chopped
Salt and pepper, to taste
Buttered bread crumbs or Parmesan cheese

Combine all ingredients; place in buttered 1½-quart casserole. Top with buttered bread crumbs or Parmesan cheese. Bake at 350° for 50 minutes. Drain. Recipe may be doubled.

ITALIAN ZUCCHINI PIE

Preheat oven to 375°   Yield: 6 servings

4 cups thinly sliced, unpeeled
  zucchini
1 cup coarsely chopped onion
½ cup margarine
2 tablespoons parsley,
  chopped
½ teaspoon salt
¼ teaspoon garlic powder
¼ teaspoon pepper

¼ teaspoon basil
¼ teaspoon oregano leaves
2 eggs, well beaten
2 cups Mozzarella cheese
1 (8-ounce) can crescent
  dinner rolls
2 teaspoons prepared
  mustard

In large skillet, cook zucchini and onion in margarine until tender, about 10 minutes. Stir in parsley and seasonings. Blend eggs and cheese in large bowl, and stir in vegetable mixture. Set aside.

Separate crescent rolls into 8 triangles. Place in ungreased (11-inch) quiche pan, (10-inch) pie pan or (12x8-inch) baking dish. Press dough over bottom and up sides to form crust. Spread crust with mustard. Pour vegetable mixture evenly into crust. Bake at 375° for 18 to 20 minutes or until knife inserted near center comes out clean. (If crust becomes too brown, cover with foil during last 10 minutes of baking.) Let stand 10 minutes before serving. Cut into wedges to serve.

MONTERREY ZUCCHINI SQUASH

Yield: 4-6 servings

4 medium zucchini
2 cups soft white bread cubes
¼ cup Parmesan cheese
1 cup grated sharp cheddar
  cheese (reserve ¼ cup
  for topping)

1 teaspoon salt
¼ teaspoon pepper
¼ teaspoon oregano
¼ teaspoon garlic powder
½ cup melted butter or
  margarine

Trim ends from squash. Parboil 5 to 7 minutes in boiling salted water, or steam squash same length of time. Cut in half lengthwise and scoop out insides. Mix remaining ingredients, adding about ⅓ of scooped-out squash. Fill drained shells. Sprinkle reserved grated cheese on top of squash, and place under broiler 5 to 6 inches. Broil until golden brown, 8 to 10 minutes. Serve immediately.

RATATOUILLE

Yield: 6 servings

½ cup olive oil
2 cloves garlic, crushed
1 onion, sliced
1 green pepper, sliced
3 medium zucchini, sliced
1 medium eggplant, cubed

2 teaspoons basil
1 teaspoon oregano
Salt and pepper, to taste
½ teaspoon dill weed,
  optional
3 fresh tomatoes, wedged

Heat oil in large skillet; add garlic, onion, green pepper and zucchini. Cook until onion is tender. Add remaining ingredients, except tomatoes, stirring occasionally. Cook 15 minutes. Add tomatoes; cover and cook 5 minutes longer. This can be served hot or cold.

VEGETABLE MEDLEY

Yield: 6-8 servings

1 stick (¼ cup) margarine
2 cups fresh green beans,
  sliced in 1½-inch lengths
2 cups carrots, sliced ⅛-inch
  thick

2 cups yellow squash, sliced
  ¼-inch thick
2 medium onions, thinly
  sliced
1 clove garlic, minced

Slice beans and carrots diagonally. Sauté in margarine for 10 minutes in 10-inch skillet. Add squash, onions and garlic. Stir-fry over medium high heat for 3 to 5 minutes. Do not overcook. Vegetables should be firm.

NOTE: May be cooked in a wok.

SUPER MIXED VEGETABLES

Preheat oven to 350°   Yield: 6 servings

1 medium zucchini,
  unpeeled, sliced thin
3 small yellow squash,
  unpeeled, sliced thin
3 slices red onion, halved
¼ cup red bell pepper, sliced
  thin
¼ cup green pepper, sliced
  thin
2 teaspoons sugar
¼ teaspoon oregano

¼ teaspoon garlic powder
¼ teaspoon black pepper
1 tablespoon raspberry
  vinegar or ½ teaspoon soy
  sauce
2 tablespoons butter or
  margarine, melted
2 medium tomatoes, peeled
  and seeded
2 tablespoons grated
  Parmesan cheese

Line a 9-inch pie plate with zucchini and yellow squash. Top with onions, red and green peppers. In separate measuring cup, combine sugar, oregano, garlic powder and black pepper. Add vinegar or soy sauce, and mix. Add melted butter, and stir to mix well. Sprinkle vegetables with spice and butter mixture. Bake covered at 350° for 40 minutes. Uncover, and add seeded tomatoes that have been sliced into 8 wedges; sprinkle with cheese. Return to oven and continue baking for 20 more minutes.

WEINKRAUT

Yield: 8 servings

2 tablespoons butter
1 small onion, finely
  chopped
2 tablespoons brown sugar
1 cup chicken broth
1½ cups dry white wine

1 small potato, grated
2 Granny Smith apples,
  pared and thinly sliced
1 quart sauerkraut
Salt, to taste

Melt butter in pot, and sauté onion lightly. Add brown sugar, stirring constantly until it dissolves. Add chicken broth, wine and remaining ingredients. Simmer on low heat for 1 hour, stirring occasionally.

NOTE: Excellent served with pork or game.

BARLEY PILAF

Yield: 10 servings

4 cups chicken stock
1⅓ cups quick cooking pearl
  barley
4 tablespoons olive oil
7 ounces vermicelli, broken
  into ½-inch pieces
⅔ cup parsley leaves
1 large onion

6 tablespoons unsalted
  butter
⅓ medium red pepper,
  seeded and diced
8 large fresh basil leaves,
  cut into fine julienne strips
Salt and freshly ground
  pepper

Bring chicken stock to a boil in a sauce pan and stir in the barley. Return to boil, then reduce heat. Cover and simmer, stirring occasionally, until barley is tender, about 12 minutes. Drain, reserving the barley and stock separately.

Heat oil in a large skillet over moderate heat. Add vermicelli and cook, stirring, until it is well browned, about 3 minutes.

Add enough water to the reserved stock to make a total of 5⅔ cups liquid. Bring to a boil in a large sauce pan; add vermicelli, and cook until tender, about 8 minutes. Drain, discarding the stock.

Chop parsley coarsely, and set aside. Chop onion coarsely. Melt butter in a skillet, and cook onion over medium low heat, stirring until soft but not brown — about 5 minutes. Add barley and vermicelli and cook, stirring until heated through. May be cooked ahead to this point. Refrigerate, and complete the pilaf just prior to serving. Place the pilaf over medium heat until heated through. Stir in parsley, red pepper, and basil. Season to taste.

BALKAN BULGAR PILAF

Preheat oven to 375°　　　　　　　　　　　　Yield: 6 servings

3 cups bulgar wheat
¼ pound butter
1 small onion, chopped

6 cups chicken broth (or 6
  cups water with 4 bouillon
  cubes)

Sauté bulgar in butter until butter is absorbed and bulgar starts to brown; add onion, and sauté a couple of minutes, stirring well. Add broth, and bring to boil. Bake in heavy casserole at 375° for 40 minutes. Stir and continue cooking for 10 minutes more.

NOTE: For added crunch and color, ½ cup each of the following may be added and stirred in during the last 10 minutes of baking: diced carrots, diced celery and ¼ cup fresh chopped parsley.

This is a good and different side dish.

LASAGNE BLANCA-VERDE

Preheat oven to 300°   Yield: 6 servings

2 pounds Ricotta cheese
2 eggs, slightly beaten
5 ounces frozen leaf spinach,
  barely cooked
6 ounces grated Parmesan
  cheese, divided
Grated nutmeg, to taste
Salt and pepper, to taste

6 tablespoons butter
6 tablespoons flour
3 cups whole milk
2 (0.35 ounce) packets
  chicken broth
3 ounces Gorgonzola cheese
1 pound lasagna noodles

Mix Ricotta with eggs, coarsely chopped spinach (be careful not to chop spinach too finely or your Ricotta mixture will turn green), a generous tablespoon of grated Parmesan cheese, a grating of nutmeg, salt and pepper to taste.

Cheese Sauce:
Melt butter in medium sauce pan, and add flour, mixing until smooth and flour is cooked. Add milk and contents of chicken broth packets. Cook and stir until thickened. Break Gorgonzola into bits, and add to sauce; stir until smooth. Taste before adding salt.

In large pan, boil lasagna noodles in water until barely cooked through. Spread out on clean dish towels to drain.

Lightly butter an 8x10-inch pan that is 2½ to 3 inches deep. Spread a thin layer of cheese sauce over bottom. In an overlapping pattern, place a single layer of lasagna noodles on top of cheese. Spread ⅓ of Ricotta mixture over noodles; then spread a layer of the cheese sauce. Sprinkle with a thin layer of Parmesan cheese. Continue layering until there are 3 layers of Ricotta and cheese sauce. Cover with aluminum foil, and bake at 300° for 30 minutes. Uncover, and bake another 30 minutes until cheese topping is golden brown.

NOTE: This dish may be refrigerated a day or two before baking or frozen for several weeks. If frozen, thaw to room temperature before baking, or it will scorch.

HUNGARIAN NOODLE BAKE

Preheat oven to 350°   Yield: 6 servings

4 ounces (2½ cups) fine
  noodles
1 cup cream style cottage
  cheese
1 cup sour cream
¼ cup finely chopped onion
1 clove garlic, minced

1 tablespoon Worcestershire
  sauce
Dash Tabasco sauce
1 tablespoon poppy seed
½ teaspoon salt
Dash pepper

Cook noodles in boiling salted water until tender; drain. Combine noodles with remaining ingredients. Bake in greased 9x13-inch baking dish at 350° for 30 minutes or until hot. (Do not overbake or it will become dry.) Sprinkle with paprika.

JEWEL'S NOODLES
(Easy)

Yield: 4 servings

1 (8-ounce) package egg
  noodles
4 tablespoons melted butter
  or margarine
½ cup chopped or sliced
  almonds

1 tablespoon poppy seed
1 tablespoon orange rind
1 tablespoon lemon rind
1 cup sour cream
Salt and pepper, to taste

Cook noodles; drain and keep warm. Mix remaining ingredients together, and stir into noodles. Serve immediately.

NOODLES ROMA

Yield: 10-12 servings

1 pound fettuccine noodles
1 bunch scallions, chopped
  fine
1 medium zucchini, sliced
8 ounces fresh sliced
  mushrooms
1 (4-ounce) can black olives,
  pitted, cut in half

¼ pound Proscuitto ham, cut
  in strips
¼ pound Genoa salami, cut in
  strips
1 large ripe tomato, finely
  chopped

Cook noodles in boiling water until tender, about 10 minutes. Drain well. Toss with remaining ingredients, and mix with the following dressing. Chill.

Dressing:
1 tablespoon Dijon mustard
2 teaspoons fresh lemon juice
5 tablespoons olive oil

1 clove of garlic, crushed
Salt and pepper, to taste

NOTE: This dish is to be served cold.

CHINESE FRIED RICE
(For leftover pork roast and rice)

Yield: 6-8 servings

2 eggs, beaten with ¼
  teaspoon water
¼ cup vegetable oil
1 cup diced, cooked pork
  roast
1 cup cooked shrimp or 1
  (4¼-ounce) can medium
  shrimp, rinsed and drained

6 scallions, chopped
1 (8-ounce) can water
  chestnuts, coarsely
  chopped
3 to 4 cups cooked white rice
2 to 3 tablespoons soy sauce
Salt, to taste

Pour beaten egg into a lightly greased 10-inch cast iron skillet. Cook and flip it over like a crepe. Remove from skillet to a paper towel. When cool, cut into small strips.

Using same skillet, pour in vegetable oil, and sauté pork, shrimp, scallions and water chestnuts until scallions are soft and meats are heated through. Add cooked rice; mix well, and add soy sauce. Stir and heat thoroughly. Add salt if needed. Stir in cooked egg strips, and mix well.

NOTE: May also be made in a wok.

GARLIC BROWN RICE

Preheat oven to 375°   Yield: 6-8 servings

3 tablespoons olive oil
1 onion, chopped fine
2 cloves garlic, minced
½ cup long-grained white
   rice, unwashed

4 cups (1 quart) chicken or
   beef consommé
1½ cups water
Salt and pepper, to taste

Simmer onion and garlic in olive oil. Add rice, and brown slowly. Add chicken or beef consommé and water. Place in 1½-quart casserole, and bake 45 minutes in 375° oven. Season with salt and pepper. Place under broiler to brown, if necessary.

RICE WITH GREEN CHILIES

Preheat oven to 350°   Yield: 6-8 servings

2 cups water
1 teaspoon salt
1 cup rice
1 (4-ounce) can green chilies,
   chopped

1 cup Monterrey Jack
   cheese, grated

Bring salted water to a boil. Pour in rice. Stir once. Cover and cook over low heat 20 to 25 minutes. Mix with remaining ingredients and place in greased casserole. Bake in 350° oven, uncovered, until bubbly, about 15 to 20 minutes.

SPANISH RICE CASSEROLE

Preheat oven to 350°   Yield: 6 servings

1 (7-ounce) package paella
   rice or Spanish rice
1 stick butter
1 (2-ounce) jar chopped
   pimento and juice

1 (2-ounce) jar mushroom
   caps and juice
1 (10½-ounce) can onion soup
1 (14½-ounce) can beef broth

In casserole, mix all ingredients together, including juices from pimento and mushrooms. Cover and bake at 350° for 1 hour or until all liquid is absorbed.

RICE CASSEROLE

Preheat oven to 350°   Yield: 6-8 servings

2 (14½-ounce) cans beef
   consommé
½ cup water
1 can mushrooms
1 cup converted rice
   (uncooked)

4 green onions, chopped
   (tops included)
1 stick melted butter or
   margarine

Mix together in 2-quart casserole. Cover casserole and bake at 350° for 45 minutes. Needs to look dry and to have stopped bubbling.

ORANGE RICE

Preheat oven to 350°   Yield: 4 servings

1 stick (½ cup) margarine
1 large onion, chopped
½ orange rind, grated
1 cup chopped celery

1 cup orange juice
1 cup water
1 cup uncooked rice

Sauté onions in margarine until transparent. Add orange rind and celery. Brown slightly. Add orange juice and water; bring to a boil. Add uncooked rice, and bake in 2-quart casserole at 350° for one hour.

NOTE: Good with pork roast or ham.

NO-FAIL RICE
(Easy)

Yield: 4 servings

1 cup rice
1½ cups water
¼ stick butter or
   margarine

Juice of ½ lemon (may use
   bottled juice)
½ teaspoon salt or to taste

Mix all ingredients together. Bring to a boil over high heat. Cover and reduce heat to low; simmer for 25 minutes. Fluff with fork.

ORIENTAL SNOW PEAS AND RICE

Yield: 6 servings

1 cup long-grained white
  rice
2 cups water
1 tablespoon butter or
  margarine
1½ teaspoons salt
1½ teaspoons cornstarch

⅓ cup chicken broth
1 tablespoon vegetable oil
2 cloves garlic, minced
1½ teaspoons soy sauce
1 pound fresh snow peas
1 (8-ounce) can sliced water
  chestnuts, drained

In a medium sauce pan, place water, butter and salt. Bring to a boil and add rice. Cover and bring to second boil and reduce heat to simmer. Cook for 25 minutes. Remove from heat and set aside.

While rice is cooking, combine cornstarch with chicken broth; mix well and set aside.

Remove stem ends of snow peas and rinse well. Drain.

Place vegetable oil in skillet and heat until hot. Add garlic and sauté until lightly browned. Add soy sauce, snow peas and water chestnuts. Stir-fry over high heat for 1 minute. Reduce heat to medium; add chicken broth mixture and stir well. Bring to a boil and stir constantly for about 1 minute or until sauce is thickened. Serve over cooked rice.

RICE PILAF

Preheat oven to 350°

Yield: 6 servings

1½ cups long grain white
  rice, unwashed
1 stick (½ cup) margarine
3 cups water
5 chicken bouillon cubes

¾ cup each chopped parsley,
  carrots and celery
½ cup green onions, chopped,
  tops also

Brown rice in margarine in heavy (iron) skillet, stirring occasionally. Place bouillon and water in sauce pan, and cook until bouillon dissolves. Add to hot browned rice. (This will really sizzle!) Remove from heat. Transfer rice mixture to 2-quart casserole dish. Bake covered at 350° for 35 minutes. Remove from oven, and fold in chopped raw vegetables until well-mixed. Return to oven for 10 more minutes. Serve hot.

NOTE: Vegetables will still be crunchy. Great with any entree.

WILD RICE WITH MUSHROOMS AND ALMONDS

Preheat oven to 325°   Yield: 6-8 servings

¼ pound butter
1 cup wild rice
½ cup slivered, toasted
  almonds

2 tablespoons chopped green
  onions
½ pound sliced mushrooms
3 cups chicken broth

Mix all the ingredients together except chicken broth. Place in a heavy frying pan, and cook until rice turns yellow, stirring constantly. Put into casserole with chicken broth; cover and bake at 325° for 1 hour.

GARLIC PESTO

Yield: 8 servings

2 (10-ounce) packages frozen
  chopped spinach
⅓ cup chopped fresh parsley
4 cloves garlic, minced
1 tablespoon dried tarragon
1 teaspoon dried basil
½ cup finely chopped
  walnuts
½ teaspoon salt
½ teaspoon pepper

¼ teaspoon anchovy paste
  (optional)
⅔ cup olive oil
¾ cup grated fresh Parmesan
  cheese
1 (16-ounce) package
  spaghetti
1 (4-ounce) jar sliced
  pimentos

Thaw spinach. Using a food processor, add spinach and next 8 ingredients. Process until smooth. Pour olive oil slowly in processor while it is still running and oil is combined with spinach mixture. Remove mixture to a medium sized mixing bowl and fold in Parmesan cheese.

Cook spaghetti according to package directions. Drain and serve on individual plates with garlic mixture. Garnish with pimento strips.

SPAGHETTI FLORENTINE

Preheat oven to 375°   Yield: 8 servings

8 ounces spaghetti
2 (10-ounce) packages frozen
  chopped spinach
½ cup chopped onion
½ cup grated Parmesan
  cheese
4 tablespoons butter,
  softened

2 eggs, slightly beaten
1 (4-ounce) jar pimento,
  chopped
3 cups sliced fresh
  mushrooms
4 tablespoons butter
2 (16-ounce) jars meatless
  spaghetti sauce

Break spaghetti into thirds, and cook according to package instructions. Cook spinach according to package instructions, adding the onion. Drain. Combine spinach, cheese, eggs, 4 tablespoons butter and pimento. Then add drained spaghetti. Place in greased 2-quart baking dish, and bake at 375° for 25 minutes, covered. Serve with Mushroom Sauce.

Mushroom Sauce:
Cook mushrooms in 4 tablespoons butter in sauce pan until tender, and add spaghetti sauce. Heat through. Serve as an accompaniment to the baked spaghetti.

TOFU AND SPINACH STUFFED MANICOTTI

Preheat oven to 350°   Yield: 4 servings

8 manicotti (pasta) shells   Boiling water

Filling:
¼ cup minced onion   1 pound fresh tofu
2 tablespoons vegetable oil   1 (10-ounce) package frozen
1 tablespoon minced parsley   spinach, thawed and
1 large clove garlic, minced   drained
½ teaspoon basil   1 egg, beaten
½ teaspoon oregano   Salt and pepper, to taste

Sauce:
3 large tomatoes   Salt
2 teaspoons vegetable oil   ⅓ cup grated Parmesan
2 tablespoons basil   cheese
2 tablespoons thyme

Cook manicotti in boiling water for 8 minutes. Drain and cool. Sauté onion in oil until clear; add parsley, garlic and seasonings. In a mixing bowl, mash tofu with potato masher, and stir in drained spinach. Stir in sautéed seasonings and egg. Mix well; add salt and pepper to taste.

Peel tomatoes, and chop finely. Put in sauce pan with oil, basil, thyme and cook, uncovered, over low to medium heat until well blended and slightly thickened, about 10 minutes. Add salt to taste.

While sauce is cooking, stuff cooled manicotti shells with tofu mixture and place shells close together in a shallow baking pan. Pour sauce over shells; sprinkle with Parmesan cheese. Cover with foil and bake at 350° for 20 minutes. Serve immediately.

CANDIED APRICOTS

(That special dish to be served with roast pork)

Preheat oven to 300°   Yield: 8-10 servings

2 (16-ounce) cans apricots,   ½ pound butter or
  drained   margarine, melted
1 small box Ritz crackers,   1 (1-pound) box light brown
  crushed fine   sugar

In a greased casserole, layer apricots, cracker crumbs and brown sugar. Start with apricots, and end with crumbs. Pour melted butter over all. Bake 1 hour at 300°.

NOTE: Recipe may be halved.

HOT CURRIED FRUIT

Preheat oven to 350°   Yield: 6-8 servings

⅓ cup butter
1 cup brown sugar, packed
4 teaspoons curry powder
1 (16-ounce) can bing
  cherries

1 (16-ounce) can pears
1 (16-ounce) can peaches
1 (20-ounce) can pineapple
  chunks

Melt butter, and add sugar and curry. Drain and dry fruit; place in 1½-quart casserole. Add butter mixture, and cover until ready to bake. Bake, uncovered, 1 hour at 350°. Serve warm.

CANDIED KUMQUATS

Yield: 1 quart

1 quart kumquats, washed
1 cup water
2 cups sugar

1 tablespoon cornstarch
1 teaspoon salt
Granulated sugar for garnish

Pierce stem ends of kumquats with a needle. Cook in water until tender. Remove kumquats, and set aside. Add sugar, cornstarch and salt to remaining water, and bring to a soft-boil stage. Using a spoon, dip kumquats to coat. Place on a rack to cool. Roll in granulated sugar. Store in a cool place on layers of waxed paper in a tightly covered container.

SCALLOPED PINEAPPLE BAKE

(Good with ham or pork)

Preheat oven to 350°   Yield: 16 servings

½ cup butter
1 cup granulated sugar
2 eggs
2 cups milk

2 (20-ounce) cans pineapple
  chunks, drained
4 cups cubed bread (Vienna
  style is best)

Cream butter and sugar. Add eggs, and beat well. Add milk, pineapple and bread. Then mix together gently. It may have curdled appearance. Pour into a buttered 12x8-inch pan. Refrigerate overnight. Bake at 350° for 1½ to 2 hours, uncovered

Meats

AFRICAN OIL PALM

Hints for Meats

Meat should be stored in the coldest part of the refrigerator.

Keep ready-to-serve meats no longer than one week. Keep cured meats no longer than two weeks.

Keep canned hams in the refrigerator. Do not freeze.

It is better to cook meat slowly as it will be more tender and juicy.

When buying steaks, do not buy them too thin; they should be at least one inch thick and not more than two inches thick. The fat should be white, medium thick and not bumpy.

Meat should be at room temperature before you place it on the grill.

It is time to turn steaks when red juice begins to appear on the uncooked side. Only turn the steak once, using a wide spatula or tongs. Do not pierce the steak with a fork. It will cause the juice to run out.

To prevent steak from curling up, score the outside of the steak at 1½-inch intervals.

Partially freezing meat will allow you to cut it easier.

Salt meat after cooking to prevent juice from being pulled to the surface of the meat.

When roasting meat, do not put flour on top of the meat, do not cover the roasting pan and do not baste.

Do not roast meat that is less than three pounds. It will dry out.

Remove fat from meat after cooking if so desired. The fat gives extra flavor to the meat and holds in the juices.

When making hamburger patties, handle them as little as possible. If handled too much, they will become tough and lose some of their juices.

When sauteeing meat in butter, it is better to combine the butter with oil. Use one teaspoon oil to two teaspoons butter. By doing this, you reach a higher temperature without burning the butter.

Use a small amount of paprika when stewing meats as it will help the meat become brown and add a rich brown color to the liquid.

Use frozen ground beef within two to three months.

Center cut meats are the most tender.

Canned foods have a shelf life of about one year, after which they start losing their nutrients and flavor. Date them when you buy them.

Crumble extra bacon and freeze to use at a later date for topping on salads, soups and baked potatoes.

After taking meat from the oven, let it set for about 15 minutes; it will be easier to carve.

STARS AND STRIPES

Yield: 4 servings

2 to 3 tablespoons vegetable oil
1 (1-inch) slice fresh ginger root, minced fine
½ pound sirloin steak, sliced thin
½ medium red pepper, seeded and cut into julienne strips
4 green onions, white and green parts, sliced diagonally
3 tablespoons soy sauce
3 carambolas (star fruit), sliced into thin stars
Cooked rice

Heat oil in wok or fry pan. Add minced ginger and stir fry briefly. Do not brown. Add steak, stirring quickly for 1 minute. Add red pepper and green onions. Stir fry 1 more minute. Add soy sauce, and stir quickly. Add carambola; stir quickly until heated through. Serve on cooked rice.

CHURRASCO

(Argentine Grilled Beef)

Yield: 6-8 servings

1 (2½ to 3 pounds) beef tenderloin, rib eye or strip steaks
¾ cup olive oil
3 to 4 tablespoons minced garlic
1 tablespoon black pepper
2 tablespoons minced fresh parsley
¼ cup vinegar
1 tablespoon salt

If using tenderloin, trim off excess fat and slice in 2-inch thick pieces. Combine olive oil, garlic, pepper, parsley and vinegar in small mixing bowl. Place meat in glass dish and pour marinade mixture over meat. Cover and refrigerate for 1½ hours. Remove from refrigerator. Turn meat and allow meat to return to room temperature. Remove meat from marinade and grill over hot coals to desired doneness. Allow about 2½ minutes per side for medium doneness. Sprinkle salt over meat just before removing from grill.

NOTE: All you need is a tossed green salad and a baked potato with this one.

NO PEEK STANDING RIB ROAST

Preheat oven to 375°   Yield: 6-8 servings

3 or 4 pound rib roast   **Salt and pepper**
1 or 2 cloves garlic, minced

Sprinkle salt, pepper and garlic on fat of roast. Place in roasting pan and bake at 375° for 1 hour. Turn off oven and do not peek. (This can be done early in the afternoon.) Thirty minutes before you sit down to dinner, turn oven back on to 375°. This makes a rare roast; 35 minutes for medium rare.

ROPA VIEJO
(Old Clothes!)

Yield: 6 servings

2 pounds skirt steak or   **1 (8-ounce) can tomato sauce**
** brisket**   **1 teaspoon salt**
⅓ cup vegetable oil   **1 bay leaf**
1 medium onion, chopped   **½ cup dry wine**
2 cloves garlic, minced   **1 (4-ounce) jar chopped**
1 large hot chili pepper,   ** pimentos**
** chopped**   **3 cups cooked rice**

Simmer the brisket or steak in large covered sauce pan until very tender. Shred the meat into small strips. Chop onions, garlic and chili pepper fine. Sauté the vegetables in oil in a Dutch oven until softened; add the meat strips and remaining ingredients, except rice. Cook, covered, over low heat for 20 minutes, stirring occasionally so it doesn't stick to bottom of pan. Remove bay leaf, and serve over cooked rice.

CUBAN BOLICHE ROAST

Yield: 6 servings

3 to 5 pound eye of round
  roast
2 to 4 chorizo (Spanish
  sausage)
2 teaspoons oregano
2 or 3 bay leaves
3 teaspoons paprika

2 or 3 cloves garlic, minced
Salt and pepper
1 (8-ounce) can tomato sauce
2 large onions
1 green pepper
Flour

Slice chorizos. Make a long cut in roast, and stuff with the chorizo sausage. Season with salt and pepper. Dredge in flour, and brown in large roasting pan, using a little olive oil. Add remaining ingredients, and cook, covered, in roasting pan over low heat or in oven at 300° for 3 hours. Serve with black beans and rice.

MEAT MARINADE FOR A 2-POUND ROAST

Yield: 1 cup

½ cup vegetable oil
2½ tablespoons chopped
  garlic
1 tablespoon seasoned
  pepper

¼ teaspoon cumin
⅛ cup vinegar
1 tablespoon salt
½ tablespoon paprika

Mix all ingredients together, and pour over roast. Refrigerate for 24 hours. Grill to desired doneness.

BARBECUE CHUCK ROAST

Yield: 6 servings

4-pound chuck roast
⅓ cup soy sauce
⅓ cup vegetable oil
⅛ cup lime juice
3 tablespoons honey

1 teaspoon crushed oregano
½ teaspoon crushed thyme
½ teaspoon crushed red
  pepper flakes
3 to 5 cloves garlic, minced

Place roast in large pan. Mix all ingredients, and pour over roast. Cover and refrigerate for 24 hours, turning every 3 to 4 hours. Drain and grill.

ROLADEN

Yield: 4 servings

1 pound round steak, well
  trimmed
Prepared mustard
Seasoned salt
Pepper
1 medium onion, finely
  chopped
½ pound bacon, cooked,
  drained and crumbled

4 dill pickle slices
1 hard-cooked egg
1½ cups water
2 beef bouillon cubes
2 tablespoons flour
½ cup burgundy wine

Cut steak into four pieces and pound with a meat mallet. Spread each piece of steak with mustard, seasoned salt and pepper. Sprinkle with onion, bacon and pickle slices. Cut egg into 8ths. Place egg at end of steak and roll up; secure with toothpicks. Brown meat rolls in skillet in bacon drippings. Remove meat and place in 1-quart casserole dish.

In a sauce pan, dissolve bouillon in boiling water, and mix flour with about ¼ cup of the bouillon mixture, stirring until smooth. Add this to bouillon, along with the wine. Continue to cook over medium heat until thickened, stirring often. Pour wine sauce over meat, and bake at 325° for 1 hour.

STEAK SUPPER IN FOIL

Preheat oven to 350°   Yield: 4 servings

2½ feet (18-inch width)
  aluminum foil
1½ pounds chuck steak (1
  inch thick)
1 envelope onion soup mix

4 large carrots, quartered
2 large onions, halved
2 large potatoes, quartered
2 tablespoons butter

Place meat in center of foil; sprinkle with soup mix; cover with vegeables. Dot with butter. Fold over foil, and secure to hold in juices. Place on baking sheet, and bake at 350° for 1 to 1½ hours.

MARINATED FLANK STEAK
(Fire up the Grill or Hibachi!)

Yield: 4-6 servings

¼ cup soy sauce
2 tablespoons vinegar
3 tablespoons honey
1½ teaspoons minced garlic
1½ teaspoons ground ginger

¾ cup vegetable oil
1½ pounds flank steak
1 green onion, chopped
  (optional)

Mix soy sauce, vinegar and honey. Blend in garlic and ginger; add oil. Pour marinade over meat, and let stand at least overnight (better if marinated 2 days) in refrigerator. Cook steak over red hot coals, about 5 minutes per side for rare. Baste occasionally with marinade during cooking. Slice thin and diagonally across meat.

PEPPER STEAK CABALLERO

Yield: 6 servings

1½ pounds sirloin steak, cut
  in strips ⅛ inch thick
1 tablespoon paprika
2 cloves garlic, minced fine
2 tablespoons butter
1 cup sliced green onions
  with tops

2 green peppers, sliced
2 large tomatoes, diced
1 cup beef broth
¼ cup water
2 tablespoons cornstarch
2 tablespoons soy sauce
3 cups hot cooked rice

Sprinkle steak with paprika, and allow to stand while preparing other ingredients. Cook steak and garlic in butter until meat is browned. Add onions and green peppers; continue cooking until vegetables are wilted. Add tomatoes and broth; cover and simmer about 15 minutes. Blend water with cornstarch and soy sauce; stir into steak, and cook until thickened. Serve over rice.

BEEF STROGANOFF

Yield: 6 servings

2 pounds round steak, ¼ inch
thick
2 tablespoons butter or
margarine
2 tablespoons onion,
chopped
2 tablespoons flour
½ cup sherry

1 (2½-ounce) can
mushrooms, drained
1 pint sour cream
2 tablespoons tomato paste
or ketchup
½ teaspoon paprika
Salt and pepper, to taste
Cooked rice or noodles

Cut meat in strips across the grain, the width of a pencil and about 1½ inches long. Heat meat with butter and onion in skillet until meat is no longer pink. Stir in flour; add sherry. Cook, stirring constantly, until sauce boils and thickens. Cover and cook slowly, stirring frequently, for about 1 hour or until meat is tender. Add remaining ingredients; heat and blend well. Adjust seasonings. Serve over rice or noodles.

BEEF ITALIAN STYLE

Yield: 4-6 servings

2 pounds round steak
2 tablespoons olive oil
2 tablespoons grated onion
1 (3-ounce) can mushrooms
1 (8-ounce) can tomato sauce
2 garlic cloves, crushed
1 teaspoon celery salt

¼ teaspoon pepper
1 bay leaf
½ cup dry red wine
1 beef bouillon cube
1 cup boiling water
2 tablespoons flour
Cooked rice or noodles

Cut steak into large cubes. Brown in oil in large, heavy skillet. Add remaining ingredients, except flour. Bring to a boil, then simmer for 2½ hours. Combine 2 tablespoons flour with ¼ cup water; stir until smooth, and add to meat mixture. Cook ten minutes. Serve over rice or noodles.

BEEF SHERRY

Preheat oven to 275°

Yield: 8 servings

3 pounds stew beef, cubed
2 (10¾-ounce) cans cream of
mushroom soup

¾ cup sherry
1 envelope dry onion soup
mix

Place uncooked cubed beef in 13½x18¾-inch baking dish. Top with combined remaining ingredients. Cover and bake at 275° for 5 hours. Uncover the last 30 minutes.

NOTE: Great served with your choice of rice.

BEEF WITH BEER

Yield: 8-10 servings

2 pounds onions, sliced
5 tablespoons melted
 margarine
3 to 4 pounds lean beef
 (chuck or round, cut into
 1½ to 2-inch squares)
All purpose flour

⅓ cup vegetable oil
1 teaspoon salt
1 teaspoon pepper
2 cloves garlic, minced
1 (12-ounce) can beer
Hot cooked noodles or rice

Sauté onion in margarine until tender. Dredge beef in flour, and brown in hot oil. Combine onion, meat, salt, pepper, garlic and beer in a large Dutch oven. Simmer, covered, about 1½ hours until meat is tender. Combine a small amount of cooking liquid and about 2 tablespoons flour; slowly add to meat mixture, stirring until smooth and thickened. Serve over noodles or rice.

BEEF BOURGUIGNON

Yield: 6 servings

3 pounds boneless sirloin
 strip steak
2½ cups burgundy wine,
 divided
½ teaspoon garlic powder
¼ teaspoon thyme
½ bay leaf
¼ cup vegetable oil
3 tablespoons flour

1 (10½-ounce) can onion soup
1½ cups water
6 carrots, cut lengthwise in
 1-inch pieces
1 (8-ounce) can small onions
½ pound fresh mushrooms or
 2 (4-ounce) can button
 mushrooms
2 tablespoons butter

Cut beef into cubes 1½ inches to 2 inches square. Combine 2 cups wine with garlic, thyme and bay leaf. Pour over steak; cover and marinate 24 hours. When ready to cook, drain, saving marinade. Dry steak on paper towels. Heat oil in heavy skillet and sear. Remove with slotted spoon. Place in large (2-quart) saucepan.

Mix flour and oil remaining in skillet. (You may have to add a bit more oil). Add reserved wine marinade, onion soup and water. Stirring constantly, cook until it reaches a high boil. Pour over steak; cover tightly and bake 2 hours at 300°. Steak should be very tender — cook longer if not. At this stage, steak may be refrigerated for 24 hours.

In the meantime, cook carrots in small amount of water, until tender. Sauté mushrooms in 2 tablespoons butter (drain canned mushrooms), and add drained canned onions. Bring casserole to room temperature, add vegetables and remaining ½ cup burgundy. Bake at 300°, covered, until heated thoroughly, about 20 to 25 minutes.

COMPANY MEAT LOAF

Preheat oven to 350°   Yield: 8 servings

3 eggs
¼ cup milk
¼ cup sour cream
1 cup soft white bread
  crumbs
¼ teaspoon thyme
¼ teaspoon salt
¼ teaspoon pepper
¼ teaspoon nutmeg

1½ pounds lean ground beef
¼ pound ground pork
¼ pound ground veal
2 tablespoons onion,
  chopped or grated
¼ teaspoon garlic powder
1 teaspoon chives
3 bacon strips

Flavoring Sauce:
½ cup chili sauce
2 tablespoons brown sugar

¼ teaspoon dry mustard

Combine eggs, milk, sour cream and bread crumbs. Let stand for 5 minutes. Add remaining ingredients, and shape loaf in loaf pan. Cover with bacon strips, and bake at 350° for 30 minutes. Pour flavoring sauce over meat loaf, and continue baking 30 minutes longer.

SICILIAN MEAT ROLL

Preheat oven to 350°   Yield: 6 servings

1½ pounds lean ground beef
½ cup tomato juice
2 eggs, beaten
½ cup soft bread crumbs
1½ teaspoons salt
½ teaspoon pepper
¼ teaspoon oregano

2 cloves garlic, minced
3 tablespoons dried parsley
  flakes
6 to 8 slices cooked ham,
  thinly sliced
2 cups (8 ounces) Mozzarella
  cheese, shredded

Mix all ingredients, except ham and cheese, kneading by hand until well blended. Mixture is patted onto a sheet of foil about 10x16-inches. Arrange ham slices on top of meat layer in an overlapping pattern, leaving a small border all around that is uncovered. Sprinkle shredded cheese over this. Roll up meat, lifting foil away as rolling proceeds (like a jelly roll). Roll the meat onto a greased (9x13 inch) baking dish, and tuck in the ends. Bake at 350° for 1 hour. Allow meat to set for 15 minutes before cutting into ½-inch slices, revealing ham and cheese.

LASAGNA
(Great make-ahead dish)

Preheat oven to 350°   Yield: 6-8 servings

1 (10-ounce) package
  lasagna noodles
1 pound ground beef
1 pound mild Italian
  sausage, remove casing
1 clove garlic, minced
1 tablespoon basil
1 teaspoon salt

1 medium onion, chopped
1 (16-ounce) can tomatoes
2 (6-ounce) cans tomato
  paste
1 teaspoon Worcestershire
  sauce
⅛ teaspoon pepper

Cook lasagna noodles according to package directions; set aside. Brown beef and sausage together in 10-inch skillet, slowly, crumbling sausage as it cooks.

Add remaining ingredients and simmer uncovered ½ hour, stirring occasionally.

Cheese Filling:

3 cups ricotta cheese or small
  curd cottage cheese
1 pound Mozzarella cheese,
  shredded

2 tablespoons parsley flakes
2 eggs, beaten
1½ teaspoons salt
½ teaspoon pepper

Combine all filling ingredients in medium-sized mixing bowl. Mix well. Place a layer of drained and cooked lasagna noodles in a 3-quart glass baking dish that has been greased.

Spread half of the meat mixture over the noodles to cover completely. Add half the cheese filling, and spread evenly over meat mixture. Continue layering with noodles, then other half of meat mixture and cheese filling.

Bake at 350° for 30 minutes. Let stand 10 to 15 minutes before serving.

NOTE: This may be frozen or refrigerated and baked at a later time. Thaw completely before baking.

AMERICAN CHOP SUEY

Yield: 4 servings

½ cup onion, finely chopped
½ cup celery, finely chopped
¼ cup soy sauce
1 pound ground chuck
1 (16-ounce) can whole
  tomatoes, chopped

½ teaspoon salt
1½ cups egg noodles, cooked
1 cup mild cheddar cheese,
  grated

Fry onions and celery until clear, and add soy sauce. In same pan, brown ground chuck and add tomatoes with juice. Mix, cover and simmer 15 to 20 minutes. Add salt and cooked egg noodles. Place mixed ingredients in casserole dish, and spread grated cheese over top. Broil until lightly browned.

"PICADINHO"
(BRAZILIAN PICADILLO)

Yield: 4 servings

2 tablespoons oil or
  shortening
1 pound ground chuck
1 medium onion, peeled and
  thinly sliced
1 medium tomato, chopped
1 clove garlic, crushed

3 to 4 teaspoons green
  olives, chopped
⅛ teaspoon oregano
⅛ teaspoon thyme
1 cup beef stock or bouillon
Salt and pepper, to taste

In a 10-inch skillet, heat oil or shortening, and stir in beef. Add next 6 ingredients, and cook, stirring until the meat is browned. Drain off fat. Add beef stock or bouillon; taste. Add salt and pepper as needed. (Salt may not be needed, especially if bouillon is used.) Cover pan, and cook over low heat until liquid is evaporated. If necessary, remove lid to hasten evaporation.

NOTE: Brazilians serve this dish over rice, sometimes with black beans.

GREEN ENCHILADA CASSEROLE

Preheat oven to 350°   Yield: 4-6 servings

1½ pounds ground beef
1 medium onion, chopped
1 teaspoon chili powder
1 (10-ounce) can enchilada
  sauce
1 (12-ounce) can evaporated
  milk
1 (10¾-ounce) can cream of
  mushroom soup

1 (4-ounce) can green chilies,
  chopped
1 (7-ounce) package tortilla
  chips
2 cups grated cheddar
  cheese

Brown meat, onion and chili powder together; drain well. In bowl, combine the enchilada sauce, milk, soup and chilies. In a deep 2-quart casserole dish, layer half of each: tortilla chips, meat, cheese and sauce. Repeat layers, leaving cheese off top. Bake at 350° for 30 to 45 minutes. Top with cheese, and bake until bubbly.

SOUTH OF THE BORDER CHILI

Yield: 6-8 servings

2 pounds ground beef
2 large onions, chopped
½ teaspoon garlic powder
1 teaspoon salt, or to taste
¼ teaspoon pepper
2 (16-ounce) cans whole
  tomatoes

1 (8-ounce) can tomato sauce
3 to 5 teaspoons chili powder
1 tablespoon cumin powder
2 (15 or 16-ounce) cans
  kidney beans
1 or 2 dashes cayenne
  pepper, for zip

Brown meat and onion together in 10-inch skillet. Add garlic, salt and pepper. Add rest of the ingredients in the order given. Stir occasionally. Cook in a crock pot for 2 to 4 hours on low heat, or large pot for same amount of time.

TAMALE PIE

Preheat oven to 350°   Yield: 8 servings

2 large onions
1 tablespoon vegetable oil
2 pounds ground beef
1 tablespoon salt
Dash pepper
1 tablespoon chili powder

1 tablespoon Worcestershire
  sauce
1 (3-ounce) can pitted black
  olives, sliced or chopped
2 cups tomato juice

Chop onions, and sauté in oil until transparent. Add meat, and cook until crumbly. Drain well. Mix all ingredients, and pour into a 9x13-inch pan. Cover with topping, and bake at 350° for 45 minutes to 1 hour.

Topping:
1 cup flour
1 cup corn meal
1 teaspoon salt

2 teaspoons baking powder
2 cups milk
¼ cup melted butter

Mix all ingredients, and spoon onto meat mixture.

STUFFED CABBAGE ROLLS
(HOLUPTSI)

Yield: 6-8 servings

1 medium to large cabbage,
 cored
1½ pounds ground beef or
 1 pound ground beef and
 ½ pound ground pork
½ cup uncooked long grain
 rice

1 medium to large onion,
 chopped
2 teaspoons salt
½ teaspoon black pepper
2 (16-ounce) cans stewed
 tomatoes

In large stock pot, add enough water to completely cover cabbage. Parboil until leaves start to spread slightly. Meanwhile, mix ground beef, rice, onion, salt and pepper together.

Drain cabbage in colander. When cabbage is cool enough to handle, take one leaf at a time and place a ball of the meat mixture on base of leaf. Starting at base, roll and fold up leaf over meatball. Place in stockpot (seam side down). After one layer is placed in pot, pour ½ can stewed tomatoes on top; sprinkle with salt and pepper. Continue layering until all meat is used up. Use rest of cabbage, placing on top of last layer of rolls. Add one tomato can of water. Cook over low heat about 2½ hours. Once or twice during cooking time, carefully lift the rolls to prevent sticking or scorching.

NOTE: These are even better heated the next day, and they freeze great. Add juice from cooking to the rolls when packing for freezing.

STUFFED GRAPE LEAVES
(Greek)

Yield: 8 servings

⅓ cup uncooked rice
1 pound ground beef or lamb
2 teaspoons ground
 cinnamon
1 teaspoon nutmeg

½ teaspoon salt
⅛ teaspoon pepper
4 teaspoons melted butter or
 margarine
1 (8-ounce) jar grape leaves

Soak rice in warm water for 15 minutes and mix with meat, spices and butter. Rinse grape leaves. Using 2 tablespoons meat mixture, roll up in grape leaf, starting at stem end with dull side up. Arrange in Dutch oven in layers. Cover in water, and sprinkle with salt and pepper. Cook over low heat 1 hour; drain well. Serve on platter or in 2½-quart casserole dish.

BURGUNDY MEAT BALLS

Yield: 6 servings

1 pound ground beef
1 medium onion, minced
½ green pepper, chopped
1 clove garlic, minced
1 cup cracker crumbs
1¼ teaspoon salt
¼ teaspoon pepper
2 eggs, slightly beaten

2 tablespoons butter or
  margarine
2 tablespoons olive oil
¾ cup burgundy wine
¾ cup V-8 juice
2 to 3 tablespoons flour or
  cornstarch

Mix meat, onion, green pepper, garlic, cracker crumbs, salt, pepper and eggs. Shape into 12 balls. Flatten slightly, and brown well in hot butter and oil. Add wine and V-8 juice. Cover and simmer 20 to 30 minutes. Remove meat to warm platter. Thicken remaining liquid with cornstarch or flour, and pour over meat balls.

NOTE: Great with buttered noodles and a tossed salad.

CRANBERRY MEATBALLS

Preheat oven to 350°

Yield: 6-8 servings

1½ pounds ground beef
½ pound ground pork or
  sausage
2 eggs, well beaten
2 slices bread, crumbled

½ teaspoon garlic powder
1 medium onion, chopped
½ cup ketchup
¼ cup dried parsley
1 teaspoon salt

Combine all ingredients and mix well. Form into balls and arrange in a shallow 9x13-inch baking dish.

Cranberry Sauce:
1 (16-ounce) can jellied
  cranberry sauce
¾ cup chili sauce

3 tablespoons brown sugar
1 tablespoon lemon juice

Combine all ingredients in sauce pan, and cook over medium heat, stirring until well blended and cranberry sauce is melted. Pour over meatballs and bake, uncovered, at 350° for 45 minutes.

POLYNESIAN MEATBALLS WITH SAUCE

Yield: 4-6 servings as Main Course
or 30 meatballs as an appetizer

1½ pounds ground beef
¾ cup quick or old fashioned
   rolled oats
1 (8-ounce) can water
   chestnuts, drained and
   finely chopped
1½ teaspoons salt

¼ teaspoon pepper
2 cloves garlic, minced
1 tablespoon soy sauce
2 dashes Tabasco sauce
1 egg
½ cup milk

Combine all the above ingredients until well blended. Shape into balls using 1 rounded teaspoon for each, if using as an appetizer, or 1 rounded tablespoon, if used as a main course. Brown in large, non-stick skillet, turning until brown on all sides. Drain off fat.

Sauce:
1 (8½-ounce) can crushed
   pineapple
1 cup brown sugar
2 tablespoons cornstarch
1 cup beef bouillon

½ cup vinegar
2 teaspoons soy sauce
⅓ cup chopped green pepper
   (optional)
¼ cup chopped onion

Drain pineapple, reserving syrup. Combine brown sugar and cornstarch in sauce pan; add reserved pineapple syrup, bouillon, vinegar and soy sauce. Bring to a boil, stirring constantly until thick and clear. Stir in green pepper, onion and pineapple. Add to meat balls, and simmer 10 minutes for large meat balls and 5 minutes for appetizer meat balls. Serve in sauce.

PEASANT STEW

Yield: 4 servings

½ cup vegetable oil
1½ pounds beef stew meat
½ cup flour
1 teaspoon salt
½ teaspoon pepper
1 teaspoon garlic powder
1 cup water

1 cup white wine
4 medium potatoes, peeled
4 carrots, peeled
4 medium onions, peeled
12 fresh mushrooms, cut in
   half

Using a Dutch oven, add oil and heat until hot. Dredge flour onto stew meat, and place pieces in pan to brown, as needed. Add salt, pepper and garlic powder. After completely brown, lower heat, and pour in water and wine. Simmer for ½ hour. Add vegetables, and continue to simmer until vegetables and mushrooms are tender (about 25 minutes). Arrange on platter.

For Gravy:
   Combine 1 cup water and 3 tablespoons flour; stir until smooth. Pour into boiling pan juices, and stir until thickened. Salt to taste. Pour into gravy bowl and serve.

   NOTE: Can be adapted to cooking in a crock pot. Simply brown meat in skillet first, then place all ingredients in crock. Cook on low for eight hours. Great for the working lady!

ARMENIAN ROAST LAMB

Preheat oven to 325°   Yield: 4-6 servings

1 (6-pound) leg of lamb
6 large potatoes
6 large carrots
3 large turnips

8 tomatoes
Salt, pepper and paprika, to
   taste

Chop all the vegetables into large chunks. Wash lamb and place fat side up in a roasting pan. Cover with vegetables, and sprinkle with salt, pepper and paprika to taste. Cover with 1 cup water. Cover and bake at 325° for 35 minutes per pound.

HERB ROASTED RACK OF LAMB

Preheat oven to 325°   Yield: 4-6 servings

¼ teaspoon ground thyme
¼ teaspoon black pepper
⅛ teaspoon onion powder
1 (8-rib) rack of lamb or
  2½ pounds lamb

½ teaspoon salt
½ teaspoon Season-all
¼ teaspoon monosodium
  glutamate

Combine seasonings; rub on lamb. Place on rack in shallow pan, fat side up. Bake at 325° for 30 minutes per pound or to desired degree of doneness. Serve hot.

NOTE: May also be used on pork roast.

LAMB CHOPS IN WINE SAUCE

Yield: 4 servings

2 tablespoons oil
1 medium onion, chopped
1 clove garlic, chopped
4 shoulder lamb chops,
  ¾ inch thick

½ teaspoon salt
¼ cup dry white wine
⅓ cup stock or bouillon
2 tablespoons tomato paste

Heat oil in 10-inch skillet; add onion and garlic. Cook 5 minutes over medium heat, stirring occasionally. Sprinkle lamb with salt. Add lamb to onion mixture, and cook over medium heat until browned on both sides. Combine wine, stock or bouillon and tomato paste; mix well. Pour over lamb mixture. Cook 40 minutes over low heat, stirring occasionally. Serve lamb with sauce.

BARBECUED LEG OF LAMB
(Use the grill!)

Yield: 12 servings

1 (7-pound) leg of lamb,
  butterflied

Marinade:
3 or 4 tablespoons olive oil   ½ teaspoon rosemary
2 tablespoons soy sauce   1 or 2 cloves of garlic, finely
Juice of ½ lemon, plus grated   minced (optional)
  peel

Rub unboned side of lamb with 1 tablespoon olive oil. Place oiled side down in a baking dish. Rub remainder of the oil plus rest of the ingredients on the top side. Cover with plastic wrap, and marinate one hour or longer — until ready to cook. When coals are right (glowing embers) place lamb on an oiled double-sided rack and barbecue. Turn every five minutes, brushing with oil, for a 45-minute period. Remove from grill to a cutting board, and let set for 10 minutes. Carve from either small end. Carve on a diagonal, as if cutting a flank steak.

NOTE: For even cooking, slash lobes of lamb in 2 or 3 places, making long cuts about 1½ inches deep.

LAMB CHOPS STUFFED WITH FETA
(Use the grill!!)

Yield: 4 servings

½ cup minced onions   2 tablespoons minced fresh
2 tablespoons olive oil   mint
2 small garlic cloves, minced   Salt and pepper, to taste
2 tomatoes   8 lamb rib chops, French-cut,
¼ pound Feta cheese   with pocket cut in center

Using a small sauce pan, sauté onions in oil until soft. Add garlic and tomatoes, and cook for three minutes. Add feta and cook until almost melted. Add mint, salt and pepper to taste. Cool. Stuff chops, and secure with a toothpick. Brush with olive oil, and grill, turning once. Cook 8 minutes for medium rare. Salt and pepper to taste. Garnish with mint.

PERSIAN PILAF

Preheat oven to 350°   Yield: 8 servings

1 tablespoon olive oil
1 pound lamb, cut in 1-inch
  cubes
⅔ cup chopped onion
½ cup chopped tomato (fresh
  or canned)
½ teaspoon salt
¼ teaspoon curry powder

¼ teaspoon ground cumin
⅛ teaspoon tumeric
2 cups long grain white rice,
  rinsed well
¼ cup butter
3 cups chicken broth or
  water

Braise lamb in oil in a large heavy pan until light brown. Add onions, and cook until softened, stirring well. Add tomato and seasonings; cooking and stirring for a couple of minutes more. Transfer the lamb mixture to a 3-quart casserole dish. Add drained rice to the top of the lamb mixture. Place butter, in pats, on top of rice, and add liquid. Cover and bake at 350° for 45 to 50 minutes.

HAM PUFF

Preheat oven to 350°   Yield: 6 servings

14 slices of bread, trimmed
7 slices American cheese
½ teaspoon dry mustard
2 cups ground cooked ham
½ cup finely chopped celery

½ cup butter, melted
4 eggs
3 cups milk
½ teaspoon salt
½ teaspoon paprika

Grease a 9x13-inch baking dish. Line bottom with half the bread. Place cheese over bread, and sprinkle with mustard. Add ham and celery; top with remaining bread. Brush generously with melted butter. Beat eggs slightly; add milk, salt and paprika. Pour over bread, and refrigerate overnight. Bake at 350° about 45 minutes.

TROPICAL HAM CASSEROLE

Preheat oven to 350°   Yield: 4-6 servings

3 cups diced, cooked ham
1 medium onion, sliced in
  thin rings
1 green pepper, sliced in
  rings
½ cup raisins
¾ cup pineapple chunks
1 cup unsweetened pineapple
  juice

⅓ cup vinegar
½ cup brown sugar (do not
  pack)
2 tablespoons cornstarch
2 teaspoons dry mustard
¼ teaspoon salt
1 teaspoon Worcestershire
  sauce
1 tablespoon soy sauce

Place ham in casserole, and arrange onion, pepper, raisins and pineapple on top. Heat juice, brown sugar and vinegar, and mix with cornstarch, mustard and salt. Add Worcestershire and soy sauce. Pour over ham, and bake at 350° for 45 minutes.

NOTE: This can be made ahead for camping or boating. Before serving, transfer to large sauce pan and reheat on burner.

HAM BROCCOLI ROLL-UPS

Preheat oven to 350°   Yield: 10 servings

20 slices cooked ham
20 slices Swiss cheese
2 (10-ounce) packages frozen
  broccoli, defrosted

3 cups sliced raw onions,
  sauteed until tender

Place cheese slice on ham slice, and roll around a stalk of broccoli. Secure each roll with a toothpick, and place in oblong pan. Spread sautéed onions over top.

Sauce:
4 tablespoons margarine
4 tablespoons flour
1 teaspoon salt

½ teaspoon basil
⅛ teaspoon pepper
2 cups milk

Melt margarine in a saucepan, and slowly add flour. Cook a few minutes. Add salt, basil and pepper. Slowly add milk, and cook until slightly thickened. Pour sauce over onions; cover and bake at 350° for 30 minutes. Remove toothpick before serving.

CAULIFLOWER HAM CASSEROLE

Preheat oven to 350°   Yield: 6 servings

1 medium head cauliflower
  (2 pounds)
2 cups cubed cooked ham
1 (3-ounce) can sliced
  mushrooms, drained
4 tablespoons butter or
  margarine
⅓ cup all purpose flour

1 cup milk
1 cup cubed sharp cheddar
  cheese
½ cup sour cream
1 cup soft bread crumbs
1 tablespoon butter or
  margarine, melted

Break cauliflower into buds. Cook, covered, in boiling salted water until tender, 10 to 12 minutes. Drain. Combine ham and mushrooms with cauliflower. In medium saucepan, melt 4 tablespoons butter and stir in flour. Add milk all at once; cook and stir until mixture thickens and bubbles. Add cheese and sour cream to sauce; stir until cheese melts. Combine with cauliflower and ham mixture. Turn into 2-quart casserole. Combine crumbs and remaining butter; sprinkle over top. Bake, uncovered, at 350° for 40 minutes.

COATINGS FOR BAKED HAM

1. Make purée by cooking 2 cups of dried apricots and 2½ cups water until soft; add 1 cup sugar. Purée in blender. Brush over ham and use for basting.

2. Mix juice of 2 oranges, ½ cup pineapple juice, ½ cup each of sugar and white corn syrup. Baste ham frequently with mixture.

HAM LOAF WITH APPLE JELLY SAUCE

Preheat oven to 350°   Yield: 8 servings

1 tablespoon butter
3 tablespoons light brown
  sugar
1 cup milk
1 egg
2 tablespoons ketchup
2 tablespoons yellow
  mustard
1 teaspoon salt
⅛ teaspoon pepper
2 cups soft white bread
  crumbs

8 cups ground cooked ham
½ pound ground pork
½ pound ground veal
2 tablespoons finely chopped
  onion
2 tablespoons chopped
  parsley
1 (20-ounce) can whole
  peeled apricots

Spread butter in bottom of 1½-quart round baking dish. Press brown sugar on top of butter. In large bowl, combine milk, egg, ketchup, mustard, salt and pepper; beat until well blended. Stir in bread crumbs; let the mixture stand several minutes. Add ham, pork, veal, onion and parsley; mix well. Spoon mixture evenly into prepared dish. Bake, uncovered, at 350° for 1 hour. Drain off excess fat. Invert loaf on hot platter.

Heat apricots over low heat while ham loaf is cooking. Drain; garnish ham loaf. Serve with apple jelly sauce.

Sauce:

1 (10-ounce) jar apple jelly
  (1 cup)
¼ cup prepared mustard

1 tablespoon prepared
  horseradish

In small saucepan over medium heat, combine jelly, mustard and horseradish. Heat, stirring constantly, until jelly melts, and sauce is hot. Makes 1¼ cups.

CHALUPAS

Yield: 8-10 servings

1 (4-pound) boneless pork
   roast (minus fat)
2 whole jalapeño peppers
1½ teaspoons oregano
2 cloves garlic, minced
2 pounds dry pinto beans,
   picked, washed and
   drained

1½ teaspoons salt
½ teaspoon black pepper
Water to cover roast, spices
   and beans

Combine roast, peppers, oregano, garlic, dry beans, salt and pepper in large stock pot. Cover with water. Cook over medium to low heat for 6 to 8 hours, stirring frequently. When ready to serve, remove pork roast from bean mixture, and shred in small pieces. Return to bean mixture, and stir well. Reheat. Place on large serving platter.

Place the following garnishes in individual bowls:

Corn chips
Hot sauce
Shredded cheddar cheese or
   Monterrey Jack cheese

Chopped onion
Shredded lettuce
Chopped tomato
Chopped avocado

Serving should be in following order: corn chips, meat and bean mixture, hot sauce, shredded cheese, chopped onion, shredded lettuce, chopped tomato and chopped avocado. Guests serve themselves from the bowls.

NOTE: Pralines are nice for after-dinner fare.

APPLE SKILLET DINNER
(Quick and easy)

Yield: 4 servings

1 pound bulk pork sausage
1 teaspoon dried leaf thyme
½ cup brown sugar, packed
¼ cup cider vinegar

4 cups shredded cabbage
2 red delicious apples, cored
 and sliced

Cook sausage and drain well. Add thyme, brown sugar and vinegar. Mix well. Add cabbage and cover. Cook 2 to 3 minutes, just until cabbage is wilted. Stir in apple slices, and cook 2 minutes longer.

SAUSAGE SPAGHETTI WITH EGGPLANT SAUCE

Yield: 8 servings

½ cup vegetable oil
1 eggplant (1 to 1½ pounds)
 peeled, cut in 1-inch cubes
1 medium onion, chopped
1 clove garlic, crushed
2 tablespoons fresh parsley
½ pound Italian sausage
1 (16-ounce) can Italian style
 tomatoes

1 (6-ounce) can tomato paste
½ cup dry white wine
1 (4-ounce) can mushrooms
1 teaspoon dried oregano
 leaves
1 teaspoon salt
1 teaspoon sugar
1 pound thin spaghetti
Grated Parmesan cheese

Heat oil over medium heat in a 4-quart Dutch oven. Add eggplant cubes, onion, garlic, parsley and Italian sausage. Cook until transparent and tender, about 5 minutes. Stir in tomatoes, paste, wine, mushrooms, oregano, salt and sugar. Break up tomatoes with fork. Reduce heat; cover and simmer 45 minutes, stirring occasionally. Serve over drained spaghetti, and sprinkle with grated Parmesan cheese.

B&B WILD RICE CASSEROLE

Preheat oven to 325°   Yield: 6-8 servings

1 cup wild rice (cook as
   directed)
¼ pound butter
2 small onions, grated
2 tablespoons flour
2 cups milk
Salt and pepper
2 chicken bouillon cubes

¼ teaspoon sage
1 (8-ounce) can mushrooms,
   drained
1 pound mild pork sausage,
   cooked and drained
1 (8-ounce) can water
   chestnuts, sliced

Sauté onions in butter until transparent. Remove onions. Stir in flour, and stir until smooth. Add milk gradually, stirring until thickened. Add bouillon cubes, seasonings, rice, mushrooms and sausage. Fold in water chestnuts. Place in casserole dish, and bake at 325° for 20 to 30 minutes.

SPANISH STYLE ROAST PORK

Preheat oven to 350°   Yield: 6 servings

3 to 6 pound pork roast
4 to 7 cloves of garlic
¾ cup chopped onions
¾ cup lime juice or mixture
   of any citrus juice
½ cup safflower oil or olive
   oil
2 chopped jalapeños

¼ cup chopped green pepper
1 tablespoon honey
2 teaspoons fresh ground
   black pepper
1 tablespoon cumin seeds
1 teaspoon oregano
1 teaspoon paprika
1 teaspoon capers

Mix all the above ingredients, except roast. Pour over roast, and keep refrigerated for 24 to 48 hours, turning roast several times. Pour off marinade before roasting. Bake at 350° for 1 hour or until meat thermometer inserted into thickest part registers 165°.

DELICIOUS PORK CHOPS

Yield: 4 servings

4 loin pork chops
1 medium onion, sliced
4 teaspoons brown sugar

1 cup ketchup
2 cups cooked rice

Place chops in skillet. Over each chop, place onion slices, a teaspoon brown sugar and ¼ cup ketchup. Cover and simmer about 50 minutes to 1 hour or until chops are falling off bone. Serve over rice.

NOTE: Great for camping or boating.

PORK CHOPS AND RICE
(Easy)

Yield: 6 servings

6 pork chops, browned
1 cup uncooked rice
2 (10½-ounce) cans beef
   bouillon

1 can water
1 green pepper
1 medium onion, chopped

Brown pork chops in skillet. Pour rice in 9x13-inch casserole baking dish. Place pork chops on top. Add bouillon, water and pepper (also onion if desired) to pan in which you browned pork chops. Stir and pour over pork chops and rice. Bake at 350° for at least 1 hour. Add water, if necessary.

VARIATIONS: (1) For added flavor, add ¼ teaspoon marjoram or thyme. (2) Add 1 (2½-ounce) jar sliced mushrooms, and use 1 (10½-ounce) can beef bouillon and 1 (10½-ounce) can French onion soup.

SPAGHETTI AND PORK CHOP CASSEROLE

Preheat oven to 350°   Yield: 4 servings

4 (1-inch) thick pork chops
1 teaspoon salt
¼ teaspoon pepper
Flour
2 tablespoons fat
8 ounces thin spaghetti
1 (10½-ounce) can condensed
   tomato soup

½ can water (use soup can as
   measure)
¼ pound processed American
   cheese
1 medium onion, minced

Sprinkle chops with ½ teaspoon salt and ⅛ teaspoon pepper; dredge with flour; brown in hot fat. Cook spaghetti 10 minutes in boiling salted water and drain. Add remaining ingredients and remaining salt and pepper. Turn into 2-quart casserole, and top with chops; cover and bake at 350° for one hour, or until tender.

EXTRA GOOD BARBECUE SPARERIBS

Preheat oven to 350°   Yield: 4-6 servings

Cut 4 pounds spareribs into serving pieces. Brown in a baking pan on top of stove, or place in hot oven to brown.

Sauce:
1 cup sliced onion
1 cup ketchup
1 cup water
2 tablespoons Worcestershire
   sauce

2 teaspoons salt
¼ cup brown sugar
2 teaspoons dry mustard
1 teaspoon paprika

Mix sauce ingredients together and cook until blended (about 20 minutes).

Pour mixture over spareribs. Cover and bake at 350° for 1¾ hours, basting ribs with sauce 2 or 3 times. Uncover and bake for 15 minutes more.

SPARERIBS HAWAIIAN

Preheat oven to 400°   Yield: 4-6 servings

4 pounds spareribs
1 (15-ounce) can tomato
  sauce
1 (20-ounce) can crushed
  pineapple

1 large onion, finely chopped
½ green pepper, diced
4 tablespoons Worcestershire
  sauce
Salt and pepper

Marinate pork or beef ribs in sauce several hours, turning once. Bake in 400° oven 40 minutes or until tender.

PORK ST. TAMMANY

Yield: 12 servings

2 (6-ounce) packages long
  grain and wild rice mix
1 cup boiling water
1 cup chopped dried apricots
4 green onions, finely
  chopped
1 cup chopped fresh
  mushrooms
½ cup chopped green pepper
4 tablespoons butter
6 tablespoons chopped
  pecans

2 tablespoons chopped fresh
  parsley
¼ teaspoon salt
¼ teaspoon pepper
⅛ teaspoon red pepper
⅛ teaspoon garlic powder
6 (1-pound) boneless pork
  tenderloins
6 slices bacon
1 (16-ounce) can apricot
  halves, drained
Fresh parsley sprigs

Cook rice according to package directions; set aside.

Pour boiling water over apricots; let stand 20 minutes to soften; drain. Sauté green onions, mushrooms and green pepper in butter until tender. Add rice, apricots, pecans, parsley and seasonings; stir until well mixed.

Cut a lengthwise slit on top of each tenderloin, being careful not to cut through the bottom and sides. Spoon one-third of stuffing into the opening of one tenderloin; place cut side of second tenderloin over stuffing. Tie tenderloins together securely with string, and place on a rack in a roasting pan. Top with two bacon slices. Repeat procedure with remaining tenderloins. Place an aluminum foil tent over tenderloins; bake at 325° for 1½ to 2 hours or until meat thermometer registers 170°. Remove foil the last 30 to 40 minutes of baking. Remove from oven; let stand 5 minutes. Remove string; slice and garnish with apricot halves and parsley.

NOTE: Recipe can be reduced by half successfully!

PORK TENDERLOIN FLORIDA

Yield: 4 servings

1 tablespoon best quality
  olive oil
4 pork tenderloins, tapered
  ends removed and
  reserved for other use
Salt and white pepper, to
  taste
2 tablespoons shallots,
  finely chopped

½ cup brandy
½ cup chicken broth
1 tablespoon cornstarch,
  dissolved in 2 tablespoons
  water
1 large mango, sliced
Watercress, for decoration

Heat oil until hot but not smoking in heavy skillet. Brown pork, which has been patted dry and seasoned with salt and white pepper. Pour off all but 1 tablespoon fat. Reduce heat, and sauté shallots. Add brandy, and cook to reduce by half. Add chicken broth and pork. Cover, reduce heat and simmer for 30 to 40 minutes or until tender. Transfer pork to serving platter. Stir cornstarch mixture into pan juices. Bring sauce to boil over moderate heat, stirring, and adjust seasoning to taste. Spoon sauce over pork on plate. Place mango slices on sauce around pork. Garnish with watercress.

VEAL NORMANDE

Yield: 4-6 servings

1½ pounds veal cutlets
3 tablespoons butter
3 tablespoons brandy
1 (10½-ounce) can cream of
  mushroom soup

⅔ cup milk
1 apple, peeled and thickly
  sliced
Cooked rice

Pound veal with mallet. In large skillet, brown veal in butter and remove from pan. Add brandy; stir to loosen brown bits. Stir in soup and milk. Add veal and apple; cook over low heat until tender, stirring occasionally. Serve with rice.

VEAL VERMOUTH

Yield: 4 servings

1 pound veal cutlets, each
   about ½ inch thick
¼ cup all-purpose flour
4 tablespoons butter or
   margarine
½ pound mushrooms, sliced
½ cup dry vermouth

2 tablespoons water
¾ teaspoon salt
⅛ teaspoon garlic powder
⅛ teaspoon pepper
Sautéed cherry tomatoes
Parsley sprigs for garnish

About 50 minutes before serving, pound veal with meat mallet. Pound cutlets to about ⅛-inch thickness. Slice cutlets into 3x2-inch pieces. On waxed paper, coat cutlets lightly with flour.

In 10-inch skillet, over medium high heat, melt butter or margarine, and cook meat, a few pieces at a time. Cook until lightly browned on both sides. Remove pieces as they brown, adding more butter if necessary.

Add mushrooms, vermouth, water, salt, garlic powder and pepper to skillet; heat to boiling. Reduce heat to low; cover and simmer 5 minutes or until mushrooms are tender. Return meat to skillet, and heat through. Stir in chopped parsley. Arrange meat on platter with sautéed cherry tomatoes. Garnish with parsley sprigs.

VEAL AND PORK CASSEROLE

Preheat oven to 350°

Yield: 4 servings

½ pound cubed veal
½ pound cubed pork
2 cups chopped celery
1½ large onions, chopped

½ cup white rice
½ cup wild rice
4 tablespoons soy sauce
4 cups boiling water

Sauté veal, pork, celery and onions. Mix all ingredients, and place in a greased casserole. Bake, covered, at 350° for 1½ hours. Serve with Mushroom Sauce.

Sauce:

1 (10¾-ounce) can cream of
   mushroom soup
1 (2½-ounce) jar sliced
   mushrooms, drained

½ cup sherry wine

Mix and heat. Do not boil.

CUBAN VEAL
(Easy)

Yield: 6 servings

3 tablespoons all-purpose
  flour
½ teaspoon salt
¼ teaspoon pepper
1½ to 1¾ pounds boneless
  veal cutlets
⅓ cup butter

¼ cup lemon juice
¾ pound lump crabmeat
1 tablespoon chopped fresh
  parsley
3 cups cooked, buttered
  noodles
Hollandaise Sauce*

Combine flour, salt and pepper; dredge veal in flour mixture. Melt butter in skillet, and brown veal on each side for about one minute. Add lemon juice and cook one more minute. Remove veal to hot platter. Remove all but one tablespoon of drippings. Add crabmeat and sprinkle with parsley. Stir crabmeat until just heated. Spoon over veal and top with Hollandaise Sauce; sprinkle with paprika if desired. Serve with buttered noodles.

See Sauces for recipe.

VEAL SCALLOPINI

Preheat oven to 350°

Yield: 6 servings

2 pounds veal shoulder or
  round (½-inch thick)
½ cup flour
1 medium onion, finely
  chopped
2 cloves garlic, minced
¼ cup butter
1 cup sliced mushrooms
1 teaspoon salt

1 teaspoon sugar
Pepper, to taste
1 (15-ounce) can tomato
  sauce or 1 (15½-ounce) can
  tomato soup with enough
  water to make 2 cups
  liquid
3 cups cooked wide egg
  noodles

Cut veal in 1½-inch squares. Dredge in flour. Melt butter in skillet. Cook veal, onion and garlic until browned. Add remaining ingredients. Stir to mix well. Turn into 2½-quart casserole. Cover and bake at 350° for 2 hours. Serve over noodles.

VEAL SPAGHETTI

Yield: 4 servings

2 medium green peppers, cut into strips
1 tablespoon vegetable oil
1 large onion, chopped
1 large carrot, grated
1 pound veal cutlets, cut into bite-size pieces

1 (14½-ounce) can whole tomatoes, undrained
¼ pound fresh mushrooms, sliced
¼ cup dry red wine
1 small clove garlic, crushed
2 cups hot cooked spaghetti

Sauté green peppers, onions and carrots in oil for 5 minutes. Brown veal in a medium size skillet until brown. (Takes just a few minutes.) Add peppers, onions, carrots and remaining ingredients, except spaghetti. Simmer over low heat, covered, for one hour. Serve over hot spaghetti.

VEAL BIRDS

Preheat oven to 350°

Yield: 6-8 servings

8 veal cutlets

Dressing:
4 cups soft dry bread, cubed
¼ cup butter, melted
Salt, to taste
Pepper, to taste
Sage, to taste
2 teaspoons baking powder

½ cup finely chopped onion
½ cup finely chopped celery
Water or wine to moisten stuffing
1 tablespoon butter
⅛ cup vegetable oil

Combine all ingredients for stuffing. Add water or wine until moistened. Roll cutlets around the stuffing mixture and skewer with toothpicks. Brown cutlets in butter and oil in a 10-inch skillet. Transfer cutlets to baking dish. Deglaze skillet with ¼ cup water, and pour scrapings and water over veal birds. Cover and bake at 350° for 1 hour. Uncover and bake for ½ hour longer or until browned.

NOTE: Serve with Rice Pilaf.*

See Vegetables for recipe.

Poultry

COCONUT PALM

Hints for Poultry

Only keep poultry in the refrigerator a day or two before cooking.

If you buy frozen poultry, watch out for brown spots; this means it has been improperly stored.

Poultry is an excellent source of protein, less fatty and less costly than other meats.

Choose poultry that is plump and has no surface defects.

When frying poultry, put the dark pieces in first as they will take longer to cook than the white pieces.

Chicken will freeze nicely for approximately six months if properly wrapped (aluminum foil or freezer wrap).

Do not stuff poultry until just before cooking or it may spoil. Also, never put poultry in the refrigerator with stuffing in it. Take stuffing out and store it in a separate dish.

To keep batter on chicken to be fried, place the chicken, with batter on it, in the refrigerator for one hour before cooking it.

The secret to a more tasty chicken salad is to cut the chicken in larger pieces.

Small chickens are done when the drumstick moves around easily, the juices are clear and the internal temperature is 185° F.

Use tongs when turning chicken. If you use a fork, all the natural juices will cook out.

If on a diet, take the skin off the chicken first before cooking. The fat is absorbed from the skin during cooking.

When cooking chicken parts on a grill, place all the chicken bone-side down. Turn all the chicken at the same time.

Do not cook chicken at too high a temperature. A low temperature keeps the bird uniformly tender and the meat more juicy.

Do not stuff a turkey too tightly; it will become hard and compact and may burst the skin from expansion.

If you brush a chicken with butter before cooking, the skin will be crisper.

Always defrost poultry in the refrigerator.

ARTICHOKE CHICKEN

Preheat oven to 375°   Yield: 8 servings

2 (2½ pound) chickens, cut
   into serving pieces
4 tablespoons butter
1 (8-ounce) package frozen
   artichoke hearts, thawed
½ cup chopped onion
⅓ cup flour

1½ teaspoons rosemary
1½ teaspoons salt
¼ teaspoon pepper
1 cup chicken broth
1 cup white wine
1 (6-ounce) can button
   mushrooms

Brown chicken in butter in skillet. Transfer to 9x13-inch casserole. Arrange artichokes around chicken. Add onions to skillet. Blend in flour, rosemary, salt and pepper. Add broth and wine, stirring until thick. Add mushrooms. Spoon over chicken. Bake, covered, at 375° for 55 to 60 minutes.

SAVORY LEMON CHICKEN

Yield: 6 servings

3 pounds chicken pieces
⅓ cup vegetable oil
⅓ cup white wine
2 teaspoons lemon and
   pepper seasonings

1 teaspoon dry mustard
½ teaspoon crushed tarragon
   leaves
½ teaspoon onion powder

Combine everything but the chicken. Shake well. Marinate the chicken in the dressing for at least 4 hours. Grill over hot coals.

CHICKEN AND DUMPLINGS

Yield: 6-8 servings

1 (3-pound) chicken	1 teaspoon pepper
2 quarts water	1 chicken bouillon cube
1 tablespoon salt	1 teaspoon seasoned salt

Place chicken and all seasonings in a 4-quart stockpot; add water to cover. Bring to a boil. Skim residue and lower heat; simmer covered about 1½ hours. Remove chicken from stockpot. Set aside to cool. De-bone.

Dumplings:
3 cups flour   6 tablespoons water
3 large eggs

Blend flour and eggs with enough water (adding a teaspoon at a time) to form a stiff dough. Pull off about ½-cup dough at a time, and place on floured waxed paper. Dust top of dough with flour, and roll thin, about ⅛-inch thick. Cut into 1½x1-inch long strips. Drop into boiling chicken stock. Boil until dumplings are tender, about 10 minutes. Add chicken, and simmer until chicken is heated through.

GOOD OLD FASHIONED CHICKEN TETRAZZINI

Preheat oven to 350°   Yield: 8-10 servings

1 chicken (preferably a hen)
1½ quarts water
1 teaspoon salt
1 stick (¼ pound) margarine
  or butter
1 celery stick
1 pound thin spaghetti
½ pound Velveeta cheese,
  grated or cubed
2 (10¾-ounce) cans cream of
  mushroom soup, undiluted

1 (4-ounce) jar pimentos,
  drained and sliced
1 medium onion, chopped
1 small green pepper,
  chopped
¼ teaspoon black pepper
1 (2.5 ounce) jar sliced
  mushrooms, drained
Paprika, for color

Use a 4-quart Dutch oven or soup pot.

Cook chicken in 1½ quarts water with salt, butter and celery stick until tender. Remove chicken from broth to cool. Discard celery stick. Reserve broth. Cook 1 pound of spaghetti in one quart boiling chicken broth (add water to broth to make one quart) for 10 minutes. Heat Velveeta cheese and undiluted cream of mushroom soup over low heat until smooth, being careful not to burn on bottom of sauce pan. De-bone chicken and cut into small bite-size pieces. Add chicken, pimentos, onion, green pepper, and black pepper to cooked spaghetti mixture; simmer for 10 minutes. Add mushrooms and cheese/soup mixture to chicken/spaghetti mixture. Stir to mix well. Pour into a 3-quart casserole dish and sprinkle top with paprika. Bake, uncovered, at 350° for 20 minutes or until bubbly.

NOTE: Great for a ladies luncheon or bazaar.

HERBED CHICKEN SOUFFLÉ

Preheat oven to 325°   Yield: 10 servings

1 (8-ounce) package herb
  seasoned stuffing mix
3 cups cooked chicken, diced
  (1 medium sized hen)
½ cup butter (melted) or
  ½ cup chicken fat

½ cup sifted flour
¼ teaspoon salt
Dash of pepper
3 cups chicken broth
6 eggs, slightly beaten

Grease a 13x9x2-inch casserole or soufflé dish. Prepare stuffing according to package directions, and spread in bottom of casserole. Add layer of diced chicken. Melt butter (chicken fat adds even more flavor) in sauce pan and blend in flour and seasonings. Stir in the broth, and cook until thick. Stir a small amount of the hot mixture into slightly beaten eggs. Blend chicken broth, sauce and eggs together gradually. Pour over chicken, and cook at 325° for 40 to 45 minutes or until knife inserted in soufflé comes out clean. Serve with Pimento Mushroom Sauce.

Pimento Mushroom Sauce:
1 (10¾-ounce) can cream of
  mushroom soup
1 cup sour cream

¼ cup milk
½ cup pimento, chopped

Combine all ingredients. Heat and ladle over soufflé while serving.

ARROZ CON POLLO

Yield: 4-6 servings

1 frying chicken, cut in serving pieces
1½ teaspoons garlic powder
2 tablespoons olive oil, divided
2 tablespoons butter or margarine, divided
1 medium onion, chopped
1 clove garlic, minced
1 green pepper, chopped
2 stalks celery, chopped

1 (8-ounce) can tomato sauce
1 cup short grained white rice
2 cups water
1 (2-ounce) jar pimentos
1 package Vigo flavoring mix
Salt and pepper, to taste
1 (8½-ounce) can tiny green peas

Rinse and skin chicken pieces.

Season chicken pieces with garlic powder, and brown in a combination of 1 tablespoon olive oil and 1 tablespoon margarine. Remove from pan, and sauté onion, garlic, green pepper and celery in remaining tablespoon olive oil and 1 tablespoon margarine. Return chicken to pan, and add tomato sauce, rice, water, pimentos, Vigo flavoring, salt and pepper. Cover and simmer 1 to 1½ hours or until rice is tender. Check chicken and rice after 30 minutes cooking time. Add more water, if necessary. After cooking 1 hour, add peas. Mix, heat and serve.

COQ AU VIN

Preheat oven to 325°   Yield: 6-8 servings

6 chicken breast halves, boned
½ cup flour
Salt and pepper, to taste
¼ teaspoon nutmeg
¼ teaspoon paprika
½ cup margarine or butter
6 green onions, chopped tops too
1 clove garlic, minced

1 bay leaf
⅛ teaspoon thyme
1 (2.5 ounce) jar sliced mushrooms, drained
1½ cups dry white wine or dry Vermouth
2 slices bacon, cooked, drained and crumbled
Cooked rice (curried, white or wild)

Dredge chicken in flour mixed with salt, pepper, nutmeg and paprika. Brown in skillet in margarine or butter. Remove chicken to a 13x9x2-inch baking dish. Add next five ingredients to skillet, and sauté 10 minutes. Add wine and stir. Pour over chicken in baking dish, and sprinkle bacon bits over top. Cover and bake at 325° for 50 to 60 minutes. Serve with curried, white or wild rice.

CUBAN CHICKEN AND YELLOW RICE

Yield: 4 servings

8 pieces of chicken
Salt, pepper and garlic salt,
  to taste
½ cup lemon or lime juice
4 tablespoons olive oil
2 medium onions, chopped
Pepper, to taste
6 cloves garlic, minced
½ cup diced ham
½ can tomato paste (3
  ounces)

1 medium green pepper,
  diced
1 cup dry white wine
2 cups uncooked yellow rice
4 cups chicken broth (use 4
  cups water and 4 bouillon
  cubes)
1 (16-ounce) can tiny peas
1 small jar pimentos,
  chopped

Sprinkle chicken with salt, pepper and garlic salt. Pour lemon juice over chicken, and marinate 4 hours, turning occasionally. Drain. Sauté chicken in olive oil for 15 minutes in a 12-inch skillet, turn chicken so that it is brown on both sides. Add onions and ground pepper to taste, garlic, ham, tomato paste and green pepper. Continue to sauté on medium heat until onions are transparent. Reduce to simmer. Add wine, and simmer 2 or 3 minutes. Add rice, and stir well so that rice is coated. Add chicken broth; stir and boil 1 minute. Cover and cook over low heat about 15 minutes. Add peas. Turn heat off and leave covered 15 minutes before serving. Garnish with pimentos.

DOMINICAN CHICKEN WITH RUM AND LIME

Yield: 6 servings

6 boneless chicken breasts,
  skinned
Juice of 2 limes
¾ cup white rum
¼ cup soy sauce

2 garlic cloves, minced
Flour
Vegetable oil for frying
6 lime wedges, for garnish

Rinse chicken, and pat dry with paper towels. Place in bowl and add lime juice. Toss chicken to cover with juice. Make a marinade sauce in a bowl by combining rum, soy sauce and garlic. Add chicken to marinade and toss. Cover and chill for 5 hours. Drain chicken, and dredge with flour. Fry chicken in hot oil (375°), turning it until it is golden brown. Transfer chicken to paper towels to drain. Serve with lime wedges.

PARTY CHICKEN

Preheat oven to 350°   Yield: 6 servings

6 boneless chicken breast halves
2 tablespoons butter
6 small ham steaks
1 (10¾-ounce) can of chicken soup, undiluted

1 (10¾-ounce) can cream of celery soup, undiluted
1 (2.5-ounce) jar sliced mushrooms, drained
½ cup chopped celery

Brown chicken breasts in butter. Place ham steaks in individual dishes or one large rectangular pan. Place chicken breasts on top of each piece of ham. Mix soup, mushrooms and celery together. Pour over chicken. Cover and bake at 350° for 1 hour.

CHICKEN BREASTS IN HAM

Yield: 6 servings

3 large skinned, boned chicken breasts, halves
¼ cup flour
½ teaspoon garlic salt
½ teaspoon paprika
¼ teaspoon chili powder
3 tablespoons butter or margarine

⅔ cup chicken broth
6 large slices deli ham, thin cut
Wooden toothpicks
Dill Mustard Sauce*

Cut chicken breasts in 6 even strips (18 total). Dredge in a mixture of flour and spices. Brown in butter; add chicken broth, cover and simmer 20 minutes or until tender. Cool. Cut each ham slice into 3 strips. Wrap 1 chicken piece with 1 ham strip, and skewer with toothpick. Cover with foil and refrigerate. May be served hot or cold, with or without Dill Mustard Sauce.

See Sauces for recipe.

FANCY FAST CHICKEN

Preheat oven to 350°   Yield: 6 servings

3 boneless chicken breasts
  (six halves)
6 slices Swiss cheese
¼ pound fresh sliced
  mushrooms (optional)

½ cup white wine
1 (10¾-ounce) can cream of
  chicken soup, undiluted
2 cups herbed stuffing mix
1 stick (¼ pound) butter

Place chicken in lightly greased 9x13-inch glass baking dish. Top each piece with slice of Swiss cheese. Lay mushrooms over the Swiss cheese. Mix can of soup with wine, and pour over chicken. Spread stuffing mix over top, and drizzle melted butter over the top. Bake at 350° for 45 to 50 minutes.

CHICKEN ALMONDINE

Preheat oven to 350°   Yield: 8 servings

3 cups cooked chicken, diced
4 hard-cooked eggs, grated
2 cups cooked rice
1½ cups chopped celery
1 small onion, chopped
1 (10¾-ounce) can cream of
  mushroom soup, undiluted

1 cup mayonnaise
2 tablespoons lemon juice
1 cup bread crumbs
2 tablespoons butter or
  margarine
1 cup slivered almonds

Mix all ingredients except bread crumbs and butter. Place in a 3-quart casserole. Moisten bread crumbs with melted butter. Sprinkle bread crumbs and almonds over top. Bake at 350° for 45 minutes. May be frozen for future use before baking. Bring to room temperature before baking, if frozen.

HOT CHICKEN SALAD

Preheat oven to 325°   Yield: 6 servings

12 slices thin bread
4 ounces margarine
2 cups chopped chicken,
   cooked
½ cup mayonnaise
1 (4-ounce) can mushrooms,
   undrained

2 hard-cooked eggs, chopped
½ cup chopped scallions
½ cup chopped ripe olives
1 cup sour cream
1 (10¾-ounce) can cream of
   chicken soup, undiluted

Cut crusts from thin bread; butter both sides. Line a 13x9-inch casserole dish with 6 slices of bread. Mix next six ingredients; spread ½ of mixture over bread. Put six slices of bread on top, then add remaining chicken mixture. Refrigerate overnight. Bring to room temperature. Spoon sour cream and chicken soup (mixed) over top. Bake at 325° for 30 to 45 minutes.

CHICKEN PARMESAN

                                        Yield: 6 servings

1 egg
2 tablespoons water
2 pounds chicken parts
½ cup Italian bread crumbs
1 tablespoon shortening
1 (10½-ounce) can tomato
   soup, undiluted

¼ cup water
¼ cup chopped onion
½ teaspoon each: basil,
   garlic powder, oregano
   leaves, crushed
Shredded Mozzarella cheese

Beat egg plus 2 tablespoons water. Roll chicken in egg mixture, then in crumbs. In a large fry pan, brown in 1 tablespoon shortening. Stir in soup, water, onion and seasonings. Cover and simmer for 45 minutes. Sprinkle with cheese and serve.

KUNG PAO CHICKEN
(Use your wok)

Yield: 4-6 servings

2 tablespoons soy sauce
1 tablespoon white wine
  vinegar
1 tablespoon dry cooking
  sherry
3 tablespoons chicken broth
2 teaspoons sugar
2 teaspoons cornstarch

1 tablespoon dry cooking
  sherry
1 teaspoon cornstarch
½ teaspoon salt
⅛ teaspoon white pepper
1½ pounds chicken breasts,
  skinned, boned and cut
  into bite-size pieces

2 tablespoons peanut oil,
  divided
4 to 6 small dry, hot chili
  peppers
½ cup cashews

2 tablespoons peanut oil
¼ teaspoon fresh ginger, or
  to taste
½ teaspoon minced garlic
2 whole scallions, chopped
  into 1½-inch lengths
1 can sliced water chestnuts

Cooked rice

NOTE: Have all ingredients chopped, measured, etc., ready to go before you start cooking. You will not have time to stop once you've started cooking in the wok. When adding oil to wok, always drizzle around the upper half.

Cooking Sauce:
   In small bowl, combine 2 tablespoons soy sauce, 1 tablespoon white wine vinegar, 1 tablespoon dry cooking sherry, 3 tablespoons chicken broth and 2 teaspoons each sugar and cornstarch. Set aside.

   In another bowl, combine 1 tablespoon sherry, 1 teaspoon cornstarch, ½ teaspoon salt and ⅛ teaspoon white pepper. Add chicken and coat well. Stir in 1 tablespoon peanut oil, and let stand 15 minutes to marinate.

   Heat wok over medium heat. Add 1 tablespoon peanut oil. Add chili peppers and nuts; stir until peppers begin to char. Remove and set aside. Add remaining 2 tablespoons oil, and increase heat to high. When oil is heated, add ginger and garlic. Stir once; add chicken. Stir fry until chicken is done. Add remaining ingredients. Stir cooking sauce. Add to wok. Cook, stirring until sauce bubbles and thickens. Serve over rice.

MEXICAN CHICKEN CASSEROLE

Preheat oven to 350°   Yield: 10 servings

1 medium onion, chopped or grated
3 tablespoons butter
1 (10¾-ounce) can cream of mushroom soup, undiluted
1 (10¾-ounce) can cream of chicken soup, undiluted

1 cup chicken broth
12 corn tortillas
1 chicken, cooked and boned
1 (4-ounce) can green chilies, chopped
1 pound Monterrey Jack cheese, grated

Cook onion in butter. Dilute soups with chicken broth; add onion. Arrange tortillas, chicken, chilies and soup mixtures in layers in large greased casserole. Make at least two layers, then top with cheese. Bake at 350° for 40 minutes.

NOTE: Can be made ahead and refrigerated, but allow a little more time to bake.

CHICKEN ENCHILADA OLÉ

*(This came from the desert of Arizona with the flavor of Mexico —
a heritage and inherited recipe.)*

Preheat oven to 350°   Yield: 4-6 servings

3 tablespoons vegetable oil
1 (1-dozen) package flour tortillas
3 chicken breasts, cooked and shredded
1 pound Longhorn cheese, grated

¼ pound Monterrey Jack cheese, grated
1 (4-ounce) can green chili peppers, cut into small slivers and seeds removed
1 large onion, chopped

Soup Sauce:
1 (10¾-ounce) can cream of mushroom soup
1 (10¾-ounce) can chicken soup
½ teaspoon oregano

¼ teaspoon cumin
¼ teaspoon sage
1 teaspoon chili powder
1 clove garlic, pressed
Salt, to taste

Heat a small amount of vegetable oil in skillet. Dip each tortilla in hot oil, just to soften. Drain on paper towel. Grease the bottom of a 2½-quart casserole. Make 2 or 3 layers of tortillas, chicken, cheeses, green chili peppers, onion and Soup Sauce. Bake at 350° for 45 minutes.

NOTE: Serve with a fruit salad that has avocado, if in season.

CHICKEN TAHITIAN

Preheat oven to 350°   Yield: 6 servings

6 chicken breasts halves
Salt and pepper, to taste
2 tablespoons vegetable oil
1 (6-ounce) can frozen
  orange juice concentrate,
  thawed and undiluted

6 tablespoons melted butter
  or margarine
1¼ teaspoons ground ginger
1¼ teaspoons soy sauce
1 (8-ounce) can pineapple
  slices, drained

Season chicken lightly with salt and pepper. Put oil in a shallow baking pan; add chicken and bake at 350° for 30 minutes. Combine orange juice concentrate, butter, ginger and soy sauce in sauce pan. Simmer 3 minutes. Baste chicken with sauce; bake an additional 35 minutes, basting frequently with sauce. Place chicken under broiler until golden brown. Garnish with pineapple slices.

SPANISH MARINATED CHICKEN

Preheat oven to 350°   Yield: 4 servings

2 chickens (halved)
1 red sweet pepper, chopped
4 to 7 cloves of garlic,
  minced
¾ cup chopped onion
¾ cup citrus juice (lime,
  orange or grapefruit)
½ cup honey
¾ cup olive oil
1 teaspoon crushed red
  pepper flakes

⅛ teaspoon saffron
1 teaspoon cumin seed
1 teaspoon coriander leaf or
  ¼ teaspoon ground
  coriander
½ teaspoon black pepper
1 teaspoon green
  peppercorns
1 teaspoon oregano
1 teaspoon paprika
Cooked yellow rice

Lay chicken pieces in a 3-quart baking dish. Mix all other ingredients together in blender. Pour over chicken; cover and refrigerate for 24 hours. Turn several times. Drain and bake at 350° for 1 hour. Serve with yellow rice.

RICE WITH CHICKEN AND SAUSAGE

Preheat oven to 400°   Yield: 6 servings

3 slices bacon cut into small
  squares
2 cups finely chopped onion
2 cloves garlic, finely minced
2 green peppers, cored,
  seeded and chopped
1 pound sweet Italian
  sausage
½ pound hot Italian sausage
4 cups chicken stock
Salt and pepper, to taste

2 cups rice
12 stuffed green olives
1 tablespoon capers
1½ teaspoon saffron
1 (3-pound) chicken, cut into
  parts
⅛ teaspoon salt
1 tablespoon paprika
¼ cup olive oil
1 cup cooked peas
Pimento for garnish

Combine bacon, onion, garlic and green peppers in a skillet; add
sausage, sliced into ½-inch lengths. Cook all together until the onions
are wilted. Spoon the mixture into an earthenware casserole, and add ¼
cup stock. Add salt and pepper to taste, plus rice, olives, capers and
saffron. Sprinkle the chicken pieces with salt and paprika. Cook in olive
oil until brown on all sides, then add to the casserole. Add remaining
stock and cover. Bake at 400° 35 to 40 minutes, stirring once during the
baking. (If rice becomes too dry, add new stock.) When rice is tender,
uncover and reduce oven heat to 300°. Add peas and cook 10 minutes
longer. Garnish with pimento.

CHINESE CHICKEN

Preheat oven to 350°   Yield: 8-10 servings

3 cups sliced celery
1 cup chopped onion
1 (4-ounce) can mushrooms
¾ cup chopped green pepper
2 tablespoons butter
4 cups white sauce*
1 (4-ounce) can pimentos,
  drained
1 (6-ounce) can toasted
  almonds

2 (8-ounce) cans water
  chestnuts, sliced and
  drained
2 (3-pound) chickens, cooked
  and cut into large serving
  pieces
1 (6-ounce) can Chinese
  noodles

Sauté celery, onion, mushrooms and green pepper in butter until soft. Add the sautéed vegetables to white sauce, along with pimento, almonds, water chestnuts and chicken. Refrigerate until 30 minutes before serving. Top with Chinese noodles, and bake at 350° for 30 minutes.

NOTE: This is especially good with the Hot Curried Fruit recipe.

See Sauces for recipe.

CHICKEN PIE

Preheat oven to 350°   Yield: 6 servings

2 tablespoons butter
2 tablespoons flour
1 teaspoon salt
⅛ teaspoon pepper
1 teaspoon thyme
½ cup light cream or ½ cup
  light evaporated milk

½ cup chicken broth
2 cups chopped chicken
1½ cups mixed frozen
  vegetables, thawed
1 medium onion, chopped
2 (8-inch) pie crusts

Melt butter over medium heat. Add flour, salt, pepper, thyme, and stir until smooth. Mix in cream and broth, stirring constantly over medium heat until it boils. Stir in chicken chunks and vegetables. Pour into pie crusts and bake at 350° for 45 minutes.

CRANBERRY CHICKEN

Preheat oven to 350°   Yield: 12 servings

24 chicken legs
Salt and pepper
1 (8-ounce) bottle Catalina
  salad dressing
1 envelope dry onion soup
  mix

1 (16-ounce) can whole
  cranberry sauce
½ cup water
Paprika

Wash chicken; dry and place in baking pan. Lightly salt and pepper. Mix together dressing, soup mix, cranberry sauce, and water. Pour evenly over chicken. Sprinkle with paprika. Cover with foil, and bake at 350° for 1½ hours.

NOTE: May use other chicken parts. This can also be used as an appetizer.

CHICKEN IN WINE

Preheat oven to 350°   Yield: 4-6 servings

3 whole boneless chicken
  breasts
Salt and pepper
2 tablespoons margarine or
  butter
1 (10¾-ounce) can cream of
  chicken soup, undiluted
¾ cup Sauterne wine

1 (5-ounce) can sliced water
  chestnuts, drained
1 (3-ounce) can sliced
  mushrooms, drained
2 tablespoons chopped green
  pepper
¼ teaspoon thyme

Sprinkle salt and pepper over chicken breasts and brown chicken slowly in margarine, in 10-inch skillet. Remove chicken, and place in 2-quart casserole. Add remaining ingredients to drippings in skillet, and heat to boiling point, stirring occasionally. Pour sauce over chicken, and cover casserole with aluminum foil. Bake at 350° for 25 to 30 minutes. Uncover, and bake 25 more minutes or until tender.

SHERRIED CHICKEN

Preheat oven to 350°   Yield: 4 servings

1 frying chicken, cut up (or
    favorite pieces)
½ cup flour
1 teaspoon salt
¼ teaspoon pepper
¼ teaspoon paprika
⅓ cup butter or margarine

⅓ cup dry white wine
1 (10¾-ounce) can cream of
    chicken or mushroom
    soup, undiluted
1 small onion, finely
    chopped
½ cup chopped celery

Dredge chicken in a mixture of flour, salt, pepper and paprika. Brown in butter. Place in casserole. Add remaining ingredients to browning pan, and heat through. Pour over chicken; cover and bake at 350° for 45 minutes.

CHICKEN DIABLO

Preheat oven to 350°   Yield: 4 servings

4 chicken breast halves
4 tablespoons margarine
½ cup honey
½ cup prepared mustard

1 teaspoon salt
1 teaspoon curry powder
Cooked rice

Wash chicken, and pat dry with paper towel. Melt butter in shallow baking pan. Stir in remaining ingredients. Roll chicken in mix to coat both sides. Arrange meaty side up in single layer. Bake at 375° for 1 hour or until chicken is done. Baste periodically. Serve over rice.

MIAMI ORANGE CHICKEN

Preheat oven to 350°   Yield: 6 servings

6 boneless breast of chicken
    halves
Salt and pepper, to taste
Garlic powder, to taste

½ cup orange marmalade
6 tablespoons butter
1 large orange, cut into 6
    slices, peeled

Wash and dry chicken pieces. Place in large flat baking dish. Sprinkle with salt, pepper and garlic powder, to taste. Spread orange marmalade on each piece of chicken. Top each piece with a tablespoon of butter. Lay an orange slice on top of butter. Cover with foil, and bake at 350° for 45 minutes. Uncover, and bake for 15 minutes more.

CAPE CORAL CHICKEN

Preheat oven to 350°   Yield: 4-6 servings

2 cups cooked chicken pieces
8 ounces medium cheddar
cheese, grated
2 cups uncooked elbow
macaroni
1 medium onion, chopped
fine
2 cups chicken broth
1 (10¾-ounce) can mushroom
soup, undiluted

1 (10¾-ounce) can cream of
celery soup, undiluted
1 soup can filled with milk
½ teaspoon salt
1 (3-ounce) can mushroom
slices, drained
Extra grated cheese for
topping

Mix all ingredients. Place in buttered 9x13-inch pan. Cover and refrigerate overnight. Sprinkle with extra cheese. Cover, and bake at 350° for 1 hour.

CHICKEN CORDON BLEU

Preheat oven to 325°   Yield: 6 servings

6 boned chicken breast
halves, flattened
Flour, for dredging
Vegetable oil and butter, for
frying
½ cup chicken broth

½ cup dry Vermouth
1 teaspoon flour
6 slices baked ham
6 slices Swiss cheese or
Mozzarella
6 large mushroom caps

Dredge chicken in flour, and brown in hot oil in a 10-inch skillet. Drain and place in oven-proof pan. Make sauce in frying pan with drippings, chicken broth, Vermouth and a little flour. Stir until smooth. Place 1 slice ham, 1 slice cheese, and a mushroom cap on each chicken breast. Cover with sauce. Bake at 325° for 20 minutes.

NOTE: May be doubled successfully.

COCONUT CHICKEN WITH GREEN PIGEON PEAS
(A Trinidad Recipe)

Yield: 6 servings

1 whole chicken (3 to 4
  pounds), skinned
1 medium onion, finely
  chopped
1 clove garlic, minced
3 scallions, finely chopped
1 teaspoon salt
½ teaspoon pepper
3 cups pigeon peas (can be
  purchased frozen)

Water
2 cloves garlic, chopped
½ onion, chopped
Salt and pepper, to taste
2 tablespoons vegetable oil
2 tablespoons brown sugar
¼ cup tomato paste
2 onions, quartered
1 whole green hot pepper
2 tablespoons coconut milk

Cut skinned chicken into serving size pieces. Season with onion, garlic, scallions, salt and pepper. Set aside for one hour. Meanwhile, place pigeon peas in pot with water to cover. Add garlic, onion, salt and pepper; cook until soft.

In heavy pot, place 2 tablespoons oil. When hot, add the brown sugar, stirring until brown. Add chicken and sauté, tossing until golden brown. Add tomato paste, quartered onions, green hot pepper and coconut milk; simmer for about 5 minutes. Add pigeon peas to chicken, and simmer until chicken is cooked. Adjust seasonings.

NOTE: Be careful not to cut hot pepper, as it will be too spicy.

EASY DUTCH CHICKEN

Preheat oven to 400°

Yield: 6-8 servings

2 small roasting chickens
2 chicken bouillon cubes
1 lime
2 teaspoons butter

½ teaspoon salt
¼ teaspoon pepper
Paprika
Chopped parsley

Wash and dry chickens. Place in roasting pan. Put 1 bouillon cube, ½ lime and 1 teaspoon butter inside each chicken. Place 1 pat of butter on top of each chicken along with salt, pepper, paprika and a small amount of chopped parsley. Cover and bake at 400° for 1 hour.

NOTE: May add whole carrots and onions or small whole potatoes to the pan around chicken, if desired.

BRANDIED ROAST CORNISH HENS
WITH PEACHES

Yield: 12 servings

Stock:

2 quarts water
1 quart chicken broth
1 cup coarsely chopped
  carrots
1 cup coarsely chopped
  onions
1 cup coarsely chopped
  celery
½ teaspoon thyme

½ teaspoon basil
2 bay leaves
½ cup tomato paste
½ cup crushed fresh
  tomatoes
1 clove garlic, split
⅛ teaspoon nutmeg
⅛ teaspoon ginger

Place all ingredients in a large pot and bring to a boil. Reduce heat and simmer for four hours, then strain. Cook strained liquid until reduced to 1½ quarts. Set aside.

Caramel:

1 cup sugar
¼ cup orange juice

¼ cup water
Juice of ½ lemon

Place all ingredients in heavy skillet and cook over medium heat, stirring occasionally, until the center of the mixture begins to turn brown. Be patient! This may take 10 minutes or so. When caramel is the color of weak coffee, remove skillet from heat, but continue to stir for about 3 minutes or until caramel is slightly cooled. Set aside. This may be done early in the day, but caramel will harden, so slowly warm the caramel before adding to the sauce.

12 Cornish hens　　　　　**Creole Meat Seasoning**

Rub hens inside and out with a liberal amount of meat seasoning. Roast at 400° for about an hour or until tender.

6 large fresh peaches, very ripe

Be sure to buy the peaches in advance to let them ripen at room temperature, if they are not ripe. Cut an X into base of each peach. Blanch in boiling water for 4 to 5 minutes. Remove peaches from water; cool and peel. Slice each peach into 8 slices just before adding to sauce.

(continued on next page)

BRANDIED ROAST CORNISH HENS
WITH PEACHES (cont.)

Sauce:

1 tablespoon vanilla extract
¾ teaspoon cinnamon
¼ teaspoon nutmeg
⅛ teaspoon ginger
¼ teaspoon oregano
¼ teaspoon basil

¼ teaspoon thyme
½ cup water
6 tablespoons cornstarch
⅓ cup ice water
48 peach slices, from above
¼ cup peach brandy

Pour reduced stock, from above, into large saucepan. Bring to a quick boil, then whisk in the caramel. Blend well. Add vanilla extract, cinnamon, nutmeg, ginger, oregano, basil, thyme, and ½ cup water. Mix well and bring to a boil. Combine cornstarch and ice water, and stir into boiling stock mixture. Bring sauce back to a boil; reduce to a simmer. Just before serving, drop peach slices into the sauce, and stir in brandy.

To Serve: Place a Cornish hen on plate and ladle ⅓ cup sauce and 4 peach slices over each.

CORNISH HENS AND WILD RICE

Preheat oven to 350°   Yield: 6 servings

1 (3-quart) glass baking dish
   (13x9x2-inches)
1 (6-ounce) box wild rice mix
1 (8-ounce) jar mushrooms,
   drained (save liquid), or
   ½ pound sautéed fresh
   mushrooms, sliced

3 Cornish hens, split
1 cup orange juice
1 cup water (mushroom
   liquid if used)
1 cup dry Vermouth
Salt and pepper, to taste
Butter

Place rice, mushrooms and herbs in glass dish. Place hen halves skin side up on top. Pour liquids over hens; salt and pepper. Place pieces of butter on top. Bake uncovered at 350° for 1 hour or until hens are brown and all liquids are absorbed.

TURKEY LASAGNA

Preheat oven to 375°   Yield: 6-8 servings

1 (10¾-ounce) can condensed
  cream of chicken soup,
  undiluted
1 (10¾-ounce) can condensed
  cream of mushroom soup,
  undiluted
1 cup finely chopped onion
1 cup chopped ripe olives
½ cup grated Parmesan
  cheese

½ cup sour cream
¼ cup mayonnaise
2 tablespoons pimento
  (optional)
½ teaspoon garlic salt
4 cups cooked, cubed turkey
4 cups shredded cheddar
  cheese, divided
6 to 8 lasagna noodles,
  cooked and drained

Grease baking dish, 9x13-inches, preferably glass. Combine all ingredients, except cheddar cheese and noodles. Spread about ⅓ turkey mixture over bottom of pan. Top with 4 noodles and then cheddar cheese. Make another layer, ending with cheese. Bake at 375° for 25 minutes or until bubbly.

TURKEY TETRAZZINI

Preheat oven to 350°   Yield: 10 servings

½ pound fresh mushrooms
1 chopped onion
1 chopped green pepper
2 tablespoons margarine or
  vegetable oil
3 cups cooked, diced turkey
1 pound spaghetti
Turkey stock or chicken
  broth

2 (10¾-ounce) cans cream of
  mushroom soup, undiluted
⅓ cup white cooking wine
½ pound grated cheddar
  cheese
1 (16-ounce) package herb
  stuffing mix
½ pound butter, melted

Sauté mushrooms, onion and green pepper in margarine or oil. Mix with cooked and diced turkey. Cook spaghetti in turkey stock, if possible. Drain and save stock. Make a sauce with the mushroom soup and wine, adding turkey stock to make 1 quart of liquid. Add grated cheese to the sauce. Combine sauce, turkey and spaghetti mixtures. Put in 4-quart casserole. Crush 1 package herb stuffing, and mix with ½ pound butter. Sprinkle on top of mixture in casserole. Bake at 350° for 45 minutes. May be frozen for future use.

ROAST TURKEY WITH GIBLET GRAVY

Preheat oven to 400°   Yield: 8 servings

1 (12-pound) turkey
2 tablespoons corn oil
2 tablespoons melted butter
1 tablespoon salt
1 teaspoon white pepper
1 cup chopped onions
1 cup chopped carrots
1 cup chopped celery

1 garlic clove, crushed
⅛ teaspoon thyme
⅛ teaspoon rosemary
⅛ teaspoon marjoram
24 peppercorns
4 whole cloves
Parsley, crabapples and
     apple slices, for garnish

Giblet Stock:
3 cups water
1 cup chopped celery

½ teaspoon salt
Turkey giblets

Giblet Gravy:
2 tablespoons flour

2 cups dry white wine

Pour oil in large open roasting pan; place pan in oven to heat. Insert meat thermometer into turkey at thickest part of thigh muscle without touching bone. Place turkey in pan, breast side up. Brush with butter, and sprinkle with salt and pepper. Roast on lowest shelf of oven at 400°. After 45 minutes reduce oven temperature to 325°. After 1 hour of roasting time, place vegetables, garlic, thyme, rosemary, marjoram, peppercorns, cloves and sprig of parsley around turkey in pan; stir vegetables to coat evenly with drippings to prevent from getting too brown. Baste turkey every 20 minutes. Continue roasting for 2½ more hours or until meat thermometer reaches 185 degrees or about 18 minutes per pound.

When turkey is done, carefully pour off juice from cavity into the roasting pan. Place turkey on platter, cover and prepare gravy.

Giblet Gravy:

Pour pan drippings and vegetables from roasting pan into medium saucepan. Skim off fat. Heat drippings and boil over high heat to reduce drippings almost by half. Mix flour and small amount of white wine until smooth. Add flour mixture, remaining wine and 2 cups of stock (made from giblets), and heat to a boil over medium heat. Simmer, uncovered, for 15 minutes. Pour gravy through strainer and return to sauce pan. Add chopped giblets and heat. Season to taste with salt. Yield: About 3 cups.

TURKEY BREAST PICCATA

Yield: 4-6 servings

1 pound thinly sliced turkey
  breast, pounded thin
½ cup flour
1 teaspoon salt
¼ teaspoon pepper
2 tablespoons vegetable oil
¼ cup butter

½ cup chicken broth
2 tablespoons lemon juice
1 small lemon, sliced very
  thin
Salt and pepper, to taste
2 tablespoons chopped fresh
  parsley

Dredge cutlets in flour mixed with salt and pepper. Heat boil and butter, and sauté cutlets for about 5 minutes over medium heat until golden brown. Transfer to warm platter. Add chicken broth to pan, simmer and stir to remove brown bits from bottom of pan. Return turkey to pan. Add lemon juice and slices of lemon. Heat only until lemons are hot. Season to taste with salt and pepper. Add parsley. Serve with sauce poured over turkey cutlets; garnish with lemon slices.

TURKEY AND RICE CASSEROLE

Preheat oven to 350°   Yield: 6 servings

1½ pounds white meat turkey
  roast, cooked
1 (6-ounce) box wild and
  white rice
4 large tart apples, peeled
  and coarsely chopped

1 medium onion, grated
1 (3-ounce) jar sliced
  mushrooms, drained
2 cups shredded Swiss
  cheese

Cook turkey roast, cool and cut into chunks or cubes. Cook rice according to box instructions. Combine remaining ingredients together, except cheese. Pour into a 2-quart casserole, and sprinkle top with Swiss cheese. Bake at 350° for 25 minutes or until cheese is melted and browned slightly.

TURKEY-ARTICHOKE PIE

Preheat oven to 350°   Yield: 4-6 servings

1 (12-ounce) package frozen
  chopped spinach
2 cups cooked white or
  brown rice
4 tablespoons butter or
  margarine
1 (9-ounce) package frozen
  artichoke hearts, thawed
1½ cups diced cooked turkey
1 cup shredded Monterrey
  Jack cheese

¼ pound mushrooms, sliced
2 tablespoons all-purpose
  flour
½ teaspoon curry powder
½ teaspoon garlic powder
1 teaspoon prepared
  mustard
1 cup milk
Salt and pepper, to taste

Cook spinach according to package directions; drain well, squeezing out all liquid. Combine spinach with rice; mix in 2 tablespoons butter. Press rice mixture evenly over bottom and sides of a well-greased 9-inch pie pan. Cover and chill ½ to 1 hour.

Blot artichokes dry, then cut each into 2 or 3 pieces. Arrange evenly over rice; top with turkey, then cheese.

Melt remaining 2 tablespoons butter in a skillet over medium heat; add mushrooms and saute until golden. Stir in flour, curry powder, garlic powder, mustard and milk; cook until bubbly. Pour over cheese and bake at 350° for 15 to 20 minutes.

TURKEY BURGERS

Yield: 4 servings

1 pound ground cooked
  turkey
1 egg, beaten
½ teaspoon salt
⅛ teaspoon pepper

1 small onion, chopped
1 clove garlic, minced fine
1 teaspoon butter
¼ cup sour cream
1 teaspoon chopped chives

Mix ground turkey with egg, salt, pepper, onion and garlic. Shape into burger patties. Heat butter in skillet, and brown patties on both sides. Cover and cook for 10 minutes or until patties are heated through. Remove from pan, and keep warm. Stir sour cream into pan to incorporate browned particles. Add chives. Taste and add additional salt and pepper, if needed. Spoon sour cream mixture over patties and serve.

Seafood

MANILA PALM

Hints for Seafood

If a fish is fresh, no indention will be made after you touch the fish.

There are several different cuts of fish:

a. Fillet: The sides of the fish are cut lengthwise.

b. Steaks: These are cross section slices from a large fish such as Halibut or Kingfish. Each steak is at least ⅝-inch thick.

c. Dressed or Pan-Dressed: This is a whole and eviscerated fish which is also scaled. Once the head, tail and fins are removed, the fish is ready for use. Trout or Grouper are good examples.

d. Drawn: This is whole, eviscerated fish. The head, tail and fins have usually been removed.

3. Fresh fish have bright, bulging eyes that are clear, pink gills and fins, and no unpleasant odor.

Ideal serving quantities:

a. One pound per person for whole fish.

b. One-half pound per person for dressed fish.

c. One-third pound per person for steaks or fillets. Before placing fish in the refrigerator, wash it in cold water, dry with a paper towel and wrap it in moisture-proof paper.

Baking a fish with its head on will keep the moisture in and help seal in the flavor.

When baking a fish, never turn it as it will fall apart. Fish is done when its flesh is no longer translucent and it flakes with a fork.

Use paprika to help brown your fish while cooking.

When dieting, choose fishes that are lower in fat content such as snapper, grouper, sole, shrimp and haddock. Mackerel, mullet, pompano, and salmon are more fatty.

When serving lobster, allow 1 to 1½ pounds of lobster per person.

Barbecued lobster is a delicious cooking approach. Place lobster on a hot grill with the tail down, and cook for 15 minutes. Baste with melted butter and turn. Cook for another three minutes until the shell is bright red.

To get fresh flavor from frozen fish, thaw the fish in milk in the refrigerator.

When buying oysters and clams, make sure the shells are closed. They are not fresh if they are open.

If you buy lobsters that are already cooked, check to see if they were cooked alive by trying to straighten out their tail. The tail should spring back into a curled position if they were cooked alive.

Use leftover head and bones from fish in soups, sauces and chowders.

One pound of raw shrimp (unshelled) will serve three people.

SHRIMP JUNIPER

Yield: 4 servings

1 pound large shrimp, in
  shells
1 tablespoon peanut oil
2 teaspoons salt
2 cloves garlic, sliced

1 teaspoon fresh-grated
  ginger
2 green onions, chopped
1 tablespoon light soy sauce
2 tablespoons gin

Have all ingredients ready. This dish must be done very quickly and over very high heat. Do not peel the shrimp.

Heat the wok or frying pan until very hot. Add the oil, salt, and garlic all at once. Throw in the shrimp, and toss it for a moment. Add the ginger and green onions, still at high heat. Toss for a moment until shrimp changes from a gray to a bright orange-pink.

When the shrimp are cooked to your taste (and this should take only a moment), pour soy sauce and gin into the pan all at once. It should make a sizzling sound. Place lid on pan immediately, and turn off heat. Serve while still hot. Each guest may peel his own shrimp, but many of us eat the shell and all. This dish is that good!

BOMBAY RICE WITH SHRIMP

Preheat oven to 350°   Yield: 6 servings

3 cups cooked rice
2 teaspoons curry powder
½ cup flaked coconut
½ cup chopped walnuts
½ cup chopped apple
1 pound cooked, cleaned
  shrimp

1 teaspoon salt
½ cup raisins
½ cup water
¼ cup chopped onion
1 (10¾-ounce) can cream of
  celery soup, undiluted

Combine all ingredients and mix well. Bake in buttered 2-quart casserole at 350° for 20 minutes

SEASHELL MACARONI AND SHRIMP

Yield: 4-6 servings

¾ cup butter
3 tablespoons dried parsley
1 to 1½ tablespoons dried
  basil
2 (4-ounce) cans cocktail
  shrimp
1 (8-ounce) box medium
  seashell macaroni

¼ teaspoon ground pepper
1 tablespoon Parmesan
  cheese
2 to 3 tablespoons dry white
  sherry wine

Slowly melt butter in an 8-inch skillet. Add parsley and basil. Drain shrimp, and rinse. Add shrimp to parsley and basil, and simmer until heated through. Sherry is added just before serving.

Meanwhile, cook macaroni in boiling, salted water. Drain and place on platter. Sprinkle ground pepper and Parmesan cheese over macaroni. Top with shrimp mixture.

NOTE: Serve with garlic bread and a salad.

SPICY BROILED SHRIMP
(Easy)

Yield: 4 servings

2 pounds shrimp, cleaned
  and deveined
2 sticks (1 cup) margarine
3 tablespoons Worcestershire
  sauce

4 tablespoons lemon juice
2 tablespoons Pickapeppa
  sauce
¼ teaspoon red pepper
1 teaspoon salt

Melt margarine in sauce pan. Add Worcestershire sauce, lemon juice, pepper sauce, red pepper and salt. Simmer 5 to 7 minutes. Place cleaned shrimp in 9x13-inch baking dish. Pour sauce over shrimp and place on middle shelf area of oven. Broil 15 minutes, turning shrimp at 5 minute intervals. Serve shrimp in sauce.

NOTE: Great served with French bread or use the sauce over cooked rice. A fruit salad is a perfect side dish.

COCONUT SHRIMP

Preheat oven to 350°   Yield: 6 servings

36 large shrimp   **Dash paprika**
1 cup flour   **1¼ cups beer**
1 teaspoon salt   **2 cups shredded coconut**
Pepper, to taste   **Vegetable oil for frying**

Clean and devein shrimp, leaving tails attached. Drain on paper towels. In medium size bowl, combine flour, salt, pepper and paprika. Gradually stir in beer; mix until well blended. Place shrimp in beer batter. Heat 1 inch oil in heavy, large sauce pan. One by one, remove shrimp from beer batter, allowing excess batter to drip off and dredge in shredded coconut. Fry in deep, hot oil until coconut begins to brown. Remove with slotted spoon and drain on paper towels.

Orange Mustard Sauce:
6 tablespoons orange   **6 teaspoons Dijon style**
   marmalade   **mustard**
6 tablespoons orange juice

Combine orange marmalade, orange juice and mustard. Serve on the side as a dipping sauce.

SHRIMP CRÊPES

Preheat oven to 425°   Yield: 6 servings

Crêpes:

½ cup cold water   ½ teaspoon salt
1 cup milk   1⅓ cups flour
3 eggs   3 tablespoons melted butter

Crêpes:

Whirl all batter ingredients in an electric blender for about 1 minute. Refrigerate at least 1 hour.

Brush a 7- or 8-inch skillet with oil; heat over moderately high heat until just beginning to smoke. Pour 3 tablespoons batter into pan, quickly tilting pan to cover bottom with a thin film. Cook crêpe 1 minute until brown; turn and cook other side. Transfer to plate. Stack crêpes using wax paper between each crêpe.

Filling:

2 cups hot medium cream   2 cups cooked shrimp
  sauce*   3 tablespoons chopped
2 tablespoons dry sherry or   scallions
  sauterne   Salt and pepper, to taste
½ cup grated Swiss cheese

Add sherry and cheese to cream sauce. Combine half the sauce with shrimp and scallions; season to taste. Place a large tablespoonful of shrimp mixture on each crêpe. Roll up and place in greased baking dish. Top with remaining sauce; sprinkle with additional cheese, and bake at 425° for 15 minutes or until hot and browned.

See Sauces for Basic White Sauce recipe.

SHRIMP, MUSHROOM,
AND ARTICHOKE CASSEROLE

Yield: 4 servings

2½ tablespoons butter
½ pound mushrooms
1½ pounds shrimp, cooked
  and deveined
1 (7½-ounce) can artichoke
  hearts, sliced (drain
  and squeeze well)

½ cup Parmesan cheese,
  grated
Paprika, for color
2 cups cooked rice

Melt 2½ tablespoons butter in skillet, and saute mushrooms. Set aside. Boil and shell shrimp. In a 2-quart casserole, make 1 layer each of artichoke hearts, shrimp and mushrooms.

Sauce:
4½ tablespoons butter
4½ tablespoons flour
¾ cup milk
¾ cup whipping cream

½ cup dry sherry
1 tablespoon Worcestershire
  sauce
Salt and pepper, to taste

Melt 4½ tablespoons butter in a sauce pan. With a wire whisk, add the flour, milk and cream; stir until thick. Add sherry, Worcestershire sauce, salt and pepper to cream sauce.

Pour sauce over layered ingredients. Sprinkle top with grated cheese, and sprinkle paprika over top for color. Cover and refrigerate overnight. Next day, preheat oven to 375°. Bake at 375° for 25 to 30 minutes. Serve over cooked rice.

SHRIMPLY DELICIOUS

Yield: 4 servings

1 pound raw, peeled,
  deveined shrimp
¼ cup all-purpose flour
1 clove garlic, minced
¾ teaspoon salt
⅛ teaspoon pepper
¼ cup vegetable oil

1 (16-ounce) can stewed
  tomatoes
½ cup chopped green chili
  peppers
¼ cup dry sherry
1½ cups cooked rice
Parsley, for garnish

Thaw shrimp, if frozen. Combine flour, garlic, salt and pepper. Roll shrimp in flour mixture. Heat oil in electric frypan to 350°. Fry shrimp until lightly browned. Add tomatoes, chili peppers, and sherry; heat thoroughly, stirring occasionally. Serve over hot, cooked rice. Garnish with parsley.

ITALIAN SCAMPI

Preheat oven to 350°   Yield: 4 servings

1 pound large shrimp,
  shelled and deveined
½ cup butter
½ teaspoon salt
6 cloves garlic, minced
2 tablespoons chopped
  parsley

1 teaspoon grated lemon
  peel
1 tablespoon lemon juice
1 cup Marsala wine
Lemon wedges

Wash shrimp, and drain on paper towels. Melt butter in 13x9x2-inch baking dish in oven. Add salt, garlic and 1 tablespoon parsley. Mix well. Arrange shrimp over butter mixture. Bake, uncovered, at 350° for 5 minutes. Turn shrimp, and sprinkle with lemon peel, lemon juice, and rest of parsley. Bake 4 minutes longer. Add Marsala wine. Bake 5 more minutes, longer if necessary to make shrimp tender. Arrange on a heated platter. Pour drippings over top or serve in a separate bowl as a sauce. Garnish with lemon wedges.

COLUMBIA SHRIMP SUPREME

                                              Yield: 4 servings

16 jumbo shrimp
Juice of ½ lemon
1 teaspoon salt
Pepper
8 strips bacon

3 eggs
½ cup milk
Flour
Vegetable oil for deep frying

Shell and devein shrimp. Squeeze lemon juice over shrimp, and sprinkle with salt and pepper. Cut each bacon strip in half. Wrap each shrimp in a piece of bacon, and skewer in place with a wooden pick. Combine eggs and milk. Dip shrimp in egg mixture, then in flour. Fry in deep fat at 350° until light brown.

SKILLET SHRIMP CREOLE

Yield: 4 servings

1 (16-ounce) can peeled
  tomatoes (drain and
  reserve liquid)
½ cup diced celery
¼ diced green pepper
¼ cup minced onion
3 tablespoons butter
¾ pound shrimp, peeled and
  cooked

1 teaspoon sugar
½ teaspoon salt
½ teaspoon pepper
1 bay leaf
¼ teaspoon chopped parsley
¼ teaspoon Worcestershire
  sauce
1½ cups minute rice,
  uncooked

Drain tomatoes, measuring liquid. Add water to liquid to make 1½ cups. Sauté celery, green pepper and onion in butter until lightly browned. Add shrimp, measured liquid, tomatoes, sugar, salt, pepper, bay leaf, parsley and Worcestershire sauce. Cover and simmer 3 minutes. Stir in minute rice. Cover and simmer an additional 5 minutes. Remove bay leaf before serving.

SHRIMP AND SCALLOP GRATIN

Preheat oven to 400°

Yield: 4 servings

1 pound raw shrimp, shelled
  and deveined
1 pound bay scallops

8 tablespoons medium dry
  sherry

Seasoned Mixture:
½ cup chopped parsley
2 chopped garlic cloves
1 tablespoon chopped
  scallion

¼ teaspoon oregano
¾ cup bread crumbs
½ teaspoon salt
Pinch of cayenne

1 stick (¼ pound) melted butter

Divide shrimp and scallops into 4 buttered gratin dishes. Sprinkle 2 tablespoons of sherry on each dish. Combine the seasonings, and sprinkle this mixture over each dish. Drizzle extra stick of melted butter over the tops. Bake at 400°, in upper third of the oven, for 12 minutes or until tops are brown.

SEAFOOD OR SHRIMP GUMBO

Yield: 6-8 servings

2 pounds raw shrimp,
  cleaned and deveined
2 tablespoons flour
4 tablespoons vegetable oil
3 cups chopped fresh okra
2 medium onions, chopped
1 (16-ounce) can stewed
  tomatoes

2 quarts water
1 teaspoon salt, or to taste
2 to 3 cloves garlic, minced
1 bay leaf
Cayenne or black pepper, to
  taste
4 cups cooked white rice

Clean and devein shrimp. Using a heavy skillet, make a dark roux of 2 tablespoons flour and 2 tablespoons oil. Stir and cook over medium heat until flour is a rich, dark brown color. Add shrimp to roux and cook, stirring constantly, for 5 minutes. Set aside. In a 4-quart Dutch oven or stock pot, add 2 tablespoons oil, the okra and onion. Stir, and cook over medium heat until okra is almost done, about 5 to 6 minutes. Add the canned tomatoes, water, salt, garlic, bay leaf, pepper, and finally the roux and shrimp. Stir to mix well. Cover and reduce heat to simmer for 30 minutes. Serve over ⅓ cup rice in individual bowls.

Seafood Gumbo
Make the above recipe except simmer for 15 minutes, then add:

½ pint oysters, with juice
1 (6-ounce) package frozen
  white crabmeat, thawed
  and picked for shell
  fragments

Cook for 15 minutes more.

CRAB SALAD CASSEROLE

Preheat oven to 325°   Yield: 8 servings

1 pound crabmeat	4 eggs, slightly beaten
8 slices bread	3 cups milk
½ cup mayonnaise	1 (10¾-ounce) can cream of
1 cup chopped celery	mushroom soup, undiluted
1 green pepper, chopped	½ to ¾ cup shredded
1 medium onion, chopped	cheddar cheese
½ teaspoon salt	

Drain crabmeat and check for shell fragments. Cut 4 slices of bread into cubes. Place in 3-quart, buttered casserole. Combine crabmeat, mayonnaise, celery, pepper, onion and salt; spread over bread. Trim crusts from remaining four slices of bread; dice and place over crab mixture. Mix eggs and milk together, and pour over bread. Cover and refrigerate several hours or overnight.

Remove from refrigerator to let casserole reach almost room temperature. Bake at 325° for 15 minutes. Remove from oven and spoon soup over top; sprinkle cheese over all, and bake for 1 hour longer.

NOTE: This may be doubled and tripled.

SPAGHETTI AND CRAB

Yield: 6 servings

¼ cup olive oil	2 teaspoons salt
½ cup chopped onion	½ teaspoon paprika
1 teaspoon chopped garlic	½ cup water
1 teaspoon chopped parsley	1 pound crabmeat, fresh or
1 teaspoon chopped celery	canned
1 cup tomatoes	¼ cup sherry
1 cup tomato sauce	8 ounces spaghetti
½ teaspoon black pepper	Grated cheddar cheese

Sauté onion, garlic, parsley and celery in olive oil until golden brown. Add tomatoes, tomato sauce, pepper, salt, paprika and water. Simmer 1 hour. Add crabmeat and sherry. Cook spaghetti according to package directions and drain. Serve with grated cheese.

MARTHA'S CRABMEAT CASSEROLE
(Easy)

Preheat oven to 350°   Yield: 4 servings

1 (6-ounce) package frozen
  crabmeat, thawed and
  drained
1 (10¾-ounce) can cream of
  mushroom soup, undiluted
1 cup milk

½ cup shredded cheddar
  cheese
2 tablespoons chopped onion
1 cup uncooked, small shell
  macaroni

Combine all ingredients. Place in 1½-quart casserole; cover and refrigerate overnight. Bake at 350° for 1 hour.

NOTE: Nice with green salad and crusty rolls.

LOBSTER CASSEROLE DELUXE

Preheat oven to 350°   Yield: 8 servings

6 lobster tails
2 (6-ounce) cans lump
  crabmeat
1 cup chopped celery
½ cup chopped onions

¼ cup chopped green pepper
1½ cups mayonnaise
2 tablespoons Worcestershire
  sauce
Buttered bread crumbs

Cook lobsters 15 minutes. Cool, then cut in bite-size pieces. Drain and rinse crabmeat, and check for shell and membrane. Combine all ingredients except bread crumbs and place in 9x13-inch greased baking dish. Sprinkle with buttered bread crumbs and bake, uncovered, at 350° for 30 minutes.

DANISH LOBSTER TETRAZZINI

Yield: 6 servings

2 (10¾-ounce) cans
  condensed cream of
  mushroom soup, undiluted
⅔ cup condensed tomato
  soup, undiluted
3 cups cooked, shelled and
  diced lobster

½ pound thin spaghetti
½ cup grated Parmesan
  cheese
½ cup grated sharp cheddar
  cheese
2 tablespoons bread crumbs

Combine and heat mushroom and tomato soups in large sauce pan.
Add lobster meat, and cook for 5 minutes. Cook spaghetti in boiling
water until firm, but tender. Drain and rinse with boiling water. Pour
spaghetti in well-greased, 2-quart casserole. Spoon lobster mixture over
spaghetti. Combine remaining ingredients, and sprinkle over top of
casserole. Bake at 375° for 15 minutes or until brown on top.

NOTE: This may be prepared ahead of time and refrigerated. Allow
25 to 30 minutes cooking time to heat from refrigerator. (Place in cold
oven!)

SCALLOPED OYSTERS WABASH

Preheat oven to 350°

Yield: 12 appetizer servings
or 4 servings as a main dish

1⅔ cups finely crushed
  saltine crackers
½ cup butter, melted
1½ pints small shucked
  oysters or 18 large oysters,
  with liquid
Freshly ground pepper, to
  taste

¾ teaspoon salt
2 tablespoons chopped
  parsley (optional)
½ tablespoon Worcestershire
  sauce
3 tablespoons milk, cream or
  half and half

Mix crumbs with melted butter. Place ½ cracker mixture in bottom of
9-inch square greased casserole. Add ½ oysters, reserving liquid; sprinkle with pepper, salt and parsley. Add remaining oysters, salt and
pepper.
Mix ⅓ cup oyster liquid with Worcestershire sauce and cream. Pour
over oysters. Top with remaining crumbs, and dot with butter. Bake at
350° until puffy and brown, about 45 minutes.

SCALLOPED OLYMPIA OYSTERS

Preheat oven to 400°   Yield: 6 servings

2 (10-ounce) cans frozen
  condensed oyster stew,
  thawed
1 quart shucked and drained
  Olympia oysters (or
  regular size)

¼ cup flour
¾ cup coarsely crushed
  saltine crackers
6 tablespoons butter
Paprika

Drain liquid from oyster stew, and reserve. Combine oysters from stew with fresh oysters; place oysters in six individual casseroles. Stir drained oyster stew in flour, gradually. Cook over low heat, stirring constantly, until mixture bubbles and thickens. Simmer for 5 minutes. Spoon hot sauce over oysters. Sprinkle tops of casseroles with cracker crumbs, and dot with butter. Bake at 400° for 15 minutes or until golden brown and bubbly. Sprinkle with paprika.

OYSTERS ROCKEFELLER

Preheat oven to 375°   Yield: 6 servings

18 fresh oysters
3 (10-ounce) boxes frozen
  spinach, thawed
1 medium onion, chopped
  fine
1 tablespoon butter
1 cup cream sauce or ½ pint
  whipping cream

½ teaspoon nutmeg
Salt and pepper, to taste
1 cup Hollandaise sauce*
2 cups Parmesan cheese,
  grated
2 or 3 ounces Pernod

Open oysters. Squeeze water out of spinach. Sauté onions in large sauce pan with a little butter until golden brown. Add spinach, and let it simmer for 10 minutes. Stir occasionally. Add cream sauce or cream, spices and Pernod. Mix everything well, and remove from heat. This can be prepared the day before and stored in the refrigerator at this point.

Place one heaping tablespoon of spinach mixture on top of each oyster in a 2½-quart casserole. Top with Hollandaise sauce, and sprinkle Parmesan cheese over all. Bake at 375° degrees for 7 to 8 minutes, until Hollandaise sauce and cheese are golden brown. Serve very hot.

*See Sauces for Hollandaise recipe.

SCALLOPS AU GRATIN

Preheat oven to 350°   Yield: 4 servings

1 pound scallops   **½ cup melted butter**
1½ cups coarse cracker   **½ teaspoon salt**
** crumbs**   **½ teaspoon pepper**
1 cup coarse bread crumbs   **2 cups half and half cream**
1 cup grated cheddar cheese

Wash scallops in cold water, halve crosswise and drain. Combine cracker crumbs and bread crumbs, plus cheddar cheese, melted butter, salt and pepper. Alternate scallops and mixture in buttered 3-quart casserole, reserving a few crumbs for the top. Pour half and half over the top, and bake at 350° for 40 to 50 minutes.

CORN AND CLAM PUDDING

Preheat oven to 300°   Yield: 6 servings

1¼ cups crumbled saltine   **1 tablespoon melted butter**
** crackers**   **2 tablespoons minced onion**
1 cup milk   **¼ teaspoon salt**
2 eggs, beaten   **½ teaspoon Worcestershire**
1 (4-ounce) can minced   ** sauce**
** clams, undrained**   **1 teaspoon sugar**
1 (10-ounce) package frozen   **½ cup grated cheddar cheese**
** creamed corn, thawed**

Combine milk and egg. Soak crackers in milk mixture until soggy. Add all other ingredients except cheese. Mix and place in a 1½-quart casserole. Bake, uncovered, at 300° for 50 minutes. Sprinkle with cheese, and bake another 10 minutes.

LINGUINE AND CLAM SAUCE
(Easy)

Yield: 2 servings

½ stick (¼ cup) butter or
  margarine
1 teaspoon vegetable oil
3 to 4 green onions, chopped
1 clove garlic, minced
1 (10-ounce) can whole
  clams, drained (reserve
  liquid)

¼ cup chopped fresh parsley
2 whole cloves
A few drops of lemon juice
2 cups cooked linguini
Parmesan cheese (optional)

Sauté onions and garlic in butter and oil until onions are transparent. Add clam juice, parsley, cloves and lemon juice. Heat thoroughly. Add clams, and heat. Serve over cooked linguine. Sprinkle with Parmesan cheese, if desired.

SEAFOOD THERMIDOR

Preheat oven to 350°

Yield: 6-8 servings

4 tablespoons butter
½ pound fresh mushrooms,
  medium to small
6 tablespoons flour
1 pint heavy cream
1 pint milk
⅛ teaspoon Dijon mustard
Salt, to taste
¼ pound Colby mild cheese,
  grated

Juice of one lemon
2 tablespoons sherry
4 pounds seafood — shrimp,
  lobster, scallops or
  crabmeat, cooked
½ cup bread crumbs
2 tablespoons butter

Sauté mushrooms in butter. Stir in flour until smooth. Gradually add cream and milk until slightly thickened. Add mustard, salt, cheese, lemon juice and sherry. Blend. Add cooked seafood. Place in greased casserole. Top with bread crumbs which have been sautéed in butter.

Bake at 350° for 20 minutes or until bubbly and top is slightly browned.

FLORIDA SEAFOOD CASSEROLE

Preheat oven to 400°   Yield: 8 servings

½ pound crabmeat
½ pound Florida lobster meat,
  chopped
1 pound shrimp, peeled and
  deveined
1 cup mayonnaise
½ cup chopped green pepper

¼ cup minced onion
½ teaspoon salt
1 tablespoon Worcestershire
  sauce
2 cups crushed potato chips
Paprika

Combine all ingredients together, except chips and paprika. Place in 3-quart casserole, and cover completely with crushed potato chips. Sprinkle with paprika, and bake at 400° for 20 to 25 minutes.

SPAGHETTI AND SEAFOOD CASSEROLE

Yield: 6 servings

¼ cup olive oil
1 tablespoon chopped
  parsley
⅔ cup chopped onion
1 (6-ounce) can tomato paste
1 cup water
2 cloves garlic, minced
1 (1-pound, 3-ounce) can
  tomatoes, undrained
1½ teaspoons salt

¼ teaspoon pepper
1½ teaspoons oregano
1 pound cooked, shelled
  shrimp or lobster, or
3 (6-ounce) cans king
  crabmeat
¼ cup sherry
1 pound package spaghetti
Grated Parmesan cheese

Sauté garlic, parsley and onion in oil until tender (about 5 minutes). Combine tomato paste with water, and stir until smooth. Add to garlic mixture along with tomatoes, salt, pepper and oregano. Bring to boil, and reduce heat. Simmer, uncovered, 45 minutes, stirring occasionally. Add seafood and sherry. Simmer, uncovered, 15 minutes.

Cook spaghetti according to package directions. Drain. Toss with seafood mixture. Turn onto platter and sprinkle with Parmesan cheese.

SEAFOOD CASSEROLE

Preheat oven to 400°   Yield: 8 servings

2 pounds uncooked scallops
1¼ cups dry white wine
¾ teaspoon salt
½ teaspoon pepper
1 bay leaf
1 stalk celery with leaves
¾ cup water
½ cup butter
½ pound mushrooms, thinly
  sliced
1 clove garlic, minced
¼ cup chopped green onion

¼ cup chopped green pepper
¼ cup flour
2 egg yolks
¼ cup heavy cream
¼ cup cooked noodles
1 pound cooked shrimp
2 (8-ounce) cans crabmeat
2 tablespoons chopped
  pimento
Cheddar cheese
¼ cup bread crumbs

Wash scallops in cold water; drain. In medium sauce pan combine scallops, wine, salt, pepper, bay leaf, celery and ¾ cup water. Bring to boil, and reduce heat. Simmer, covered, 10 to 12 minutes or until scallops are tender. Drain and reserve liquid. Remove and discard bay leaf and celery. Chop scallops coarsely. Melt 4 tablespoons butter in a medium skillet; sauté mushrooms for 5 minutes. Add garlic, onion and green pepper; sauté 5 minutes or more until tender. Set aside. In medium sauce pan melt remaining butter. Remove from heat; stir in flour until smooth. Gradually stir in reserved liquid from scallops. Bring to boiling point, stirring constantly. Reduce heat, and simmer 1 minute. In a small bowl, mix yolks slightly with cream. Stir some hot sauce into egg mixture, then pour back into rest of sauce. Cook, stirring, over low heat 6 minutes or until thickened.

Add noodles, scallops, vegetables, shrimp, crabmeat and pimento to sauce. Place in a 3-quart casserole dish. Sprinkle with cheese and crumbs. Bake until lightly browned and bubbly, about 20 to 25 minutes.

BAKED RED SNAPPER WITH
SOUR CREAM STUFFING

Preheat oven to 350°   Yield: 6 servings

3 to 4 pound red snapper (cleaned, scaled, head removed)
1½ teaspoons salt

Sour Cream Stuffing (recipe follows)
2 tablespoons vegetable oil

Wash and dry fish. Sprinkle inside and out with salt. Stuff fish loosely with Sour Cream Stuffing. Close opening with small skewers or toothpicks. Place in well-greased baking pan. Brush with vegetable oil. Bake at 350° for 40 to 60 minutes or until fish flakes easily with fork. Baste occasionally with drippings. Remove skewers and serve.

Sour Cream Stuffing:
¾ cup chopped celery
½ cup chopped onion
¼ cup vegetable oil
1 quart dry bread cubes
½ cup sour cream

¼ cup peeled and diced lemon
2 tablespoons grated lemon rind
1 teaspoon salt
1 teaspoon paprika

Cook celery and onion in oil until tender. Combine all ingredients, and mix thoroughly. Makes a little over 1 quart stuffing.

SNAPPER PARMESAN

Preheat oven to 350°   Yield: 6 servings

3 tablespoons margarine or butter, melted
2 pounds snapper fillets
1 large lemon

Salt and pepper, to taste
¼ cup grated Parmesan cheese
¼ teaspoon basil
Paprika, for color

Pour melted butter or margarine in 2½-quart baking dish. Place fillets in greased baking dish. Squeeze lemon juice over fillets, and let rest ½ hour. Salt and pepper fillets, and sprinkle with cheese, basil and paprika. Bake at 350° for 30 minutes. If not browned, turn on broiler for a few seconds.

CATALAN RICE WITH FISH

Yield: 6 servings

1 large onion, chopped
½ cup vegetable oil
1 cup uncooked rice
1 (16-ounce) can tomatoes
1 (10-ounce) can clams, with juice
1 cup water
1 cup dry sherry
½ pound shrimp, shelled and deveined
2 cloves garlic, minced
⅛ teaspoon saffron

Salt and pepper, to taste
½ lobster, sliced in bite-size pieces
1 pound Florida snapper fillet, cut in 2-inch pieces or grouper or grunt
1 cup cooked green peas
3 pimentos, quartered
½ cup chopped parsley
½ cup minced scallions
Dash of Tabasco sauce (optional)

Sauté onion in oil; add rice and cook until slightly yellow. Add tomatoes and clams with juice plus 1 cup water and sherry. Stir. Add shrimp, garlic, saffron, salt and pepper. Stir well; simmer for 10 minutes. Add lobster; stir again; simmer 5 minutes. Add fish pieces, and cook 10 minutes or until fish is tender. Stir very carefully so as not to break fish apart. Add peas and pimentos. Sprinkle with parsley and scallions. You may add a dash of Tabasco.

FANCY BAKED FISH FILLETS

Preheat oven to 350°   Yield: 4 servings

2 medium onions, chopped
2 stalks celery, chopped
2 medium tomatoes, chopped
¼ cup butter or margarine
½ cup tomato juice
2 tablespoons white wine
3 cloves garlic, crushed

1 bay leaf
1 to 1½ pounds fish fillets (snapper, yellowtail, grouper)
Salt and pepper, to taste
2 cups cooked rice

Sauté onions, celery and tomatoes in butter until onions are tender. Add tomato juice, wine, garlic and bay leaf. Cook over medium high heat for 3 minutes. Place fillets in greased 2-quart baking dish. Season to taste with salt and pepper. Pour sauce over fish. Bake at 350° for 20 minutes or until fish flakes easily. Serve over hot cooked rice.

FISH HOLLANDAISE

Preheat oven to 350°　　　　　　　　　　Yield: 4 servings

1½ pounds fish fillets of your
　choice
Salt and pepper, to taste
1 medium onion, sliced thin
　into rings
Lime juice

Hollandaise sauce*
1½ ounces dry white wine
Dry bread crumbs
Chives or chopped green
　onions with tops (optional)

Place fish in a 2-quart casserole dish. Salt and pepper, to taste. Arrange onion rings on top, and squeeze lime juice sparingly over fish. Bake at 350° for 20 to 25 minutes or until fish flakes easily. Remove from oven and pour Hollandaise sauce over fish. Dribble jigger of wine over all. Sprinkle with bread crumbs, green onions, and place under broiler for a couple of minutes until heated through.

See Sauces for Hollandaise recipe.

GROUPER MEUNIERE
(Easy)

Yield: 4 servings

1¼ pounds grouper fillets
Salt and pepper, to taste
3 tablespoons milk
¼ cup flour
¼ cup peanut or vegetable oil

4 tablespoons butter
Juice of ½ lemon or lime
4 slices of lemon or lime
2 tablespoons finely chopped
　parsley

Sprinkle fillets with salt and pepper to taste. Dip fillets in milk in a flat dish. Dredge with flour, shaking to remove excess. Heat oil in skillet large enough to hold fillets in one layer. Add fish, and cook on high heat until golden brown (about 1½ minutes). Turn and brown the other side. Transfer to warm platter. Pour off fat from skillet. Wipe out skillet and add butter; heat until foamy and starts to brown. Sprinkle fish with lemon juice, and pour butter over all. Garnish with lemon or lime slices and chopped parsley.

BARBECUED DOLPHIN

Yield: 4-6 servings

1½ pounds dolphin, cut in
   serving pieces
1 stick butter, melted

2 tablespoons lime juice
Garlic salt, to taste
Pepper, to taste

In 2-quart casserole dish, marinate fish in melted butter mixed with lime juice for at least 1 hour. When ready to cook, sprinkle garlic salt and pepper on fish pieces. Brush with marinade. Cook quickly over hot coals. Brush often with butter mixture.

NOTE: Dolphin is not to be confused with "Flipper" the porpoise. Sometimes this fish is called Mahi Mahi.

Desserts

FISHTAIL PALM

Hints for Desserts

It is better to use cake flour than all-purpose flour for making cakes.

Melted chocolate should be cooled before adding to ingredients with eggs. This prevents the eggs from cooking before the mixture is placed in the oven.

When rolling out pie crusts, do not use too much flour on the rolling pin or pastry sheet. It will toughen the dough. Also, do not handle the dough too much.

To keep bugs out of your flour, place a bay leaf in the bag or store flour in the refrigerator.

Cake flour is the only flour that needs to be sifted.

To prevent a skin from forming on puddings or custards, place wax paper or plastic wrap over the top of them after cooking.

To dust chocolate cake pans, use cocoa instead of flour so as not to have white on the outside of the cake.

To make sure cake is done, insert a toothpick in the center. If it comes out clean, the cake is finished. Tops of cakes may appear sticky when done in the microwave, but the toothpick should still come out clean.

Set the oven 25 degrees less when using glass baking dishes.

Stale cookies make a terrific topping when made into crumbs in the blender and then sprinkled over ice cream, puddings and custards.

Use kitchen shears to cut marshmallows, dried fruit and figs.

When cooking cupcakes in the microwave, line the microwave muffin pans with paper and only fill the cups half full.

For a great dessert, pour creme de menthe over vanilla ice cream and add nuts.

To test if custard is done, insert a knife along the side of the dish. If the knife comes out clean, the custard is finished.

To keep brown sugar soft, keep it in an airtight container.

Custard and cream pies should not be frozen; they will separate.

Store marshmallows, covered, in the refrigerator so they will not dry out.

BUSY DAY CAKE

Preheat oven to 350°   Yield: 12 servings

1½ cups boiling water
1 cup rolled oats
½ cup butter or margarine
1 cup brown sugar, packed
   well
1 cup granulated sugar

2 eggs
1 teaspoon vanilla
1½ cups all purpose flour
1 teaspoon soda
½ teaspoon salt
1 teaspoon cinnamon

Pour boiling water over rolled oats, and let stand 20 minutes in large mixing bowl. Cream together butter, brown sugar and granulated sugar. Add eggs, vanilla and oatmeal mixture. Mix until well blended. Sift flour, measure and sift again with soda, salt and cinnamon. Add gradually to creamed mixture, beating on medium speed of electric mixer until well blended. Turn batter into a well-buttered 9x13-inch pan and bake at 350° for 30 to 40 minutes or until cake tester is clean. Spread with caramel topping, evenly, over cooled baked cake. Broil 2 to 3 minutes or until topping is caramelized. Cut in squares to serve.

NOTE: May be cut smaller for tea cakes and placed in individual cupcake papers.

Caramel Topping:
2 teaspoons melted butter
   or margarine
½ cup brown sugar

⅓ cup light cream
1 cup coconut
½ cup chopped nuts

Combine the above ingredients in order listed, and spread over cake.

CHRISTMAS CAKE

Preheat oven to 325°   Yield: 10-12 servings

2 sticks butter or margarine
3 cups sugar
6 eggs
4½ ounces rum
½ pint sour cream

¼ teaspoon soda
3 cups sifted flour
¾ cup chopped pecans
Confectioners sugar, for
   garnish

Have all ingredients at room temperature.

Using a large mixing bowl and electric mixer, cream butter and sugar. Add eggs, one at a time, and beat after each addition. Add rum. In a separate small bowl, combine sour cream and soda. Add sour cream, soda and flour to mixture, alternately, ending with flour. Add chopped nuts. Pour batter into greased and floured 10-inch tube pan. Bake at 325° for one hour and 15 minutes. Cool, inverted, on cake plate. When cool, cover cake, and let stand for a day or two. Before serving, sprinkle confectioners sugar over cake.

NOTE: This cake is great for parties. It is best made several days before serving.

HAZELNUT TEA CAKE

Preheat oven to 325°   Yield: 1 (9-inch) cake

1 cup (2 sticks) butter,
   softened
⅔ cup brown sugar
1½ teaspoons vanilla
1 teaspoon mace
3 large eggs, separated
1½ cups all purpose flour

1 teaspoon baking powder
¼ teaspoon salt
1 cup light cream
2 tablespoons sugar
1 cup lightly toasted
   hazelnuts, crushed (use
   blender or food processor)

Have all ingredients at room temperature.

Butter and flour 9-inch bundt pan. Cream together butter, brown sugar, vanilla and mace until light and fluffy. Beat in egg yolks, one at a time. On plate or wax paper, sift together flour, baking powder and salt. Mix this into the creamed mixture alternately with the light cream. Beat together egg whites and sugar until mixture forms soft peaks. Stir ⅓ beaten whites into batter. Mix in crushed hazelnuts, then fold in the remaining egg whites.

Pour into prepared bundt pan. Bake at 325° for 40 to 45 minutes or until firm to touch and shrinks from sides of the pan. Let cool in pan before turning out on wire rack.

OLD CUTLER HOLIDAY CAKE

Yield: 12-16 servings

Cake:
2 (18¼-ounce) boxes white
cake mix

Mix and bake, according to package directions, in 4 (9-inch) round cake pans that have been greased and floured.

Filling:
8 egg yolks
1½ cups sugar
½ cup butter
4 ounces shredded coconut

1 cup chopped pecans
1 cup chopped candied red
  cherries
1 cup seedless raisins
⅓ cup bourbon

Combine egg yolks, sugar and butter. Cook over medium heat in medium sauce pan, stirring constantly until thickened. Add coconut, pecans, cherries, raisins and bourbon. Spread between cake layers.

Frosting:
1½ cups sugar
1 tablespoons dark corn
  syrup
¼ cup water

½ teaspoon salt
2 egg whites, well beaten
1 teaspoon vanilla
2 tablespoons bourbon

Bring sugar, syrup, water and salt to a boil until it thickens. Remove from heat. Add hot syrup mixture to egg whites in a thin stream, beating constantly until very thick. Fold in vanilla and bourbon. Frost entire cake, and garnish with a few whole red cherries.

DANNY'S FRUIT CAKE

Yield: 12-16 servings

4 cups shelled pecans
¾ pound candied cherries
1 pound candied pineapple
½ pound butter
1 cup sugar

5 large eggs
1¾ cups all purpose flour
½ teaspoon baking powder
½ teaspoon vanilla
½ teaspoon lemon extract

Chop nuts and fruits into medium size pieces; dredge with ¼ cup flour. Cream butter and sugar together until light and fluffy. Add well-beaten eggs, and blend well. Sift remaining flour and baking powder together; fold into egg and butter mixture. Add vanilla and lemon extracts. Mix well. Add fruits and nuts, mixing well. Grease a 10-inch tube pan. Line bottom with heavy brown paper, and grease again. Pour batter into prepared pan. Place in COLD oven and bake at 250° for 3 hours. Cool in pan on cake rack.

MINCEMEAT FRUIT CAKE

Preheat oven to 350°

Yield: 12-16 servings

2½ cups unsifted flour
1 teaspoon baking soda
2 eggs, slightly beaten
1 (28-ounce) jar mincemeat

1 (14-ounce) can sweetened
  condensed milk
2 cups mixed candied fruit
1 cup chopped pecans

Grease a 9-inch tube pan, and line bottom of pan with wax paper, then grease again. Sift together flour and soda in a large bowl, and combine with remaining ingredients. Pour into prepared pan. Bake 1 hour and 50 minutes at 350° or until knife inserted comes out clean. Cool 15 minutes, and serve with rum sauce.

Rum Sauce:
1 (3-ounce) package cream
  cheese
1 egg
1 cup confectioners sugar
2 tablespoons butter

1 teaspoon lemon juice
1 cup heavy cream, whipped
  stiff
2 tablespoons dark rum

In a medium size bowl, beat cream cheese until light. Add egg, sugar, butter and lemon juice; mix until blended. Fold in whipped cream and rum. Chill.

NEW YEAR'S APPLE CAKE

Preheat oven to 350°　　　　　　　　　　　Yield: 10-12 servings

4 large tart apples
1 cup sugar
⅔ cup butter, melted
1 cup chopped pecans
2 eggs, lightly beaten
2 teaspoons vanilla

2 cups sifted flour
2 teaspoons baking soda
2 teaspoons cinnamon
2 teaspoons allspice
1 teaspoon cardamom
½ teaspoon salt

Peel, core and chop apples.

Grease two 8- or 9-inch cake pans. Combine apples, sugar, butter and nuts in medium mixing bowl. Add vanilla and eggs. Sift dry ingredients, and add to apple mixture, stirring only briefly. Divide batter between pans. Bake at 350° for 40 to 50 minutes or until knife inserted comes out clean. Cool on rack.

NOTE: This cake is moist and can be eaten with fingers. It is delicious made a week ahead and refrigerated so flavors mellow. Serve at room temperature.

LINKROMS KAKE
(Norwegian Cardamom Loaf)

Preheat oven to 325°　　　　　　　　　　　Yield: 2 loaves

2 cups sugar
½ cup butter or margarine
3 eggs
3 cups flour

½ teaspoon baking soda
1 teaspoon baking powder
3 cardamom pods
1 cup milk

Cream butter and sugar in medium sized mixing bowl. Add eggs, and mix well. Combine flour, soda and baking powder. Peel cardamom pods to remove seeds; crush seeds and add to flour mixture, and stir until well mixed. Fold flour into creamed mixture, and add milk. Mix until well blended, and pour into greased and floured loaf pan. Bake at 325° for 55 to 60 minutes.

BROWN SUGAR POUND CAKE

Preheat oven to 350°   Yield: 10-12 servings

1 cup butter or margarine
½ cup vegetable shortening
1 pound light brown sugar
1 cup granulated sugar
5 eggs
3 cups flour

½ teaspoon salt
1 teaspoon baking powder
1 cup milk
1 teaspoon vanilla
1 cup chopped walnuts

Beat together butter and shortening in large mixing bowl. Gradually add brown and white sugars, creaming until light and fluffy. Beat in eggs, one at a time. Sift together flour, salt and baking powder, and add alternately with milk and vanilla. Stir in nuts. Pour batter into a greased and floured 10-inch tube pan. Bake at 350° for 1¼ hours or until done. Cool 10 minutes; remove from pan, and pour glaze over hot cake.

Glaze:

1 cup sifted confectioners
   sugar
2 tablespoons butter or
   margarine

6 tablespoons coffee cream
½ teaspoon vanilla
½ cup chopped walnuts

Cream sugar and butter; add cream. Stir in vanilla and nuts. Blend well. Pour over hot cake.

COCONUT POUND CAKE

Preheat oven to 325°   Yield: 12-16 servings

1 cup shortening
2 cups sugar
1 teaspoon vanilla
1 teaspoon almond flavoring
6 eggs

2 cups flour
1 teaspoon salt
1 (7-ounce) can flaked
  coconut

Cream shortening and sugar until light and fluffy. Add flavorings, and mix well. Add eggs, one at a time, beating well after each addition. Sift flour and salt together, and add to creamed mixture. Fold in coconut. Bake in well-greased and floured 10-inch tube pan or bundt pan at 325° for about 1 hour and 10 minutes or until cake tests done.

Glaze:
1½ cups granulated sugar
¾ cup boiling water

3 teaspoons almond flavoring

Combine all ingredients in a medium sauce pan, and bring to a boil. Boil one minute. Pour ¾ of the mixture over the baked cake while still in cake pan. Return cake to oven, and bake at 325° for 3 minutes. Remove cake from pan when cool. Turn cake onto cake plate, and pour remaining ¼ glaze over cake.

AEROBICS DROP-OUT CAKE

Yield: 12-15 servings

1 (1-pound) box yellow cake
  mix
1 (20-ounce) can crushed
  pineapple, including juice
¾ cup sugar
3 cups milk

2 (3-ounce) packages instant
  vanilla pudding
1 (8-ounce) carton whipped
  topping
¾ cup flaked coconut

Using a (10x17x1-inch) sheet cake pan, bake cake according to box directions. While cake bakes, boil pineapple with sugar over medium heat in medium sauce pan for about 5 minutes or until mixture is syrupy. When cake is done, poke holes in top of cake with toothpick, and pour the pineapple mixture on top, making sure that entire cake is covered.

After cake is completely cooled, mix 3 cups milk with 2 boxes of instant pudding, and spread over entire cake. Mix whipped topping with coconut, and spread over cake. Chill cake in refrigerator.

NOTE: Cake is better if made at least 24 hours before serving.

ECLAIR CAKE

Yield: 14-16 servings

1 (1 pound) box graham
   crackers
2 (3-ounce) boxes instant
   French vanilla pudding

3½ cups milk
1 (8-ounce) container
   whipped topping

Line bottom of 9x13-inch glass baking dish with whole graham crackers. Make pudding using 3½ cups milk. Fold in whipped topping. Spread half the mixture over crackers. Layer again with crackers, then rest of pudding mixture. Finish with layer of crackers. Chill for 2 hours.

Cocoa Glaze:
3 tablespoons butter or
   margarine
2 tablespoons cocoa
1½ cups confectioners sugar

2 teaspoons white corn syrup
2 teaspoons vanilla
3 tablespoons milk

Make cocoa glaze by melting butter over low heat in sauce pan. Add cocoa, and mix well. Remove from heat, and add remaining ingredients. Beat well, and frost cake immediately.
Refrigerate frosted cake for 24 hours.

PLUM GOOD CAKE

(Easy and moist)

Preheat oven to 325°

Yield: 10-12 servings

2 cups self rising flour
2 cups sugar
1 cup vegetable oil
1 cup chopped nuts
4 eggs, room temperature
2 (4½-ounce) jars baby food
   plums

1 teaspoon cloves
1 teaspoon cinnamon
1 teaspoon vanilla
Confectioners sugar for
   garnish

Grease and flour 10-inch bundt pan. Combine all ingredients in large mixing bowl, and mix by hand until well blended. Bake at 325° for 1 hour. Let cool 15 minutes, and remove from pan. Sift confectioners sugar on top if using for festive event.

NOTE: Freezes well and may be used right out of the freezer.

ITALIAN CREAM CAKE

Preheat oven to 350°   Yield: 16 servings

1 stick (¼ pound) butter or
   margarine
½ cup shortening
2 cups sugar
5 eggs, separated
2 cups cake flour

1 teaspoon soda
1 teaspoon vanilla
1 cup buttermilk
1 (3½-ounce) can flaked
   coconut
1 cup chopped nuts

Cream butter, shortening and sugar together in large mixing bowl. Separate eggs. Add egg yolks, flour, soda, vanilla and buttermilk to creamed mixture. Beat egg whites until soft peaks form. Fold in coconut, chopped nuts and beaten egg whites. Grease and flour 3 (9-inch) round cake pans. Pour batter equally into pans, and bake at 350° for 20 minutes or until done. Cool and remove from pans. Ice with the following:

Icing:
⅔ stick margarine
1 (3-ounce) package cream
   cheese

1½ teaspoons vanilla
1⅓ pounds confectioners
   sugar

Cream margarine and cream cheese together. Add vanilla and confectioners sugar. Beat with electric mixer until smooth and of spreading consistency. Ice between layers and sides of cake, then ice top. Sprinkle nuts on top.

NOTE: May add nuts to icing before spreading on cake.

KEY LIME CAKE

Preheat oven to 325°   Yield: 8-10 servings

1 (1-pound) box lemon cake
   mix
1 (3-ounce) package instant
   lemon pudding

1 cup water
1 cup vegetable oil
4 eggs
3 tablespoons lime juice

Combine all ingredients in a large mixing bowl, and mix until smooth. Grease and flour 10-inch bundt pan. Pour batter in prepared pan, and bake at 325° for 40 minutes. Cool, and remove from pan. Glaze with the following:

Glaze:
½ cup confectioners sugar   3 tablespoons lime juice

Combine, and spread on top of cake.

ORANGE FLUFF CAKE

Preheat oven to 325°   Yield: 8-10 servings

6 eggs, separated
1 cup sugar
4 tablespoons orange juice

1 cup flour
¼ teaspoon cream of tartar

In medium mixing bowl, beat egg yolks with 1 cup sugar, orange juice, and flour. In separate small mixing bowl, beat egg whites with cream of tartar until soft peaks form. Fold beaten egg whites into flour mixture. Grease and flour 10-inch tube pan or bundt pan. Pour batter into prepared pan, and bake at 325° for 1 hour.

Icing:
¼ pound confectioners sugar
1 teaspoon butter
½ teaspoon grated orange rind

Orange juice for spreading
consistency

Combine sugar, butter and orange rind. Add orange juice gradually until of spreading consistency.

RUM CHOCOLATE CAKE

Preheat oven to 350°   Yield: 12-14 servings

1 (18-ounce) box chocolate
  cake mix with pudding
3 eggs
⅓ cup vegetable oil

½ cup water
½ cup dark rum
½ cup slivered almonds,
  optional

Grease and flour 2 (9-inch) layer cake pans. Combine all ingredients in large mixing bowl. Blend well, then beat at medium speed on electric mixer for 2 minutes. Turn, equally, into prepared pans. Bake at 350° for 30 minutes or until tester inserted in center comes out clean. Cool in pans 10 minutes. Remove, and finish cooling on racks. Split layers in half horizontally.

Filling:
1 pint heavy cream
⅓ cup unsweetened cocoa
½ cup confectioners sugar

1 teaspoon vanilla
½ cup dark rum

Combine cream, cocoa, sugar and vanilla in large bowl. Beat until stiff. Fold in rum. Spread filling between layers and over top. Keep chilled. Serve cold.

PEANUT BUTTER CAKE

Preheat oven to 350°   Yield: 24 servings

⅔ cup shortening
⅔ cup peanut butter
2½ cups sugar
3 beaten eggs
3¼ cups sifted flour

2½ teaspoons baking soda
2¼ teaspoons baking powder
2½ cups buttermilk
1 tablespoon vanilla

Cream together shortening, peanut butter and sugar. Add beaten eggs. Sift flour, baking soda and baking powder; add to creamed mixture alternately with buttermilk, beating after each addition. Blend in vanilla. Pour into greased and lightly floured 13x9-inch pan. Bake at 350° for 35 minutes or until done.

Peanut Butter Icing:
1 cup margarine
2 cups chunky peanut butter
4 cups sifted confectioners
   sugar

1 tablespoon vanilla
⅔ to 1 cup unsweetened
   pineapple juice

Cream together margarine and peanut butter. Add confectioners sugar, vanilla and enough pineapple juice to make spreading consistency. Frost peanut butter cake.

CHOCOLATE PASTRY CAKE

Preheat oven to 425°   Yield: 9-12 servings

2 (4-ounce) packages sweet
  cooking chocolate
½ cup sugar
½ cup water
1½ teaspoons instant coffee
  granules

2 teaspoons vanilla
1 (9- or 10-ounce) package
  piecrust mix (2 sticks)
2 cups whipping cream

In medium sauce pan, combine chocolate, sugar, water and instant coffee. Cook over low heat, stirring constantly, until smooth. Add vanilla; cool to room temperature. Blend ¾ cup of the chocolate sauce into piecrust mix; divide the pastry into six equal parts. Press each part over bottom of an inverted 8x1½-inch round cake pan to within ½ inch of edge. (Do in relays according to the number of pans you have.)

Bake at 425° for 5 minutes or until done. If necessary, trim edges to even them. Cool; then run the tip of a knife under edges of layers to loosen. Lift off carefully.

Whip cream until it begins to hold soft peaks. Fold in the remaining chocolate sauce. Stack baked pastry, spreading chocolate cream between layers and over top. Chill at least 8 hours or overnight.

LEMON "CHEESE" CAKE

Preheat oven to 350°   Yield: 8-10 servings

1 cup butter
2 cups sugar
3 eggs
1 teaspoon vanilla

1 teaspoon lemon extract
3 cups flour
½ teaspoon soda
1 cup buttermilk

Cream butter and sugar. Add eggs, one at a time, beating after each addition. Add vanilla and lemon extract. Mix. Alternately, add flour and soda with buttermilk until well blended. Bake in 4 (9-inch) round cake pans. Bake at 350° for 25 minutes or until light brown. While still warm, frost with lemon cheese frosting.

Lemon "Cheese" Frosting:
1½ cups sugar
3 lemons, juice and grated
  rind

2 tablespoons butter
4 eggs
*See note

Beat eggs slightly, and add other ingredients. Place in top of double boiler, and cook over boiling water until thick, stirring constantly. Place frosting between layers and on top of cake.

NOTE: This recipe does not have cheese. It just tastes like it.

CHOCOLATE MOUSSE CAKE

Preheat oven to 325°   Yield: 6-8 servings

**7 ounces semi-sweet
  chocolate squares
¼ pound unsalted butter
7 eggs, separated
¾ cup sugar**

**1 teaspoon vanilla
⅛ teaspoon cream of tartar
¼ cup sugar
Whipped cream or whipped
  topping**

Using double boiler, melt the chocolate squares and butter. Beat egg whites until light and fluffy; add the ¾ cup of sugar a little at a time. Add chocolate mixture and vanilla to egg yolks. Meanwhile, beat egg whites and cream of tartar until soft peaks form. Add ¼ cup sugar, one tablespoon at a time, and beat until stiff.

Fold egg whites carefully into chocolate mixture. Pour ¾ of the batter into a greased 8x3-inch springform pan. Bake at 325° for 50 minutes.

Cover remaining batter and refrigerate. When baked portion is cooled, spread refrigerated portion on top and cool. Decorate with whipped cream or topping.

MIAMI CHOCOLATE CAKE

Preheat oven to 350°   Yield: 40-50 squares

2 cups sugar
2 cups flour
1 teaspoon soda
½ teaspoon salt
2 sticks (½ pound) butter or
   margarine

4 tablespoons cocoa
1 cup water
½ cup sour cream
2 eggs
1 teaspoon vanilla

Combine sugar, flour, soda and salt in mixing bowl. Melt butter in sauce pan. Add cocoa, and mix well. Add water to cocoa mixture, and bring to a boil. Stir chocolate mixture into flour mixture. Mix well. Add sour cream, eggs and vanilla. Bake in large jelly roll pan (13x17x1-inch) at 350° for 15 to 20 minutes.

Icing:
1 stick (¼ pound) butter or
   margarine
4 tablespoons cocoa
6 tablespoons sour cream

1 (1-pound) box confectioners
   sugar
1 teaspoon vanilla
¼ cup chopped nuts

Melt butter in sauce pan, and add cocoa, one tablespoon at a time. Stir until smooth, and add sour cream. Bring to a boil, and add confectioners sugar, vanilla and nuts. Spread on cake while cake is hot in pan.

WHISKEY CAKE

Preheat oven to 350°   Yield: 12 servings

1 (1-pound) box butter
  flavored cake mix
1 (3-ounce) package instant
  vanilla pudding mix
4 eggs
½ cup vegetable oil
1 cup milk
2 ounces bourbon
½ teaspoon vanilla

1 teaspoon almond extract
1 cup finely chopped nuts
4 ounces maraschino
  cherries, well drained
1 tablespoon citron, chopped
  (optional)
Confectioners sugar, for
  garnish

Combine all of the above ingredients, except powdered sugar, in large mixing bowl. Beat until well mixed, about 3 minutes. Pour into greased and floured bundt pan, and bake at 350° for one hour.

Icing:
¼ cup butter or margarine   1 cup sugar
½ cup bourbon

Combine above ingredients in medium sauce pan. Heat to boiling point. Pour over cake while still hot. Let set for 30 minutes in pan, and invert on cake plate. Dust with confectioners sugar.

ALMOND TORTE

Preheat oven to 350°   Yield: 10-12 servings

2 cups sugar
½ cup butter
3 eggs, separated
1 whole egg
½ teaspoon salt

5 tablespoons milk
1 teaspoon vanilla
1 cup flour
1 teaspoon baking powder

Cream together 1 cup sugar and butter; add egg yolks and one whole egg. Add salt, milk and vanilla. Mix flour and baking powder together; gradually add to egg mixture, stirring until smooth. Divide batter into two well-greased and floured 9-inch round cake pans. Beat egg whites until stiff, and add 1 cup sugar gradually, continuing to beat until glossy.

Carefully spread meringue over batter to within 1½ inches of edge of pans. Bake at 350° for 30 minutes.

Topping:
3 tablespoons sugar
1 tablespoon cornstarch
⅛ teaspoon salt
1 cup half and half
½ teaspoon almond extract

1 cup whipping cream,
    whipped, or 1 (8-ounce)
    container of whipped
    topping
¼ cup toasted slivered almonds

Mix sugar, cornstarch, salt and half and half in sauce pan. Cook over medium heat, stirring constantly until thickened. Add almond extract, and stir to mix well. Cool. Combine cooled mixture with whipped cream or whipped topping, and cover stacked cake layers. Sprinkle top with toasted slivered almonds.

LEMON MOUSSE

Yield: 8 servings

1⅓ cups vanilla wafer
    crumbs, divided
5 egg whites
1 cup sugar

½ cup lemon juice
Grated rind of 1 lemon
½ pint whipping cream

Cover bottom of 9-inch square pan with 1 cup vanilla wafer crumbs. Beat egg whites until stiff peaks form. Gradually add sugar, lemon juice and grated lemon rind. Whip cream until soft peaks form. DO NOT OVERBEAT. Fold whipped cream into egg and lemon mixture, and pour over vanilla wafer crumbs. Sprinkle entire top with remaining ⅓ cup vanilla wafer crumbs, and cover with plastic wrap. Freeze. Remove from freezer when ready to serve, and let stand 5 minutes before slicing and serving.

MANGO MOUSSE

Yield: 4 servings

1 mango, puréed
2 egg yolks
⅓ cup sugar
4 egg whites, room
   temperature

1 cup heavy cream, stiffly
   beaten
Grand Marnier or brandy,
   to taste

Combine pureed mango and egg yolks in mixing bowl, and beat slightly. In a separate bowl, beat the egg whites and ½ the sugar until whites begin to solidify. Slowly add remaining sugar, and beat until stiff. Do not overbeat. Fold mango mixture and egg whites together. Fold in whipped cream, Grand Marnier or brandy. Spoon into parfait type glasses, and refrigerate several hours or overnight. Garnish with chocolate curl.

MANGO ICE CREAM PIE

Yield: 6-8 servings

1 (8-inch) graham cracker
   crust
1 pint vanilla ice cream,
   softened
1½ cups chopped mangoes

1 (3-ounce) package peach
   gelatin
1 (8-ounce) container
   whipped topping

Drain fruit, and add enough hot water to juice to make 1 cup liquid. Dissolve peach gelatin in hot liquid, and add softened ice cream. Stir until dissolved, then refrigerate until it becomes the consistency of stiff egg whites. Add fruit, and pour into pie shell. Refrigerate — do not freeze. Top with whipped topping before serving.

FRUIT SALAD PIE

Yield: 12-14 servings

2 (8-inch) graham cracker
   crusts
1 (14-ounce) can sweetened
   condensed milk
½ cup lemon juice
1 (12-ounce) carton whipped
   topping

2 (11-ounce) cans drained
   mandarin oranges
2 (8-ounce) cans drained
   crushed pineapple
1 cup chopped pecans or
   walnuts

Combine condensed milk and lemon juice. Fold in whipped topping.
Drain oranges and pineapple, and add to mixture. Add nuts. Pour into
pie crusts. Freeze. To serve, allow to stand at room temperature about 10
minutes or until defrosted enough to cut.

BUTTERMILK PIE

Preheat oven to 350°   Yield: 16 servings

1¾ sticks margarine, soft or
   melted
3¾ cups sugar
½ cup flour

6 whole eggs
1½ teaspoons vanilla
1 cup buttermilk
2 (9-inch) unbaked pie shells

Add sugar and flour to margarine. Blend well. Add eggs, vanilla and
buttermilk. Pour into 2 pie shells. Bake at 350° for 40 minutes.

PUMPKIN SUPREME

Preheat oven to 350°   Yield: 16 servings

1½ cups graham cracker
  crumbs
¾ to 1 cup sugar
¼ cup margarine or butter
3 eggs, beaten
1 (8-ounce) package cream
  cheese, softened
½ cup sugar

¾ cup milk
2 (3-ounce) packages instant
  vanilla pudding
2 cups pumpkin
⅛ teaspoon nutmeg
⅛ teaspoon cinnamon
1 cup whipped topping
⅓ cup chopped pecans

Mix graham crackers, ¾ to 1 cup sugar and margarine together. Press into a 9x13-inch pan. Combine eggs, cream cheese and ½ cup sugar. Pour over crumb crust, and bake at 350° for 20 minutes. Cool.

Mix milk and instant pudding together. Stir in pumpkin, nutmeg and cinnamon. Fold in whipped topping. Spread pumpkin mixture on top of cooled mixture. Decorate with additional whipped topping and chopped pecans. Chill.

GERMAN APPLE TART

Preheat oven to 400°   Yield: 14-16 servings

2 unbaked pie crusts
3½ cups thinly sliced Granny
  Smith apples, peeled
½ cup sugar
3 tablespoons golden raisins
3 tablespoons chopped
  pecans
½ teaspoon cinnamon

½ teaspoon grated lemon
  peel
2 teaspoons lemon juice
1 egg yolk, beaten
1 teaspoon water
Whipped cream or whipped
  topping

Place one prepared crust in a 10-inch springform pan. Press in bottom and up sides of pan; trim edges. Combine apples, sugar, raisins, pecans, cinnamon, lemon peel and lemon juice. Place in pan, starting at the outside edge and working toward the center, overlapping slightly. Cut remaining crust into ½-inch wide lattice strips. Arrange strips in lattice design over apple mixture. Trim and seal edges. In small bowl, combine egg yolk and water; gently brush over lattice. Bake at 400° for 40 to 60 minutes or until golden brown, and apples are tender. Cover tart with foil during last 15 minutes of baking, if necessary, to prevent excessive browning. Cool; remove sides of pan. Serve with whipped cream or whipped topping.

EASY CHEESY APPLE PIE

Preheat oven to 375°   Yield: 6-8 servings

Crust:

1 cup flour
¼ cup oats
1½ teaspoons sugar
½ teaspoon salt

⅓ cup vegetable oil
¼ cup milk
1 teaspoon almond flavoring

Filling:

6 medium apples, peeled and
  sliced
1 (3-ounce) package vanilla
  pudding

1 cup shredded cheddar
  cheese

Topping:

⅓ cup flour
⅓ cup sugar

¼ cup oats
3 tablespoons butter (soft)

Mix all crust ingredients, and press into bottom and sides of a 9-inch pie pan. Put apple slices and pudding in a plastic bag, and coat all slices. Put into crust. Top with shredded cheese. Mix topping ingredients with a fork until crumbly, and sprinkle on top of cheese. Bake at 375° for 45 to 50 minutes. Good served warm.

NOTE: It looks like it will overflow, but it doesn't.

APRICOT ICE CREAM PIE

Yield: 8-10 servings

1 (7½-ounce) box vanilla
  wafers
½ cup slivered almonds
1 teaspoon almond extract

1 stick margarine, melted
2 pints vanilla ice cream
1 (12-ounce) jar apricot
  preserves

Crush the vanilla wafers to a very fine crumb texture. Add almonds, almond extract and melted margarine. In a buttered 8- or 9-inch spring-form pan, layer as follows: ⅓ of the crumb crust to line the bottom of pan; 1 pint of the ice cream; ½ of the apricot preserves; ⅓ of the crumb crust, sprinkled over top, then the other pint of ice cream; the other half of the apricot preserves, and the last third of the crumb crust. Freeze. Unmold to serve and slice.

MANGO BAVARIAN PIE

Yield: 8 servings

1 envelope unflavored
  gelatin
¼ cup cold water
1 cup canned, unsweetened
  pineapple juice

¼ cup sugar
¾ cup mango purée
1 cup heavy cream
9-inch baked pie shell

Soften gelatin in cold water. Dissolve sugar in pineapple juice in medium saucepan over medium heat, stirring constantly. Beat all ingredients except whipped cream until blended. Chill until partially set. Fold in whipped cream, and pour into pie shell. Chill.

CHOCOLATE CHIFFON PIE

Yield: 6-8 servings

1 (9-inch) baked pie shell
1 stick (¼ pound) butter or
  margarine
½ cup sugar
2 (1-ounce) squares
  unsweetened chocolate

2 eggs
1 teaspoon vanilla
½ cup walnuts
1 (8-ounce) container
  whipped topping

Blend butter and sugar. Melt chocolate in top of double boiler over moderate heat. Let cool, and add to butter mixture. Add 1 egg, and beat for 5 minutes. Add second egg, and beat for 5 more minutes. Add walnuts and vanilla, and pour into pie shell. Top with whipped topping. Refrigerate until ready to serve.

MILLIONAIRE'S LIME PIE

Yield: 8-10 servings

1 (14-ounce) can sweetened
  condensed milk
1 (6-ounce) can frozen
  limeade concentrate
2 tablespoons lemon juice
  (may be bottled)

1 (8-ounce) container frozen
  whipped topping
1 (9-inch) baked pastry shell
  or graham cracker crust

Blend first three ingredients. Fold in whipped topping (thawed). Pour into crust and chill thoroughly.

KEY LIME PIE

Preheat oven to 350°   Yield: 8 servings

5 egg yolks
1 (14-ounce) can sweetened
**   condensed milk**
⅓ cup key lime juice

1 (9-inch) unbaked graham
**   cracker pie crust**
1 (8-ounce) container
**   whipped topping**

Combine eggs, milk and lime juice. Pour into pie crust and bake at 350° for 20 minutes. Cool and refrigerate for at least 2 hours before serving. Top with whipped topping.

ANGEL LIME PIE
(Heavenly!)

Yield: 6-8 servings

3 eggs, separated
½ teaspoon cream of tartar
1½ cups sugar

1 lime, juiced and grated peel
¼ cup water
1 cup heavy cream, whipped

Beat egg whites until frothy; add cream of tartar; beat until stiff. Add one cup sugar gradually, beating constantly. Beat until glossy. Spray pie pan well with vegetable cooking spray. Line bottom and sides of 9-inch pie pan with this meringue. Place in cold oven, and bake at 300° for 1½ hours. Cool.

Beat egg yolks until thick and light. Add remaining ½ cup sugar, lime juice, peel and water. Cook in top of double boiler over hot water, stirring constantly, until thick. Cool. Spread half the whipped cream in the meringue shell; add the lime filling, spreading evenly. Top with remaining whipped cream. Chill 24 hours.

NOTE: Make this the day before serving.

FLORIDA ORANGE PIE

Preheat oven to 400°   Yield: 6-8 servings

1 cup sugar
5 tablespoons cornstarch
2 tablespoons grated orange
   rind
1 cup fresh orange juice
1 cup orange sections, cut
   into pieces

3 eggs, separated
1 tablespoon lemon juice
1 tablespoon butter
1 (8-inch) pie shell, baked

Combine sugar, cornstarch, rind, orange sections and juice. Cook over low heat, stirring until clear. Add small amount of hot mixture to beaten egg yolks. Return to hot mixture, and cook 5 minutes longer. Remove from heat, and blend in lemon juice and butter. Pour into baked pie shell. Make sure that both filling and pie shell are about the same temperature, either hot or cold. Make a meringue of the 3 egg whites by beating the whites until they form soft peaks. Gradually add 2 tablespoons of sugar until stiff peaks are formed. Spread on pie, and bake at 400° for 10 to 12 minutes or until lightly browned.

SWEET POTATO PIE

Preheat oven to 425°   Yield: 6-8 servings

2 cups cooked and mashed
   sweet potatoes
½ cup brown sugar
¼ teaspoon salt
1 teaspoon cinnamon

¼ teaspoon nutmeg
4 eggs, separated
½ cup melted butter, cooled
2 cups milk
1 (9-inch) unbaked pie shell

Combine potatoes, sugar, salt, cinnamon and nutmeg. Beat egg yolks, and add to cooled, melted butter. Mix with potato mixture; add milk, and mix again. Beat egg whites until stiff, and fold into potato mixture. Pour into pie shell, and bake at 425° for 15 minutes. Reduce heat to 375°, and bake for 25 minutes more. Cool.

GREAT STRAWBERRY PIE

Yield: 6-8 servings

1 (9-inch) baked pie shell
1 quart fresh strawberries,
    cleaned
1 cup sugar

3 tablespoons cornstarch
1 cup heavy cream, whipped
    and slightly sweetened

Mash ½ of the strawberries. Slice the remaining berries in half. Mix sugar with cornstarch. Add to mashed berries. Cook slowly over low heat 10 minutes or until mixture thickens. Place sliced berries in pie shell. Pour cooked berries over all. Cool thoroughly. Top with whipped cream. Decorate with a few reserved whole berries.

STRAWBERRY PIE

Yield: 6-8 servings

1 (9-inch) baked pie shell
1½ cups sugar
¼ cup cornstarch
¼ teaspoon salt
1 package strawberry
    gelatin

1½ cups water
1 tablespoon butter
1 quart whole strawberries,
    cleaned
½ pint whipping cream,
    whipped

Combine sugar, cornstarch, salt, gelatin and water in sauce pan. Cook, stirring until thickened and clear. Remove from heat. Add butter. Cool. Add strawberries. Pour into baked pie shell. Chill. Top with whipped cream.

TRES LECHES
(Nicaraguan dessert)

Preheat oven to 350°   Yield: 12 servings

6 eggs, separated   2 cups flour
2 cups sugar   ½ cup milk
3 teaspoons baking soda   1 teaspoon vanilla

Beat egg whites until foamy; slowly add the sugar. Add yolks, one by one, while still beating. Add baking soda, flour, milk and vanilla. Butter a 9x13-inch pan. Pour the mixture in, and bake at 350° for 35 minutes. When cake is done, take a fork and poke holes all over the top. You need to do this so the cake will absorb the following mixture.

Topping:
2 (14-ounce) cans sweetened   1 (13-ounce) can evaporated
   condensed milk   milk
4 egg yolks

Blend well and pour over the cake until evenly distributed.

4 egg whites   Candied cherries for garnish
1 cup sugar

Beat egg whites until foamy. Gradually add 1 cup sugar, beating until sugar is completely dissolved. Pour over last layer. Decorate cake with cherries. Refrigerate.

SPANISH FLAN

Preheat oven to 350°   Yield: 12 servings

2 cups sugar   1 cup milk
5 large eggs   2 teaspoons vanilla
1 (13-ounce) can evaporated   ⅛ teaspoon salt
   milk

Heat 1 cup sugar over medium heat, stirring constantly until golden brown. Pour slowly into 9-inch tube pan, turning to coat bottom and sides. Cool.

Beat eggs, milk and vanilla. Slowly add 1 cup sugar and salt. Pour into tube pan. Place in large pan filled with water to cover half of tube pan. Bake at 350° for 1½ to 2 hours. Remove; cool on rack 2-3 hours, then refrigerate overnight. To remove flan, place in pan of hot water 10 minutes. Flip onto plate.

PIE IN THE SKY

Preheat oven to 325°   Yield: 6-8 servings

1 (9-inch) baked pie shell

Meringue:

2 egg whites   ¼ teaspoon cinnamon
¼ teaspoon salt   ½ cup sugar
½ teaspoon vinegar

Beat egg whites until stiff. Add salt and vinegar, and beat until mixed. Gradually add cinnamon and sugar while beating. Beat until stiff but not dry. Spread over bottom of pie shell and up sides. Bake at 325° for 12-15 minutes. Cool.

Filling:

1 (6-ounce) package chocolate   1 pint whipping cream
   morsels   1 teaspoon sugar
2 egg yolks   ¼ teaspoon vanilla
¼ cup hot water

In top of double boiler, melt the chocolate morsels over hot, not boiling, water. Beat 2 egg yolks with hot water, and then blend into melted chocolate. Spread 3 tablespoons chocolate mixture over meringue. Chill remaining chocolate until cool and slightly thickened. Whip 1 pint whipping cream, and add 1 teaspoon sugar and ¼ teaspoon vanilla. Spread half the whipped cream over meringue. Add chocolate mixture to balance of whipped cream. Add to pie; chill at least 4 hours.

FUDGE PIE

Preheat oven to 325°   Yield: 6-8 servings

Crust:

¼ cup soft margarine   ¼ cup sugar
1 tablespoon flour   1 cup finely chopped pecans

Mix ingredients together, and press into 9-inch pie pan.

Filling:

½ cup soft margarine   2 (1-ounce) squares baking
1 cup sugar   chocolate, melted and
1 teaspoon vanilla   cooled
½ teaspoon baking powder   ⅓ cup sifted flour
3 eggs   ⅛ teaspoon salt

Combine all ingredients, and beat until smooth. Turn into pie shell, and bake at 325° for 35 to 45 minutes. Filling will be slightly moist.

NOTE: Best served with vanilla ice cream or whipped topping.

HAWAIIAN PIE

Yield: 12-14 servings

2 (9-inch) baked pie shells   3 bananas, sliced
1 (20-ounce) can crushed   ½ cup chopped pecans
   pineapple   1 cup shredded coconut
1 cup sugar   1 (12-ounce) container
2 tablespoons flour   whipped topping

Place undrained pineapple, sugar and flour in sauce pan. Cook over medium heat, stirring constantly until thick. Let cool. Line bottom of baked pie shells with banana slices. Sprinkle with chopped nuts; add cooled pineapple mixture. Sprinkle with coconut. Mound with whipped topping. Refrigerate.

NOTE: Make one for you and one for a favorite neighbor. Great for bridge parties or any get-together. Men love it!

PEANUT PIE

Yield: 14-16 servings

2 (9-inch) baked pie shells
1 cup confectioners sugar
1 (3-ounce) package cream
  cheese
4 heaping tablespoons
  crunchy peanut butter

2 (12-ounce) containers
  whipped topping
Salted cocktail peanuts,
  chopped for garnish

With electric mixer, cream together sugar and cream cheese until light and fluffy. Add peanut butter, and beat well. Add 1 container of whipping topping; fold and mix well. Divide between 2 baked pie crusts. Top with other container of whipped topping and garnish with chopped salted peanuts. Freeze. Remove from freezer 10 minutes before serving.

NOTE: Make one for your favorite neighbor and one for your family to enjoy.

MERINGUE FOR PIE

Yield: 1 (9-inch) pie topping

1 tablespoon cornstarch
2 tablespoons cold water
½ cup boiling water

1 tablespoon lemon juice
3 egg whites
6 tablespoons sugar

In a small pan, mix cornstarch and cold water. While stirring, pour in ½ cup boiling water. Boil over medium heat, stirring constantly, for about 2 minutes. Cool to room temperature. Add lemon juice to egg whites, and beat until they form soft peaks. Gradually add sugar, beating until firm and glossy. Add cornstarch mix, and beat until well blended. Place on top of your favorite cream pie, and lightly brown in 400° oven.

BLUEBERRY KUCHEN

Preheat oven to 400°   Yield: 8 servings

1 cup plus 2 tablespoons
  flour, divided
⅛ teaspoon salt
2 tablespoons sugar
⅔ cup sugar

½ cup margarine, slightly
  softened
1 tablespoon white vinegar
5 cups blueberries, divided
⅛ teaspoon cinnamon

Combine 1 cup flour, salt and 2 tablespoons sugar. Cut in margarine until crumbly. Sprinkle with vinegar and mix. With floured fingers, press dough into springform 9-inch cake pan, about ¼ inch thick on bottom and 1 inch high around sides. Add 3 cups berries. Mix remaining 2 tablespoons flour with ⅔ cup sugar and cinnamon. Sprinkle over berries. Bake at 400° for 50 to 60 minutes or until crust is browned and the filling bubbles. Remove from oven to rack. Sprinkle with remaining 2 cups berries. Cool. Remove rim of pan. Serve with whipped cream.

CREAM CHEESE FLAN

Preheat oven to 350°   Yield: 8 servings

¾ cup sugar
¼ cup water
Non-stick coating spray
1 (8-ounce) package cream
  cheese

1 (14-ounce) can sweetened
  condensed milk
1 cup evaporated milk
5 eggs
1 teaspoon vanilla

Caramelize ¾ cup sugar in heavy skillet over medium heat. Add the ¼ cup water to the caramelized sugar a little at a time, stirring after each addition. Spray a 9- or 10-inch pie plate with the coating spray, and dribble the caramelized sugar over the bottom of the pan. Cut the cream cheese into chunks, and place in a blender. Add milks. Blend until smooth, and add eggs, one at a time, blending well after each. Add the vanilla, and blend until mixed.

Pour the cream cheese mixture over the top of the caramelized sugar, and place pie pan in larger pre-heated pan of hot water to cover ½ the side of pie pan, and bake at 350° for 1 hour.

Cool slightly, and refrigerate for several hours. Invert on glass plate when ready to serve.

OLD ENGLISH PLUM PUDDING
(An Award Winner!)

Yield: 24 servings

1 pound suet (ground)
5½ cups fresh bread crumbs
2⅓ cups sifted flour
¾ cup white raisins
1¼ cups currants
2 cups peeled and grated
    apples
1 cup chopped pecans
Grated rind and juice of 1
    orange and 1 lemon

1½ cups brown sugar
3 cups mixed citron
1 tablespoon each of
    cinnamon, nutmeg, ginger
1⅔ teaspoons salt
1 cup dark raisins
1 fifth (750 milliliters) dark
    rum
4 eggs

Place the suet and all the above ingredients (except the rum and eggs) into a large bowl. Mix well. Add a few tablespoons of rum every few days for one month, until rum is all used. Keep bowl covered with a cloth and leave in a cool place. Stir every day. On the day of cooking, add well-beaten eggs. Place in a greased and floured pudding mold. Mold must have a lid, or cover tightly with foil. Place mold in a large pot of boiling water. Cover and simmer for 6 to 8 hours. Add water if water level goes down too far. Let stand 1 hour before serving. Leave in mold to refrigerate. Heat in oven at 250° for 1 hour before serving. Serve with rum sauce.

Rum Sauce:
1 (3-ounce) package cream
    cheese
1 egg
1 cup confectioners sugar

2 tablespoons butter
1 teaspoon lemon juice
1 cup heavy cream, whipped
2 tablespoons dark rum

In a medium size bowl, beat cream cheese until light. Add egg, sugar, butter, lemon juice, and beat well. Fold in whipped cream and rum until blended. Chill.

NOTE: Make this recipe around Thanksgiving so it will be ready in time for Christmas.

LEMON CHARLOTTE

Yield: 6-8 servings

1 cup boiling water
2 tablespoons sugar
⅛ teaspoon salt
1 (3-ounce) package lemon
   gelatin
2 tablespoons lemon juice

2 cups heavy cream
1 tablespoon lemon peel
½ pint puréed strawberries
   or raspberries
2 tablespoons sugar

Combine boiling water, sugar and salt with gelatin. When cool, add lemon juice. Refrigerate. When it begins to congeal, whip with beater until light and foamy. Whip cream until soft peaks form; add lemon peel, and fold into gelatin mixture. Pour into glass bowl, and place in refrigerator until firm.

NOTE: Serve in individual glass dishes, and pour a few tablespoons puréed strawberries or raspberries that have been combined with 2 tablespoons sugar over each serving.

FLORIDA FRAPPE

Yield: 4-6 servings

½ cup fresh orange juice
¼ cup fresh lemon juice
½ teaspoon grated lemon
   rind

1 cup lemon sherbet
10 crushed ice cubes
1 to 2 tablespoons dry sherry
   (optional)

Using blender, combine orange juice, lemon juice and rind. Blend 5 seconds. Add sherbet and 10 crushed ice cubes. Blend about 1 minute or until frothy. Blend in sherry quickly. Serve in wine glasses.

APPLE CRISP
(Easy!)

Preheat oven to 375°   Yield: 6 servings

4 cups sliced tart apples
½ cup all purpose flour
⅔ cup packed brown sugar
¾ teaspoon ground
   cinnamon

½ cup oats
¾ teaspoon ground nutmeg
⅓ cup butter
Nuts and raisins (optional)

Arrange apples in greased 8-inch square pan. Mix remaining ingredients. Sprinkle over apples. Bake at 375° until topping is golden brown, and apples are tender, about 30 minutes. Serve warm with vanilla ice cream or whipped sweetened heavy cream.

GRAPEFRUIT ALASKA

Preheat oven to 500°   Yield: 4 servings

2 ruby red grapefruit   2 tablespoons sugar
4 tablespoons grenadine   1 pint raspberry sherbet
  syrup, divided   ⅛ teaspoon salt
2 large egg whites

Cut each grapefruit in half, crosswise. With a slender grapefruit knife, cut around sections to free membranes. Flick out seeds. Remove sections to a bowl; add 2 tablespoons of the grenadine. Mix lightly; chill. With kitchen scissors, remove membranes from grapefruit shells; chill upside down on a cookie sheet. Near serving time, thoroughly drain grapefruit sections, and store in refrigerator again. (Juice is not used in this recipe.) At serving time, beat egg whites with salt until stiff. Gradually beat in remaining 2 tablespoons grenadine, then the sugar; continue to beat until stiff peaks are formed. Scoop the sherbet into shells, and add grapefruit sections. Spread with meringue, bringing down to cut edges to make perfect seal. Bake at 500° until meringue is browned, 1½ to 3 minutes. Serve immediately.

MIAMI CITRUS DELIGHT

Yield: 8-10 servings

4½ cups sugar   1½ tablespoons grated
1½ cups water   orange rind
1¼ cups lemon juice   1½ cups heavy cream,
2¼ cups orange juice   whipped
4½ bananas, mashed   5 egg whites, beaten until
1½ teaspoons grated lemon   stiff but not dry
  rind

Combine the sugar and water in a saucepan. Bring to a boil, stirring until sugar dissolves. Boil five minutes. Let cool. Add lemon juice, orange juice, bananas, lemon rind and orange rind to the syrup. Cool. Fold in the whipped cream and egg whites. Freeze in serving glasses until firm. Remove from freezer 30 minutes before serving. Garnish with thin orange slices.

NOTE: This recipe may be reduced by half successfully, using 3 egg whites.

FROZEN STRAWBERRY DESSERT

Preheat oven to 350°   Yield: 12-15 servings

1 cup flour
¼ cup brown sugar
½ cup chopped walnuts
½ cup butter, melted
2 egg whites
1 cup sugar (⅔ cup if using
   frozen strawberries)

2 cups sliced fresh
   strawberries or 10-ounce
   package frozen
   strawberries
2 tablespoons lemon juice
1 cup whipping cream,
   whipped

Combine flour, brown sugar, walnuts and butter. Spread evenly in ungreased 13x9-inch pan. Bake at 350° for 20 minutes, stirring occasionally. Reserve ½ cup baked crumbs for topping. Spread remaining crumbs in pan. Combine egg whites, sugar, berries and lemon juice in large bowl. Beat on highest speed until stiff (about 10 minutes). Fold in whipped cream. Spoon over crust. Top with remaining crumbs. Freeze 6 hours or overnight.

PECAN PICK UPS

Preheat oven to 350°   Yield: 24 servings

Crust:
3-ounce package cream
   cheese

1 cup flour
1 stick butter (¼ pound)

Filling:
¾ cup dark brown sugar,
   firmly packed
½ cup finely chopped pecans

1 teaspoon vanilla
1 tablespoon melted butter
1 egg

Mix all ingredients for crust until smooth. Chill. Put small amount in each small (1⅜-inch bottom) muffin tins, and press evenly around sides and bottom. Prepare filling, mixing all ingredients together. Put 1 teaspoon into each pastry lined tin. Bake at 350° for 30 minutes.

MEXICAN WEDDING COOKIES

Preheat oven to 325°   Yield: 24 cookies

2 sticks (½ pound) butter or
    margarine
8 tablespoons confectioners
    sugar

2 teaspoons vanilla
2 cups flour
2 cups chopped pecans

Cream together butter, sugar and vanilla. Add flour gradually and then nuts. Form into balls. Bake at 325° for 30 minutes on ungreased cookie sheet. Cool slightly, and sprinkle with confectioners sugar.

AUSTRALIAN CRISP COOKIES

Preheat oven to 300°   Yield: 48 cookies

½ stick (4 ounces) butter or
    margarine
1 tablespoon white corn
    syrup
2 tablespoons boiling water

1½ teaspoons baking soda
1 cup sugar
1 cup rolled oats
1 cup coconut
1 cup flour

Melt butter over low heat and add syrup. Add boiling water and soda. Combine remaining ingredients, and add syrup mixture. Stir to blend well. Mixture will be dry. Drop by teaspoonfuls on a greased cookie sheet. Bake at 300° for 20 minutes. Cool and store.

CHINESE CHEWS

Preheat oven to 350°   Yield: 48

1 (1-pound) box light brown
  sugar
1 stick (¼ pound) margarine
3 eggs

2 cups self rising flour
1½ teaspoons vanilla
1 (7½-ounce) can coconut
1 cup chopped nuts

Combine ingredients in order given. Place in 9x13-inch baking pan. Bake at 350° for 20 minutes or until brown and it rises and falls. Turn oven off, and leave pan in oven for 3 more minutes. Allow to cool before cutting into squares.

WALNUT DATE DOUBLE DECKER

Preheat oven to 350°   Yield: 36

Crust:
1¼ cups sifted flour
⅓ cup sugar

½ cup butter

Combine flour, sugar and butter. Blend to fine crumbs. Pack into bottom of greased 9-inch square pan. Bake at 350° for 20 minutes or until edges are lightly browned.

Filling:
⅓ cup light brown sugar,
  packed
⅓ cup granulated sugar
2 eggs
1 teaspoon vanilla
2 tablespoons flour

1 teaspoon baking powder
¼ teaspoon salt
¼ teaspoon nutmeg
1 cup chopped walnuts
1 (8-ounce) package pitted
  dates, chopped
Confectioners sugar

Combine sugars, eggs and vanilla. Beat together well. Sift flour with baking powder, salt and nutmeg. Add to sugar mixture. Stir in walnuts and dates. Turn batter into pan over baked crust. Bake at 350° for 20 more minutes. Cool in pan. Sprinkle top with confectioners sugar, and cut into bars.

NOTE: Freezes well.

LEMON BUTTER SNOW BARS

Preheat oven to 350°   Yield: 16

Crust:
½ cup butter   1⅓ cups flour
¼ cup sugar

Cream butter and sugar. Blend in flour. Press into 8-inch square pan. Bake at 350° for 15 to 20 minutes, until golden brown around the edges.

Filling:
3 tablespoons lemon juice   2 tablespoons flour
¼ teaspoon baking powder   ¾ cup sugar
2 eggs   Confectioners sugar

Combine the above ingredients, except confectioners sugar, mixing well. Pour onto crust. Bake at 350° for 15 minutes. Cool slightly, and sprinkle with confectioners sugar.

SOUR CREAM COOKIES

Preheat oven to 350°   Yield: 6 dozen

½ cup margarine   1 teaspoon nutmeg
1½ cups sugar   1 teaspoon baking soda
2 eggs   ⅔ cup sour cream
2⅔ cups flour   1 teaspoon vanilla
¼ teaspoon salt

Cream margarine and sugar. Add eggs, and beat. Sift flour, salt, nutmeg and soda together, and add to egg mixture. Add sour cream and vanilla. Drop by teaspoon onto greased baking sheet, and bake at 350° for 12 minutes or until light golden brown.

NOTE: These are better the second day if you can keep them that long.

CHOCOLATE ALMOND BARS

Preheat oven to 350°   Yield: 6 dozen

4 cups flour	**2 cups slivered almonds**
3 cups brown sugar	**12 ounces chocolate chips**
2⅔ cups butter, divided	

This recipe is for preparation with a food processor but could be easily converted. Using the metal blade, combine the flour with 2 cups of the brown sugar and half the butter for about 15 seconds. Press mixture, followed by the almonds, into two 13x9-inch baking pans. Bake at 350° until lightly browned, about 15 minutes. Meanwhile, melt remaining butter in a small sauce pan. Add remaining brown sugar, and cook over medium heat until mixture bubbles. Simmer until syrupy, about 1 minute. Pour evenly over almonds, and bake 15 minutes more. Remove from oven, and distribute chocolate chips to cover. Let stand until melted, about 5 minutes. Swirl chocolate over top for a marbled effect. Cut into small pieces; let cool until chocolate has hardened before removing.

NOTE: These are like toffee — more a candy than a cookie.

PECAN CLUSTERS

Yield: 3 dozen

4 cups brown sugar	**2 cups toasted pecan halves**
4 tablespoons cold water	**1 stick (¼ pound) butter**

Boil sugar and water for 1½ minutes. Add pecans and butter; mix. Cook for 2 minutes. Remove from range, and drop in clusters on waxed paper. Store in waxed paper-lined sealed container.

PEPPERMINT WAFER DESSERT

Yield: 9-12 servings

½ pound peppermint stick candy	**2 tablespoons cold water**
½ cup light cream	**1½ cups heavy cream, whipped**
½ tablespoon (½ envelope) unflavored gelatin	**1 (9- or 10-ounce) box chocolate wafers, divided**

Crush candy; add light cream. Heat in double boiler until candy dissolves. Soften gelatin in cold water; add to hot mixture. Chill until partially set, and fold in whipped cream. Break chocolate wafers in half and stand them around inside edge of 9x9x2-inch pan. Place layer of wafers in bottom of pan. Spread with half the gelatin mixture. Top with second layer of wafers. Spread with remainder of mixture. Top with wafers. Chill 12 hours; cut into squares.

MANGO MAGIC

Yield: 6-8 servings

3 cups ripe mangoes
1 tablespoon lemon juice

1 cup sweetened condensed
milk

Mix in blender. Place in ramekins or dessert cups. Chill in refrigerator for several hours.

ELEGANT PEARS

Yield: 4-6 servings

1 (29-ounce) can pears,
   drained
1 cup port wine

3 tablespoons brown sugar
Sour cream or vanilla ice
   cream (optional)

Melt sugar in wine. Pour over pears. Chill. Serve with dollop of sour cream or ice cream.

STRAWBERRIES ROMANOFF

Yield: 10 servings

3 quarts fresh strawberries
1 quart vanilla ice cream

1½ cups heavy cream,
   whipped with 1 tablespoon
   sugar
½ to ¾ cup Grand Marnier

Wash and hull berries; leave whole unless too big to eat gracefully. Put into serving bowl. Cover with plastic wrap until serving time. Soften ice cream out of refrigerator ½ hour, and mix with whipped cream until soft. Stir in Grand Marnier. Keep refrigerated until serving time. Do this several hours ahead. To serve, pour mixture over berries, reserving a few to garnish.

ORANGE POSITANO

(A great way to turn surplus oranges into a fancy dessert)

Yield: 16 servings

8 oranges, peeled
4 cups sugar
3 cups water

1 cup Grand Marnier
Whipped cream or whipped
 topping for garnish

Prepare a syrup by bringing to a boil the sugar, water and Grand Marnier. Continue to boil until mixture has thickened slightly.

Place oranges in bowl, and pour slightly cooled syrup over them. Allow to cool. When ready to serve, slice each orange into rounds on salad plates, and top with whipped cream or whipped topping.

WHOLE STRAWBERRIES WITH FRENCH CREAM

Yield: 6-8 servings

1 cup heavy cream
1/3 cup confectioners sugar
1/2 cup sour cream
1/2 teaspoon grated fresh
 orange rind

2 pints strawberries, rinsed
 and hulled
Grated dark sweet or milk
 chocolate

Beat heavy cream until stiff. Fold in sugar, sour cream and orange rind. Serve as topping for whole strawberries, or mix together. Sprinkle with grated chocolate.

PLANTAINS WITH CREAM AND RAISINS
(Easy!)

Yield: 8 servings

4 ripe plantains
2 tablespoons vegetable oil
⅔ cup raisins

1 (12-ounce) container
   frozen whipped topping,
   thawed

Peel and slice plantains in ¼-inch thick circles, and fry in vegetable oil in a medium sized skillet until dark brown in color. Place a layer of the fried plantains in a 9-inch square dish. Then layer half the whipped topping, and sprinkle half the raisins over top of this. Repeat. Serve while the plantains are still warm.

INDEX

ORDER BLANK

The Guild of the Museum of Science, Inc.
3280 S. Miami Avenue
Miami, FL 33129

Please send me _____ copies of **MAKE IT MIAMI**
@ $20.00 per copy for Florida residents ($16.95 a copy plus Florida sales
tax, shipping & handling).

@ $19.00 per copy for out-of-state residents ($16.95 plus shipping).

Enclosed is my check for $ _____ , payable to **MAKE IT MIAMI.**

SHIP TO:

Name _____

Street _____

City _____ State _____ Zip _____

ORDER BLANK

The Guild of the Museum of Science, Inc.
3280 S. Miami Avenue
Miami, FL 33129

Please send me _____ copies of **MAKE IT MIAMI**
@ $20.00 per copy for Florida residents ($16.95 a copy plus Florida sales
tax, shipping & handling).

@ $19.00 per copy for out-of-state residents ($16.95 plus shipping).

Enclosed is my check for $ _____ , payable to **MAKE IT MIAMI.**

SHIP TO:

Name _____

Street _____

City _____ State _____ Zip _____